Lecture Notes
in Business Information Processing

T0237861

Series Editors

Jan Mendling

Metrics for Process Models

Empirical Foundations
of Verification, Error Prediction,
and Guidelines for Correctness

 Springer

Author

Jan Mendling
Humboldt-Universität zu Berlin
Institut für Wirtschaftsinformatik
Spandauer Str. 1, 10178 Berlin, Germany
E-mail: contact@mendling.com

Library of Congress Control Number: 2008938155

ACM Computing Classification (1998): H.4, J.1, D.2

ISSN   1865-1348
ISBN-10   3-540-89223-0 Springer Berlin Heidelberg New York
ISBN-13   978-3-540-89223-6 Springer Berlin Heidelberg New York

Springer is a part of Springer Science+Business Media

springer.com

© Springer-Verlag Berlin Heidelberg 2008
Printed in Germany

Typesetting: Camera-ready by author, data conversion by Markus Richter, Heidelberg
Printed on acid-free paper   SPIN: 12540204   06/3180   5 4 3 2 1 0

To Leni and to my family

.

Preface

Business process modeling plays an important role in the management of business processes. As valuable design artifacts, business process models are subject to quality considerations. The absence of formal errors such as deadlocks is of paramount importance for the subsequent implementation of the process. This book develops a framework for the detection of formal errors in business process models and for the prediction of error probability based on quality attributes of these models (metrics). We focus on Event-driven Process Chains (EPCs), a widely used business process modeling language due to its extensive tool support. The advantage of this focus is firstly that the results of this book can be directly translated into process modeling practice. Secondly, there is a large empirical basis of models. By utilizing this large stock of EPC model collections, we aim to bring forth general insights into the connection between process model metrics and error probability. In order to validate such a connection, we first need to establish an understanding of which model attributes are likely connected with error probability. Furthermore, we must formally define an appropriate notion of correctness that answers the question of whether or not a model has a formal error. As a prerequisite to answering this question, we must define the operational semantics of the process modeling language formally.

Contributions

This book presents a precise description of EPCs, their control-flow semantics and a suitable correctness criterion called EPC soundness. Furthermore, we identify theoretical arguments on why structural metrics should be connected with error probability and provide an empirical validation of this connection. To be more concise, this book provides the following technical contributions.

Formalization of the OR-join: The semantics of the OR-join have been debated for more than a decade. Existing formalizations suffer from either a restriction of the EPC syntax (see [78, 247, 238, 4, 101]) or from non-intuitive behavior (see [325, 218, 11, 465]). In Chap. 2, we formalize the EPC semantics concept as proposed elsewhere [267]. In comparison to other approaches this novel formalization has the advantage of not being restricted to a subset of EPCs. Moreover, it provides intuitive semantics for blocks of matching OR-splits and joins since they cannot deadlock. As a proof of concept, we implemented a plug-in for ProM that calculates the reachability graph. In this way, this novel semantics definition contributes to research on the specification of business process modeling languages.

Verification of process models with OR-joins and multiple start and end events: Verification techniques for process models with OR-joins and multiple start and end events suffer from one of two problems: Firstly, they build on an approximation of the actual behavior, e.g., by considering a relaxed notion of soundness [101], by involving user decisions [109] or by approximating relaxed soundness with invariants [440]. Therefore, they do not provide a precise answer to the verification problem. Secondly, some verification approaches for semantics definitions (see [88, 464]) suffer from the previously mentioned non-intuitive behavior. While this is not the result of the verification problem itself, none of these approaches has been tailored to cope with multiple start and end events. In Chap. 3, we specify a dedicated soundness criterion for EPC business process models with OR-joins and multiple start and end events. We also define two verification approaches for EPC soundness: one as an explicit analysis of the reachability graph and a second based on reduction rules to provide a better verification performance. Both approaches were implemented as a proof of concept. In this way, we contribute to the verification of process models with OR-joins and multiple start and end events. Importantly, we also extend the set of reduction rules for business process models.

Metrics for business process models: Metrics play an important role in the operationalization of various quality-related aspects in software engineering, network analysis, and business process modeling. Several authors use metrics to capture different aspects of business process models that are presumably related to quality (see [244, 320, 308, 348, 72, 37, 67, 74, 241, 356, 275, 276]). Unfortunately, business process-specific concepts such as sequentiality, decision points, concurrency, and repetition are hardly considered while simple count metrics are often defined. There also appears to be little awareness of related research, possibly owing to the fact that process model measurement is conducted in separate disciplines such as software process management, network analysis, Petri nets theory, and conceptual modeling. In Chap. 4, we provide an extensive list of metrics for business process models and provide links to previously isolated research. Beyond that, we provide a detailed discussion of the rationale and limitations of each metric to serve as a predictor for error probability. We formulate a hypothesis for each metric based on whether it is positively or negatively correlated with error probability.

Validation of metrics as error predictors: Until now, there has been little empirical evidence for the validity of business process model metrics as predictors for error probability. Some empirical work has been conducted; however, it has always maintained a different focus: *Lee and Yoon* investigate the empirical relationship between parameters of Petri nets and their state space [243, 244]. *Canfora et al.* empirically evaluate the suitability of metrics to serve as predictors for maintainability of the process model [67]. *Cardoso* analyzes the correlation between the control flow complexity metric with the perceived complexity of process models [73]. Of most significance to this book is an analysis of the SAP Reference Model in which *Mendling et al.* test a set of simple count metrics as error predictors [275, 276]. In Chap. 5 we use logistic regression for the test, which is similar to the analysis of the SAP Reference Model. We consider both the broader set of metrics from Chap. 4, a precise notion of EPC soundness as defined in Chap. 3, and a much broader sample of EPC models from practice. The results show not only that certain metrics are indeed a good predictor for error probability, but also that simple count metrics fail to capture important aspects of a process model.

So little research on information systems and conceptual modeling combines design science and behavioral science research paradigms that there is clearly a need for more empirical insight [306]. Since the previously listed contributions cover both design and behavioral aspects, we consider the main contribution of this book to be the innovative and holistic combination of both these research paradigms in an effort to deliver a deeper understanding of errors in business process modeling.

Structure

This book is organized in six chapters. Beginning with a general overview of business process management, we continue with semantics of EPCs and the verification of soundness before discussing metrics for business process models which are subsequently validated for their capability to predict error probability.

Chapter 1 – *Business Process Management:* In this chapter, we discuss the backgrounds of business process management and define important related terms. We also sketch the importance of business process modeling and the role of errors in the business process management lifecycle.

Chapter 2 – *Event-driven Process Chains (EPC):* This chapter gathers state-of-the-art work on EPCs. Building on the foundations of prior work, we establish a novel syntax definition and a novel semantics definition for EPCs. Our semantics are based on transition relations that define both state changes and context changes. We then present an algorithm to calculate the reachability graph of an EPC based on the transition relations and a respective implementation as a plug-in for ProM. The major motivations for these novel semantics are semantic gaps and non-intuitive behavior of existing formalizations.

Chapter 3 – *Verification of EPC Soundness:* This chapter presents an EPC-specific version of soundness as a criterion of correctness for EPCs. We propose two different approaches for the verification of soundness: one based on the reachability graph and another based on reduction rules. While the first approach explicitly considers all states and transitions that are represented by an EPC, there is a problem with state explosion due to the maximum number of states growing exponentially with the number of arcs. In order to avoid a performance problem we introduce a set of reduction rules. This set extends prior work with new reductions for start and end components, delta components, prism components and homogeneous EPCs. This approach is tested by reducing the SAP Reference Model and shows that the reduction is *fast*, provides a *precise* result for almost all models, and finds *three times as many errors* as other approaches based on relaxed soundness.

Chapter 4 – *Metrics for Business Process Models:* This chapter discusses the suitability of business process model metrics predicting error probability from a theoretical point of view. Revisiting related research in the area of network analysis, software measurement, and metrics for business process models, we find that several aspects of process models have not yet been combined in an overall measurement framework. Based on theoretical considerations we present a set of 15 metrics related to size and 13 metrics that capture various aspects of the structure and the state space of the process model. For each of the metrics we discuss their presumable connection with error probability and formulate respective hypotheses.

Chapter 5 – *Validation of Metrics as Error Predictors:* In this chapter, we conduct several statistical analyzes related to the connection of metrics and error probability. The results of the correlation analysis and the logistic regression model strongly confirm the hypothetical impact direction of the metrics. We then derive a logistic regression function, based on a sample of approximately 2000 real EPC business process models, that correctly classifies 90% of the models from a second independent sample.

Chapter 6 – *Implications for Business Process Modeling:* Here we present a summary of the findings and offer an outlook on future research. A major result is a set of seven guidelines of process modeling. Beyond that, we discuss the implications for the business process modeling process, respective tool support, EPCs as a business process modeling language, and teaching of business process modeling.

Acknowledgements

The major share of this book stems directly from my doctoral thesis, submitted to the Vienna University of Economics and Business Administration (WU Wien) in May 2007. I would like to thank my supervisors, Prof. Dr. Gustaf Neumann and Prof. Dr. Wil van der Aalst. In October 2003 I began working at the Institute of Information Systems and New Media. Prof. Neumann provided me with a creative work environment where I could further develop my ideas and academic writing skills. He was open and supportive in all matters, particularly when it came to modifying the topic of my thesis. In 2004 I met Prof. van der Aalst at a conference and he agreed to be my second supervisor. His feedback was extraordinarily helpful for the formalization of my concepts.

Additionally, I would like to thank Prof. Dr. Markus Nüttgens for fueling my interest in business process modeling and EPCs, and for his continuous support since my diploma thesis in Trier, Germany; Prof. Dr. Walter Schertler and Prof. Dr. Axel Schwickert for serving as references for my application to WU in Vienna; Prof. Dr.

Carlos de Backer for being a role model in teaching information systems and explaining IT concepts in Dutch; and Prof. Dr. Hans Czap for his efforts in establishing the Diplomstudiengang Wirtschaftsinformatik at the University of Trier. I would like to thank all my former colleagues at the Institute of Information Systems and New Media and the Institute of Management Information Systems at the Vienna University of Economics and Business Administration (WU Wien) for providing a friendly work environment. Finally, thanks to Prof. Dr. Michael Rosemann and A/Prof. Dr. Arthur ter Hofstede and all my colleagues at the BPM group at the Queensland University of Technology Brisbane for their inspirations.

I was happy to discuss research and to collaborate on different paper projects with several excellent people: Wil van der Aalst, Paul Barborka, Alberto Brabenetz, Jan vom Brocke, Jorge Cardoso, Malu Castellanos, Remco Dijkman, Boudewijn van Dongen, Marlon Dumas, Rik Eshuis, Florian Gottschalk, Michael Genrich, Michael Hafner, Lukas Helm, Mitra Heravizadeh, Jörg Hoffmann, Arthur ter Hofstede, Thomas Hornung, Cirano Iochpe, Alex Kokkonen, Georg Köldorfer, Agnes Koschmider, Marcello La Rosa, Kristian Bisgaard Lassen, Jean Michael Lau, Ralf Laue, Ana Karla Alves de Medeiros, Joachim Melcher, Jürgen Moormann, Michael Moser, Michael zur Muehlen, Martin Müller, Gustaf Neumann, Jörg Nitzsche, Markus Nüttgens, Cristian Pérez de Laborda, Karsten Plößer, Andreas Pinterits, Adrian Price, Michael Rausch, Jan Recker, Manfred Reichert, Hajo Reijers, Michael Rosemann, Frank Rump, Bernd Simon, Carlo Simon, Guido Sommer, Mark Strembeck, Gerald Stermsek, Lucinéia Heloisa Thom, Roger Tregear, Irene Vanderfeesten, Eric Verbeek, Barbara Weber, Ingo Weber, Ton Weijters, Fridolin Wild, Uwe Zdun, and Jörg Ziemann. Thank you for sharing your insights with me. I also thank Kalina Chivarova for gathering some of the EPC models of the holdout sample in her bachelor thesis. A special thanks goes to Herbert Liebl, who had the nice idea of generating SVG graphics from the error analysis and highlighting the errors in the EPC models. I would also like to thank Jesse Holt for proof-reading the manuscript. Finally, thanks to Yoseba Peña, who coined the title of my thesis.

July 2008   Jan Mendling

Contents

List of Acronyms

ACM	Association for Computing Machinery
AD	Anno Domini
AND	Logical and-operator
ARIS	ARchitecture of Integrated Information Systems
BPEL	Business Process Execution Language for Web Services
BPM	Business Process Management
BPMN	Business Process Modeling Notation
BWW	Bunge-Wand-Weber
CASE	Computer Aided Software Engineering
CC	Cyclomatic complexity, cyclomatic number
CCD	Cyclomatic complexity density
CDIF	CASE Data Interchange Format
C-EPC	Configurable Event-driven Process Chain
CFC	Control-flow complexity
COCOMO	Constructive Cost Model
CPN	Colored Petri Nets
DOM	Document Object Model
ebXML	Electronic Business XML
ECC	Essential cyclomatic complexity
EPC	Event-driven Process Chain
EPK	Ereignisgesteuerte Prozesskette
EPML	Event-driven Process Chain Markup Language
ERD	Entity-relationship diagram
ERP	Enterprise Resource Planning
ET	Entscheidungstabellen-operator
FSM	Finite State Machine
GHz	Giga-Hertz
GI	Gesellschaft für Informatik e.V., German Informatics Society
GoM	Guidelines of Modeling
GQM	Goal-Question-Metric

GXL	Graph Exchange Language
HTML	Hypertext Markup Language
ID	Identifier
IEC	International Electrotechnical Commission
iEPC	Integrated EPC
IEEE	Institute of Electrical and Electronics Engineers
IFC	Information Flow Complexity
ISO	International Organization for Standardization
IT	Information technology
IWi	Institut für Wirtschaftsinformatik
KIM	Kölner Integrationsmodell
KOPeR	Knowledge-based organizational process redesign
LoC	Lines of Code
LTL	linear temporal logic
MI	Multiple Instantiation
modEPC	Modified Event-driven Process Chain
OASIS	Organization for the Advancement of Structured Information Standards
oEPC	Object-oriented Event-driven Process Chain
OR	Logical or-operator
ProM	Process Mining tool of TU Eindhoven
rEPC	Real-time Event-driven Process Chain
RG	Reachability Graph
SAP	Systeme, Anwendungen und Produkte in der Datenverarbeitung
SCOOP	System for Computerization of Office Processing
SEQ	Sequence-operator
SNA	Social network analysis
SPSS	Statistical Package for the Social Sciences
SQL	Structured Query Language
SVG	Scalable Vector Graphics
TAM	Technology acceptance model
Tcl	Tool command language
tDOM	Tool command language Document Object Model
UML	Unified Modeling Language
UML AD	Unified Modeling Language Activity Diagram
US	United States
Wf. nets	Workflow nets
WfMC	Workflow Management Coalition
Woflan	WOrkFLow ANalyzer
WS-CDL	Web Services Choreography Description Language
xEPC	Agent-oriented Event-driven Process Chain
XHTML	Extensible Hypertext Markup Language
XML	Extensible Markup Language
xoEPC	Extended Object Event-driven Process Chain
XOR	logical exclusive or-operator

XOTcl   Extended Object Tool command language
XPDL   Extensible Markup Language Process Definition Language
YAWL   Yet Another Workflow Language
yEPC   Yet another Event-driven Process Chain

1

Business Process Management

The recent progress of Business Process Management (BPM) is reflected by the figures of the related industry. Wintergreen Research estimates that the international market for BPM-related software and services accounted for more than USD $1 billion in 2005 with a tendency towards rapid growth in the subsequent couple of years [457]. The relevance of business process modeling to general management initiatives has been previously studied in the 1990s [28]. Today, Gartner finds that organizations that had the best results in implementing business process management spent more than 40 percent of the total project time on discovery and construction of their initial process model [265]. As a consequence, Gartner considers Business Process Modeling to be among the Top 10 Strategic Technologies for 2008.

Despite the plethora of popular and academic textbooks [164, 95, 196, 378, 27, 380, 248, 7, 9, 257, 49, 213, 233, 170, 407, 415, 199, 405, 447, 227, 408] as well as international professional and academic conference series such as the BPM conference [13, 106, 5, 115, 23], there are several fundamental problems that remain unsolved by current approaches. A particular problem is the lack of research regarding the definition of good design. What few contributions there are reveal an incomplete understanding of quality aspects. Business process modeling as a sub-discipline of BPM faces a particular problem in that modelers who have little background in formal methods often design models without understanding the full implications of their specification (see [336]). As a consequence, process models designed on a business level can rarely be reused on an execution level since they often suffer from formal errors such as deadlocks. Formal errors can, however, be identified algorithmically with verification techniques. In contrast, inconsistencies between the real-world business process and the process model can only be detected by talking to stakeholders. The focus of this book will be on formal errors. Since the costs of errors increase exponentially over the development life cycle [306], it is of paramount importance that errors are discovered as early as possible. A large amount of work has been conducted in an attempt to resolve this weak understanding by providing formal verification techniques, simulation tools, and animation concepts. Several of these approaches cannot be applied, however, if the business process modeling language in use is not specified appropriately. Furthermore, this research area does not address the root of the problem: as long as we do not understand why people introduce errors in a process model, we will never be able to improve the design process.

This chapter provides an overview of business process management and business process modeling. Section 1.1 elaborates on the background of business process management through a historical classification of seminal work. Section 1.2 defines business process management and illustrates the business process management life cycle. Section 1.3 discusses modeling from a general information systems point of view and derives a definition for business process modeling. Section 1.4 distinguishes between formal verification and external validation of business process models and emphasizes the need to understand why formal errors are introduced in business process models. Finally, Section 1.5 concludes the chapter with a summary.

1.1 History of Business Process Management

In the last couple of years, there has been a growing interest in business process management from industry as well as from business administration and information systems research. In essence, business process management deals with the efficient coordination of business activities within and between companies. As such, it can be related to several seminal works on economics and business administration. *Henri Fayol*, one of the founders of modern organization theory, recommended a *subdivision of labor* in order to increase productivity [122, p.20]. *Adam Smith* had already illustrated its potential benefits by analyzing pin production [406]. Subdivision of labor, however, requires *coordination* between subtasks. Business process management is concerned with coordination mechanisms in order to leverage the efficient creation of goods and services in a production system based on such subdivision of labor. The *individual tasks* and the *coordination between them* are, therefore, subject to optimization efforts. *Frederick Taylor* advocated the creation of an optimal work environment based on scientific methods to leverage the most efficient way of performing individual work steps. In the optimization of each step, he proposed to "select the quickest way", to "eliminate all false movements, slow movements, and useless movements" and to "collect into one series the quickest and best movements" [421, p.61]. The efficient coordination of business processes is demonstrated by the innovation of the assembly line system: its inventor *Henry Ford* proudly praised the production cycle of only 81 hours "from the mine to the finished machine" in his factories to illustrate the efficiency of the concept [130, p.105].

In academia, *Nordsieck* was one of the first to distinguish between structural and process organization [321, 322]. He described several types of workflow diagrams for things such as subdivision and distribution of labor, sequencing of activities, or task assignment [321]. In his work, *Nordsieck* identifies the order of work steps and the temporal relationship of tasks as the subject of process analysis with the overall goal of integrating these steps [322] and distinguishes between five levels of automation: free course of work, contents bound course of work, order bound course of work, temporally bound course of work, and beat bound course of work [322].

The decades after World War II saw a discussion about the potential of information systems to facilitate automation of office work [246, 80]. In the 1950s, these ideas seemed still quite visionary [311]. Later, in the early 1970s, it became apparent that information systems would indeed become a new design dimension in an organizational setting (see [145, 166, 148]), but research of the time mainly focused on the structural aspects (such as the relational data model [82] and query languages that later evolved to SQL [29, 30, 76]) without paying much attention to behavioral aspects such as processes. At that time, the logic of business processes used to be hard-coded into applications and were, therefore, difficult to change [189, 310]. Prototypes for office automation during the late 1970s were the starting point for a more explicit control over the flow of information and the coordination of tasks. The basic idea was to build electronic forms for clerical work that was normally handled via paper. In his doctoral thesis, *Zisman* [472, 471] used Petri nets [335] to specify the clerical work steps of an office agent and introduced a respective prototype system called SCOOP. A comparable approach was presented by *Ellis* [117], who modelled office procedures as Information Control Nets, a special kind of Petri nets consisting of activities, precedence constraints, and information repositories. An overview of further work on office automation is provided in [118].

Although the business importance of processes received some attention in the 1980s [338] and new innovations were introduced in information system support of processes (e.g. system support for communication processes [455] based on speech act theory introduced by [34, 390]), it was only in the early 1990s that workflow management prevailed as a new technology to support business processes. An increasing number of commercial vendors of workflow management systems benefited from new business administration concepts and ideas such as process innovation [95] and business process reengineering [164]. On the other hand, these business programs relied heavily on information system technology, especially workflow systems, in order to establish new and more efficient ways of doing business. In the 1990s, the application of workflow systems, in particular those supporting information systems integration processes, profited from open communication standards and distributed systems technology that both contributed to interoperability with other systems [139]. The Workflow Management Coalition (WfMC), founded in 1993, is of special importance for this improvement [185]. The historical overview of office automation and workflow systems given in [310, p.93] illustrates this breakthrough nicely. This period also saw an increase in scientific publications on workflow technology and process specification (see [119, 139, 75, 196, 386, 327, 326, 346, 3, 453, 248]) and intra-enterprise processes remained the major focus of business process management through until the end of the 1990s [97].

Since the advent of the eXtended Markup Language (XML) and web services technology, application scenarios for business process integration have become much easier to implement in an inter-enterprise setting. Current standardization efforts mainly address interoperability issues related to such scenarios (see [292, 280, 277]). The common industry interest in facilitating the integration of interorganizational processes leverages the specification of standards for web service composition (e.g. the Business Process Execution Language for Web Services

(BPEL) [91, 26, 24]), for web service choreography (the Web Service Choreography Description Language (WS-CDL) [209]), or for interorganizational processes based on ebXML and related standards (see [183] for an overview). The integration of composition and choreography languages is currently one of the main research topics in this area [270, 451].

Today business process management is an important research area that combines insights from business administration, organization theory, computer science and computer supported cooperative work. It remains a considerable market for software vendors, IT service providers and business consultants.

1.2 Definition of Business Process Management

Since the beginning of organization theory, several definitions for business processes have been proposed. As early as the 1930s, *Nordsieck* described a business process as a sequence of activities producing an output. By this definition an activity is the smallest separable unit of work performed by a work subject [322, pp.27-29]. Along these lines *Becker and Kugeler* [48] propose the following definition:

> "A process is a completely closed, timely and logical sequence of activities which are required to work on a process-oriented business object. Such a process-oriented object can be, for example, an invoice, a purchase order or a specimen. A business process is a special process that is directed by the business objectives of a company and by the business environment. Essential features of a business process are interfaces to the business partners of the company (e.g. customers, suppliers)."

As *Davenport* puts it [95, p.5], a "process is thus a specific ordering of work activities across time and place, with a beginning, an end, and clearly identified inputs and outputs: a structure for action." *Van der Aalst and Van Hee* add that the order of the activities is determined by a set of conditions [9, p.4]. It is important to distinguish here between the business process and several individual cases. Consider a business process such as car production. This process produces cars as an output. The production of one individual car that is sold to customer John Smith is one case. Accordingly, each case can be distinguished from other cases and a business process can be regarded as a class of similar cases [9].

Several categorization schemes were proposed in relation to business processes and information systems support. As an extension of *Porter*'s value chain model (see [338]), *Van der Aalst and Van Hee* distinguish between production, support, and managerial processes [9, p.9]. *Production processes* create products and services of a company that are sold to customers. These processes are of paramount importance as they generate income for the company. *Support processes* establish an environment in which the production processes go smoothly. Therefore, they do not only include maintenance activities, but also marketing and finance. *Managerial processes* direct and coordinate production and support processes. They are primarily concerned with defining goals, preconditions and constraints for the other processes. *Leymann and*

Roller provide a classification scheme[1] for processes based on their *business value* and their *degree of repetition* [248]. They use the term *"production process"* to refer to those processes that have both a high business value and a high degree of repetition. *Administrative processes* are also highly repetitive but of little business value. Furthermore, *collaborative processes* are highly valuable but hardly repeatable. Finally, *ad hoc processes* are neither repetitive nor valuable. *Leymann and Roller* conclude that information systems support should focus on production processes. In particular, workflow management systems are discussed as a suitable tool. Further definitions and classifications can be found, for example, in [264, 251, 114].

Business process management can be defined as the set of all management activities related to business processes. In essence, the management activities related to business processes can be idealistically arranged in a life cycle. Business process management life cycle models have been described in [9, 310, 114]. In the remainder of this section, we mainly follow the life cycle proposed in [310, pp.82-87] because it not only includes activities but also artifacts, and because it consolidates the life cycle models for business process management reported in [176, 134, 420, 317]. This life cycle shares the activities analysis, design and implementation with the general process of information systems development identified by [448]. The life cycle comprises the management activities of analysis, design, implementation, enactment, monitoring and evaluation. The solid arcs represent the typical order of these activities (see Figure 1.1). Organizations differ in the level of sophistication in which they support these phases and the smooth transition between them. A related model of business process management maturity is discussed in [363].

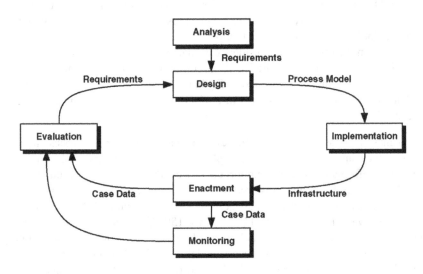

Figure 1.1. Business process management life cycle

---

[1] The authors refer to the GIGA group who originally introduced the scheme.

Analysis: The business process management life cycle begins with an analysis activity (see Figure 1.1). This analysis covers both the environment of the process and the organization structure. The output of this step is a set of requirements for the business process such as performance goals or intentions [352].

Design: These requirements drive the subsequent design activity. The design includes the identification of process activities, the definition of their order, the assignment of resources to activities and the definition of the organization structure. These different aspects of process design are typically formalized as a business process model [93, 139, 381, 9]. This model can be tested in a simulation if it meets the design requirements.[2]

Implementation: The process model is then taken as input for implementation. In this phase, the infrastructure for the business process is set up. This includes training of staff, provision of a dedicated work infrastructure or the technical implementation and configuration of software. If the process execution is to be supported by dedicated information systems, the process model is used as a blueprint for the implementation.

Enactment: As soon as the implementation is completed, the actual enactment of the process can begin. In this phase the dedicated infrastructure is used to handle individual cases covered by the business process. The enactment produces information such as consumption of time, resources and materials for each handled case. This data can be used as input for two subsequent activities: monitoring and evaluation.

Monitoring is a continuous activity that is performed with respect to each individual case. Depending on process metrics, for instance maximum waiting time for a certain process activity, monitoring triggers respective counteractions if such a metric indicates a problematic situation.

Evaluation, on the other hand, considers case data on an aggregated level. The performance results are compared with the original requirements and sources of further improvement are discussed. Evaluation thus leads to new requirements that are taken as input in the next turn of the business process management life cycle.

The business process management life cycle reveals that business process models play an important role in the design, implementation and enactment phases, especially when information systems support the process enactment. As a result, they are valuable resources for continuous process improvement, quality management, compliance management, knowledge management, end-user training, ERP system selection, and software implementation [165, 93, 95, 159, 359]. Current market research supports this relevance: approximately 90% of participating companies in a survey conducted or considered business process modeling [333]. This trend is partially motivated by new legislation including the Basel II recommendations on banking laws

---

[2] Note that zur Muehlen considers simulation as a separate activity related to evaluation [310, p.86] but this view neglects the fact that simulation is always done to evaluate different design alternatives.

and regulations and the Sarbanes-Oxley Act in the United States. In practice, software tools play a decisive role in performing the various management activities in an efficient and effective manner. There are several commercial and academic tools which support different life cycle activities (see [9, Ch.5]). The Workflow Management Coalition has proposed 5 interfaces in a reference model in order to link these tools [184]. The availability of tools is critical to the modeling of business processes in a correct and consistent way.

1.3 Definition of Business Process Modeling

Before defining business process modeling, we need to discuss the term "modeling" in a more general manner. *Nordsieck* has emphasized that "the utilization of symbols enables the model not only to replace or to complement natural language for the representation of complex matters, but to reveal the notion of the subject matter often in a more comprehensive way as with any other form of representation" [321, p.3]. The most important features of a model are brevity, clarity, precision and its graphic quality [321, p.3]. *Stachowiak* defines a model as the result of a simplifying mapping from reality that serves a specific purpose [414]. According to this definition, there are three important qualities a model should possess: First, a mapping that establishes a representation of natural or artificial originals that can be models itself; second, only those attributes of the original that are considered relevant are mapped to the model while the rest are skipped. Therefore, the model provides an abstraction in terms of a homomorphism in a mathematical sense [232]. Finally, the model is used by the modeler in place of the original at a certain point in time and for a certain purpose. This means that a model always involves pragmatics [343].

A weakness of *Stachowiak*'s concept of a model is that it implies an epistemological position of positivism.[3] This is criticized in [388], where the authors propose an alternative position based on insights from critical realism and constructivism.[4] This position regards a model as a "result of a construct done by a modeler" [388, p.243]. As such, it is heavily influenced by the subjective perception of the modeler. This makes modeling a non-deterministic task (see [293]) that requires standards in order to achieve a certain level of inter-subjectivity. The Guidelines of Modeling (GoM) [50, 388, 51] define principles that serve this standardization purpose. They are applicable for either epistemological positions or positivism and constructivism because both the choice for a certain homomorphism (positivist position) and the perception of the modeler (constructivist position) introduce subjective elements.

The Guidelines of Modeling (GoM) [50, 388] include six particular principles for achieving inter-subjectivity of models. The first three define necessary preconditions for the quality of models (correctness, relevance, and economic efficiency) and the other three are optional (clarity, comparability, and systematic design).

---

[3] Positivism is the philosophical theory that establishes sensual experience as the single object of human knowledge.

[4] In contrast to positivism, constructivism regards all knowledge as constructed. Therefore, there is nothing like objective knowledge or reality.

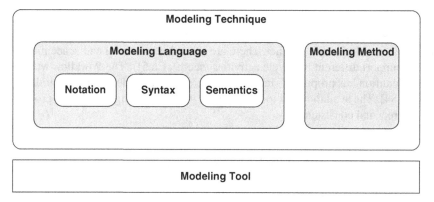

Figure 1.2. Concepts of a modeling technique

Correctness: A model must be syntactically correct. This requirement demands the usage of allowed modeling primitives and their combination according to pre-defined rules. A model must also be semantically correct. It must, therefore, be formally correct and consistent with (the perception of) the real world.

Relevance: This criterion demands that only interesting parts of the universe of discourse are reflected in the model. It is, therefore, related to the notion of completeness as proposed in [46].

Economic Efficiency: This guideline introduces a trade-off between benefits and costs of putting the other criteria into practice. For example, semantic correctness might be neglected to a certain extent if achieving it is prohibitively expensive.

Clarity: This is a highly subjective guideline demanding that the model must be understood by the model user. It is primarily related to layout conventions or the complexity of the model.

Comparability demands consistent utilization of a set of guidelines in a modeling project. It refers to naming conventions amongst other things.

Systematic Design: This guideline demands a clear separation between models in different views (e.g. statical aspects and behavioral aspects) and defined mechanisms to integrate them.

Following this line of argument, the explicit definition of a modeling technique appears to be a useful means to address several of these guidelines. A *modeling technique* consists of two interrelated parts: a modeling language and a modeling method[5] (see Figure 1.2). The *modeling language* consists of three parts: syntax, semantics and, optionally, at least one notation. The *syntax* provides a set of constructs and a set of rules how these constructs can be combined. A synonym is

---

[5] Several authors use heterogeneous terminology to refer to modeling techniques. Our concept of a modeling language is similar to grammar in [448, 449, 450] who also use the term method with the same meaning. In [207], a modeling method is called "procedure" while the term "method" is used to define a composition of modeling technique plus related algorithms.

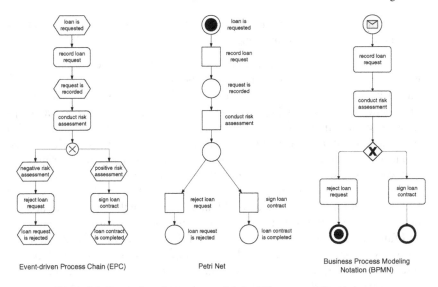

Figure 1.3. Examples of process models in different modeling languages

modeling grammar [448, 449, 450]. *Semantics* bind the constructs defined in the syntax to a meaning. This can be done in a mathematical way, for example by using formal ontologies or operational semantics. The *notation* defines a set of graphical symbols that are utilized for the visualization of models [207]. As an example, Figure 1.3 shows the same loan approval business process in different modeling notations: namely Event-driven Process Chains (EPCs), Petri nets and Business Process Modeling Notation (BPMN). The *modeling method* defines procedures by which a modeling language can be used [450]. The result of applying the modeling method is a model that complies with a specific modeling language[6]. Consider entity-relationship diagrams (ERDs) as defined in [77]. Since they define a modeling language and a respective modeling method, ERDs are a modeling technique. Entities and Relationships are syntax elements of its language. They are used to capture certain semantics of a universe of discourse. The notation represents entities as rectangles and relationships as arcs connecting such rectangles and carrying a diamond in the middle. Respective procedures, like looking for nouns and verbs in documents, define the modeling method. In practice, *modeling tools* are of crucial importance for the application of a modeling technique: they support the specification of models, the redundancy controlled administration of models, multi-user collaboration and model reuse via interfaces to other tools [359]. A recent comparison of business process modeling tools is reported in [25].

There are different approaches to providing a foundation for the correctness and relevance of what is to be put into a process model (see [398]). The following paragraph sketches ontology, speech act theory, the workflow patterns, and metamodeling as four alternative foundations. These four approaches are chosen as examples for

---

[6] Instead of model, *Wand and Weber* use the term "script" (cf. [448, 449, 450]).

their wide-spread application in information systems research. Further foundations
and evaluation techniques for modeling languages are discussed in [398].

- *Ontology* is the study of being. It seeks to describe what is in the world in terms of
  entities, categories and relationships. It is a prominent sub-discipline of philosophy. *Wand and Weber* were among the first to adopt ontology for a foundation of
  information systems modeling (see [448, 449]). They make two basic assumptions: as information systems reflect what is in the real world they should also
  be modelled with a language that is capable of representing real-world entities;
  and that the ontology proposed by *Bunge* [66] is a useful basis for describing the
  real world. The so-called *Bunge-Wand-Weber* (BWW) model proposed by *Wand
  and Weber* includes a set of representation constructs that are deemed necessary
  and sufficient for describing real-world things including their properties and behavior. These constructs should thus be available for modeling a specific domain
  and fulfilling certain consistency criteria [449]. An overview of applications of
  the BWW model is given in [345]. For examples of other ontological models
  refer to [450, 158]. Recently, ontology languages such as OWL [263] have become popular for defining domain ontologies to be used as a component of the
  semantic web [54].
- *Speech act theory* is a philosophy of language first proposed by *Austin* [34] and
  subsequently refined by *Searle* [390]. It emphasizes that language is not only
  used to make statements about the world that are true or false but also utilized to
  do something. A priest, for example, performs a speech act when he pronounces
  a couple husband and wife. The language action perspective has extended this
  view after determining that speech acts do not appear in isolation, but that they
  are frequently part of a larger conversation [455]. *Johannesson* uses this insight to
  provide a foundation for information systems modeling based on conversations
  built from speech acts [200]. Coming from the identification of such conversations, *Johannesson* derives consistent structural and behavioral models. Both the
  foundations in ontology and in speech act theory have in common that they imply
  two levels of modeling: a general level that is based on abstract entities that the
  respective theory or philosophy identifies, and a concrete level where the modeler
  identifies instances of these abstract entities in his modeling domain.
- *Workflow Patterns:* Business process models capture different aspects such as
  activities, control flow, organizational entities, functional goals and information
  consumed and generated by activities [93, 461, 107, 208]. The heterogeneity
  of business process modeling languages (see [292]) has motivated research into
  generic patterns that need to be described in a model. The work by *Van der Aalst,
  Ter Hofstede, et al.* identifies different patterns for control flow [12, 368], data
  [371], resources [370], exception handling [369] and instantiation [98]. These
  patterns have been used in various evaluations of process modeling languages.
  For an overview refer to [367].
- *Metamodeling* frees modeling from philosophical assumptions by extending the
  subject of the modeling process to the general level. The philosophical theory
  of this level, such as an ontology, is replaced by a metamodel. The difference to

an ontological foundation is that a metamodel does not claim any epistemologi-cal validity. Essentially, the metamodel identifies the abstract entities that can be used in the process of designing models. In other words, the metamodel repre-sents the modeling language (see [31, 207, 232]). The flexibility gained from this meta-principle comes at the cost of relativism; as a metamodel is meta relative to a model, it is a model itself. Therefore a metamodel can also be defined for the metamodel and it is called metametamodel. This regression can be continued ad infinitum without ever reaching an epistemological ground.[7] Most modeling frameworks define three or four modeling levels (see UML's Meta Object Fa-cility [329], CASE Data Interchange Format (CDIF) [129] or Graph Exchange Language (GXL) [456]). The definition of a modeling language based on a meta-model is more often used than the explicit reference to a philosophical position. Examples of metamodeling can be found in [332, 331, 129, 378, 380, 32, 31, 33]. Several tools like MetaEdit [410, 212], Protegé [323] or ADONIS [203] sup-port metamodeling in such a way that modeling languages can be easily defined by the user. For the application of the meta principle in other contexts refer to [315, 419].

The meta-hierarchy provides a means to distinguish different kinds of models. A model can never be a metamodel by itself, however; it can only be relative to the model for which it defines the modeling language. Models can also be distin-guished depending on the mapping mechanism [419, p.21]: *Non-linguistic* models capture some real-world aspects as material artifacts or as pictures. *Linguistic* mod-els can be representational, verbal, logistic or mathematical. Focusing on business administration, *Kosiol* distinguishes descriptive models, explanatory models and de-cision models [226]. Descriptive models capture objects of a certain area of discourse and represent them in a structured way. Beyond that, explanatory models define de-pendency relationships between nomological hypotheses. These serve as empirically valid general laws to explain real-world phenomena. Finally, decision models sup-port the deduction of actions: this involves the availability of a description model to formalize the setting of the decision, a set of goals that constraint the design situation and a set of decision parameters.

The terms *business process model*, *business process modeling language*, and *business process modeling* can thus be defined as follows:

- A *business process model* is the result of mapping a business process. This busi-ness process can be either a real-world business process as perceived by a mod-eler or a conceptualized business process.
- *Business process modeling* is the human activity of creating a business process model. Business process modeling involves an abstraction from the real-world business process because it serves a certain modeling purpose. Therefore, only those aspects relevant to the modeling purpose are included in the process model.

---

[7] This negation of a theoretical foundation of a modeling language has some similarities with approaches that emphasize that models are not mappings from the real world but products of negotiations between different stakeholders, as in [181, 402].

- *Business process modeling languages* guide the procedure of business process modeling by offering a predefined set of elements and relationships for business processes. A business process modeling language can be specified using a meta-model. In conjunction with a respective method, it establishes a business process modeling technique.

This definition requires some explanation. In contrast to [414], it does not claim that the business process model is an abstraction and serves a purpose. These attributions involve some problems about whether a model always has to be abstract or to serve a purpose. Instead, the procedure of business process modeling is characterized in such a way that it is guided by abstraction and a purpose in mind. This is important as a model is not just a "representation of a real-world system" (as *Wand and Weber* put it [448, p.123]), but a design artifact in the sense of *Hevner et al.* [180] that itself becomes part of the real world as soon as it is created. Beyond this, business process models can be characterized as linguistic models that are mainly representational and mathematical. The representational aspect points to the visual notation of a business process modeling language, while the mathematical notion refers to the formal syntax and semantics. In practice, business process models are often used for documentation purposes [96]. They can, therefore, be regarded as descriptive models for organization and information systems engineers. They also serve as explanatory and decision models for the people who are involved in the actual processing of cases. In this book, the focus is on the descriptive nature of business process models.

1.4 Business Process Modeling and Errors

It is a fundamental insight of software engineering that design errors should be detected as early as possible (see [60, 450, 306]). The later that errors are detected, the more work must be redone and the more design effort has been wasted. This also holds for the consecutive steps of analysis, design, and implementation in the business process management life cycle (see [360, 361, 336]). In the design phase, process models are typically created with semi-formal business process modeling languages while formal executable models are needed for the implementation. This problem is often referred to as the gap between business process design and implementation phase (see [312]). Therefore, the Guidelines of Process Modeling stress correctness as the most important quality attribute of business process models [51].

In order to provide a better understanding of potential errors in business process models, it is proposed to adapt the information modeling process as identified by *Frederiks and Van der Weide* [132]. This process can also serve as a framework for discussing business process modeling in the analysis and design phase of the business process management life cycle. Furthermore, it covers several steps to provide quality assurance in the modeling phase which is of paramount importance for the success of modeling projects (see [360, 361]). Figure 1.4 gives a business process modeling process mainly inspired by [132] and consisting of eight steps. In accordance with *Van Hee et al.* [174], it is proposed to first verify the process model (Step 6) before validating it (Step 7-8).

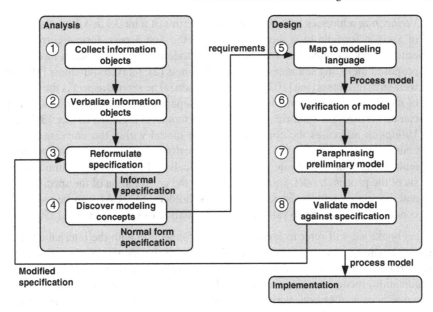

Figure 1.4. Business process modeling process in detail, adapted from [132].

The business process modeling process starts with collecting information objects relevant to the domain (*Step 1*). Such information objects include documents, diagrams, pictures and interview recordings. In *Step 2*, these different inputs are verbalized to text that serves as a unifying format. This text is rearranged according to some general guideline of how to express facts (*Step 3*) yielding an informal specification. The following step (*Step 4*) takes this informal specification as a basis to discover modeling concepts from and to produce a normalized specification. This normal form specification is then mapped to constructs of the process modeling language (*Step 5*) in order to create a business process model. These models have to be verified for internal correctness (*Step 6*) before they can be translated back to natural language (*Step 7*) in order to validate them against the specification (*Step 8*). In Steps 6-8 the order of activities follows the proposal of *Van Hee et al.* [174]. It is a good idea to first verify the internal correctness of a model before validating it against the specification, as this prevents incorrect models from being unnecessarily validated.

The business process modeling process points to two categories of potential errors based on the distinction of verification and validation. This distinction follows the terminology of the Petri nets community (see *Valmari* [436, pp.444]), the conceptual modeling community (see *Hoppenbrouwers, Proper, and Van der Weide* [187]) and the software engineering community (see *Boehm* [59], *Sommerville* [413]). Different terms for similar concepts are used in *Soffer and Wand* [412].

- *Verification* addresses both the general properties of a model and the satisfaction of a given formula by a model. Related to the first aspect, formal correctness criteria play an important role in process modeling. Several criteria have been proposed including soundness for Workflow nets [2], relaxed soundness [101] or well-structuredness (see [102] for a comparison). The second aspect is the subject of model checking and involves issues like separation of duty constraints, which can be verified, for example, by using linear temporal logic (LTL) (see [337]).
- *Validation* addresses the consistency of the model within the universe of discourse. As it is an external correctness criterion, it is more difficult and more ambiguous to decide. While verification typically relies on an algorithmic analysis of the process model, validation requires the consultation of the specification and discussion with business process stakeholders. SEQUAL can be used as a conceptual framework to validate different quality aspects of a model [250, 228].

In this book, we will refer to *formal errors* in connection with the internal correctness of business process models. Formal errors can be identified via verification. Furthermore, we use the term *inconsistencies* to refer to a mismatch of model and specification. Inconsistencies are identified by validation. Generally speaking, *error detection* is related to both verification and validation [436, p.445]. We also focus on *error detection related to verification* and, in particular, to the question which combination of model elements affects the verification of a correctness criterion for a business process model.

While there has been empirical work on different aspects of conceptual modeling [399, 39, 256, 138], little such work has been conducted on formal errors of business process models in practice. One reason for this is that large repositories of business process models capture specific and valuable real-world business knowledge of industrial or consulting companies. Confidentiality concerns present a serious problem for academia since practical modeling experience can hardly be reflected in a purely theoretical way. *Thomas* [422] calls this the "dilemma" of modeling research. One case of a model that is, at least partially, publicly available is the SAP Reference Model. It has been described in [92, 211] and is referred to in many research papers (see [127, 235, 281, 362, 427]). The extensive database of this reference model contains almost 10,000 sub-models, 604 of them being non-trivial EPCs [92, 211]. The verification of these EPC models has shown that there are several formal errors in the models (see [473, 109, 110, 275]). In [275] the authors identify a lower bound for the number of errors of 34 (5.6%) using the relaxed soundness criterion. In another survey, *Gruhn and Laue* [154] analyze a collection of 285 EPCs mainly taken from master theses and scientific publications. From these 285 models 30% had trivial errors and another 7% had non-trivial errors. These first contributions highlight that errors are indeed an issue in business process models.

1.5 Summary

In this chapter, we discussed the backgrounds of business process management and defined important terms related to it. We also sketched the importance of business process modeling for the business process management life cycle. Since process models are created in the early design phase, they should be free from errors in order to avoid expensive rework and iterations in subsequent phases. In the following chapters, we concentrate on Event-driven Process Chains (EPCs) which are frequently used for business process modeling. Based on a formal semantics definition, we identify verification techniques to detect errors.

2

Event-Driven Process Chains (EPC)

This chapter provides a comprehensive overview of Event-driven Process Chains (EPCs) and introduces a novel definition of EPC semantics. EPCs became popular in the 1990s as a conceptual business process modeling language in the context of reference modeling. Reference modeling refers to the documentation of generic business operations in a model such as service processes in the telecommunications sector, for example. It is claimed that reference models can be reused and adapted as best-practice recommendations in individual companies (see [230, 168, 229, 131, 400, 401, 446, 127, 362, 126]). The roots of reference modeling can be traced back to the Kölner Integrationsmodell (KIM) [146, 147] that was developed in the 1960s and 1970s. In the 1990s, the Institute of Information Systems (IWi) in Saarbrücken worked on a project with SAP to define a suitable business process modeling language to document the processes of the SAP R/3 enterprise resource planning system. There were two results from this joint effort: the definition of EPCs [210] and the documentation of the SAP system in the SAP Reference Model (see [92, 211]). The extensive database of this reference model contains almost 10,000 sub-models: 604 of them non-trivial EPC business process models. The SAP Reference model had a huge impact with several researchers referring to it in their publications (see [473, 235, 127, 362, 281, 427, 415]) as well as motivating the creation of EPC reference models in further domains including computer integrated manufacturing [377, 379], logistics [229] or retail [52]. The wide-spread application of EPCs in business process modeling theory and practice is supported by their coverage in seminal text books for business process management and information systems in general (see [378, 380, 49, 384, 167, 240]). EPCs are frequently used in practice due to a high user acceptance [376] and extensive tool support. Some examples of tools that support EPCs are *ARIS Toolset* by IDS Scheer AG, *AENEIS* by ATOSS Software AG, *ADONIS* by BOC GmbH, *Visio* by Microsoft Corp., *Nautilus* by Gedilan Consulting GmbH, and *Bonapart* by Pikos GmbH. In order to facilitate the interchange of EPC business process models between these tools, there is a tool neutral interchange format called EPC Markup Language (EPML) [283, 285, 286, 287, 289, 290, 291].

The remainder of this chapter is structured as follows: Section 2.1 gives a brief, informal description of EPC syntax and semantics and introduces the notation by the help of an example. Section 2.2 discusses several approaches to EPC syntax formalization and consolidates them in one definition. Section 2.3 presents various extensions that were proposed for EPCs. Section 2.4 covers different approaches to formal semantics of EPCs and introduces the semantics definition that is used later in this book. A respective implementation of these semantics in ProM is also described. Finally in Section 2.5, EPCs are compared to other business process modeling languages. The chapter concludes with a summary in Section 2.6.

2.1 EPC Notation

The Event-driven Process Chain (EPC) is a business process modeling language for the representation of temporal and logical dependencies of activities in a business process (see [210]). It is utilized by Scheer [378, 380, 384] in the Architecture of Integrated Information Systems (ARIS) as the central method for the conceptual integration of the functional, organizational, data and output perspective in information systems design. EPCs offer *function type* elements to capture activities of a process and *event type* elements describing pre-conditions and post-conditions of functions. Some EPC definitions also include *process interface type* elements. A process interface is a syntax element that links two consecutive EPCs. At the bottom of the first EPC, a process interface points to the second EPC while at the beginning of the second there is a process interface representing the preceding EPC. Syntactically, it is treated like a function since it represents a subsequent process that can be regarded as a business activity. There are three kinds of *connector types* including AND (symbol $\wedge$), OR (symbol $\vee$) and XOR (symbol $\times$) for the definition of complex routing rules. Connectors have either multiple incoming and one outgoing arc (join connectors) or one incoming and multiple outgoing arcs (split connectors). As a syntax rule, functions and events have to alternate either directly or indirectly when they are linked via one or more connectors. OR- and XOR-splits after events are not allowed since events cannot make decisions. Control flow arcs are used to link these elements.

The informal (or intended) semantics of an EPC can be described as follows: The AND-split activates all subsequent branches in concurrency; the XOR-split represents a choice between one of several alternative branches; the OR-split triggers one, two or up to all of multiple branches based on conditions. In both cases of the XOR- and OR-split, the activation conditions are given in events subsequent to the connector. Accordingly, splits from an event to multiple functions are forbidden with XOR and OR as the activation conditions do not become clear in the model. The AND-join waits for all incoming branches to complete and then propagates control to the subsequent EPC element. The XOR-join merges alternative branches. The OR-join synchronizes all active incoming branches. This feature is called non-locality since the state of all transitive predecessor nodes is considered.

Figure 2.1 shows an EPC model for a loan request process as described in *Nüttgens and Rump* [325]. The start event *loan is requested* signals the start of the process and the precondition to execute the *record loan request* function. After the post-condition *request is recorded*, the process continues with the function *conduct*

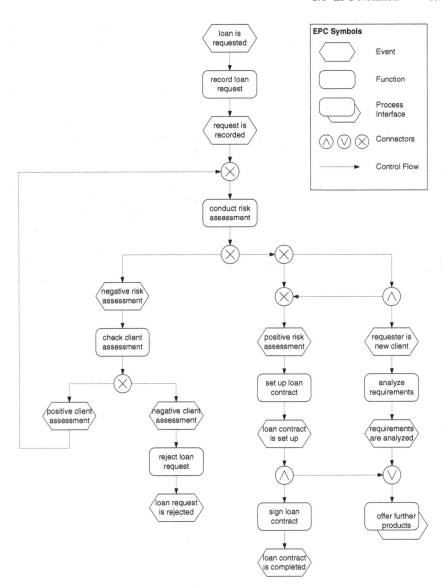

Figure 2.1. EPC for a loan request process [325]

risk assessment after the XOR-join connector. The subsequent XOR-split connector indicates a decision. In case of a *negative risk assessment*, the function *check client assessment* is performed. The following second XOR-split marks another decision: in case of a *negative client assessment* the process ends with a rejection of the loan request; in case of a *positive client assessment* the *conduct risk assessment* function is executed a second time under consideration of the positive client assessment. If the risk assessment is not negative, there is another decision point to distinguish new clients and existing clients. In case of an existing client, the *set up loan contract* function is conducted. After that, the AND-split indicates that two activities have to be executed: the *sign loan contract* function and the *offer further products* subsequent process (represented by a process interface). If the client is new, the *analyze requirements* function has to be performed in addition to setting up the loan contract. The OR-join waits for both functions to be completed if necessary. If the *analyze requirements* is not executed, it continues with the subprocess immediately. The *offer further products* process interface basically triggers a subsequent process (see Figure 2.2) for repeatedly offering products until the offering process is completed.

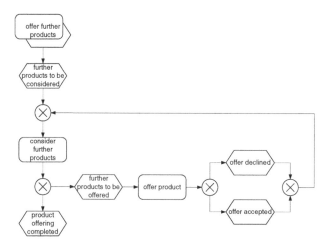

Figure 2.2. EPC for offering further products

2.2 EPC Syntax

There is not just one but several approaches towards the formalization of EPC syntax. This is due to the original EPC paper introducing them in an informal way (see [210]). This section gives a historical overview of EPC syntax definitions and joins them into one definition. Please note that we first discuss only standard control flow elements. Extensions are presented in Section 2.3.

2.2.1 Approaches to EPC Syntax Formalization

In *Langner, Schneider, and Wehler* [236, 238], the authors provide a graph-based formalization of EPC syntax distinguishing four types of nodes: function, event, connector and process interface. Arcs connect elements of these four node types in such a way that the EPC is a simple, directed and coherent graph. The authors define the following constraints: There are no arcs between elements of the same type; the cardinality of predecessor and successor sets is less or exactly one for events and exactly one for functions and process interfaces; and the border of the EPC graph consists of event type elements only.

Keller and Teufel [211, pp.158] provide a formal definition of EPCs in their book on the SAP Reference Model. Beyond the four element types (function, event, process interface and connector) they introduce a concept of model hierarchy depending on hierarchical (or hierarchically ranked) functions. Those hierarchical functions represent a call to a subprocess. The authors also identify additional constraints for the EPC graph: connections between connectors must be acyclic and EPCs have at least three nodes: one start event, one end event and one function.

The syntax formalization by *Van der Aalst* [4] defines the notion of a path in order to distinguish event-function connectors and function-event connectors. If a connector c is on a path of several consecutive connectors, it is an event-function connector if all paths to it via other connectors start with events and all paths from it via other connectors lead to functions. Function-event connectors are defined analogously. It is an additional constraint that each connector is either an event-function or a function-event connector.

In the doctoral thesis of *Rump* [366, pp.79], the EPC syntax definition is separated into two parts: a flat EPC schema and a hierarchical EPC schema. The definition of a flat EPC schema essentially reflects the element types and properties as described above. In addition, *Rump* introduces an initial marking of an EPC. This initial marking must be a subset of the power set of all start events and each start event must be included in at least one initial marking. A hierarchical EPC schema contains one or more flat EPC schemas and a hierarchy relation that maps hierarchical functions and process interfaces to EPCs. The hierarchy relation must establish an acyclic graph. A similar syntax definition is presented in [325].

The alternation between events and functions with several connectors in between was first enforced by the definition of *Van der Aalst*, yet all paths between the elements have to be considered. *Mendling and Nüttgens* provide a syntax definition based on two arc types: event-function arcs and function-event arcs [284]. As a constraint, event-function arcs must have either events or event-function connectors as source nodes and functions or event-function connectors as target nodes. A similar constraint must hold for function-event arcs. An advantage of this definition is that EPC syntax validation does not require path expansion for each connector in a chain.

While the different syntax formalizations cover an extensive set of properties, there is one syntax problem which is not addressed. Figure 2.3 shows an EPC that has two undesirable properties. First, there is no path from a start node to reach the nodes $e1$, $f1$, and $c1$. There is also no path from the nodes $e2$, $f2$, and $c4$ to an end

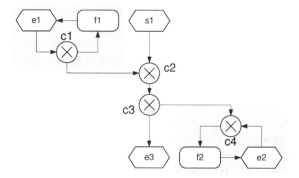

Figure 2.3. An EPC with nodes that have no path from a start event and that have no path to an end event

node. Since such a structure is not meaningful, we will also require that each node of an EPC must be on a path from a start to an end node.

Table 2.1 summarizes the presented approaches towards EPC syntax formalization. Further work related to EPC syntax is listed in [325]. The following section provides a formal EPC syntax definition that consolidates the different approaches.

Table 2.1. Overview of approaches to EPC syntax formalization

	[236]	[211]	[4]	[366]	[284]
Cardinality Constraints	+	+	+	+	+
Fnct.-Event Alternation	+/-	+/-	+	+	+
No Connector cycles	-	+	-	+	+
Hierarchy	-	+	-	+	+
No Hierarchy cycles	-	-	-	+	+
Initial Marking	-	-	-	+	+
Nodes on start-end-path	-	-	-	-	-

2.2.2 Formal Syntax Definition of Flat EPCs

The subsequent syntax definition of flat EPCs essentially follows the presentation in [325] and [284]. If it is clear from the context that a flat EPC is discussed, the term EPC will be used instead for brevity. Please note that an initial marking as proposed in [366, 325] is not included in the syntax definition, but discussed in the context of EPC semantics in Section 2.4.4.

Definition 2.1 (Flat EPC). *A flat $EPC = (E, F, P, C, l, A)$ consists of four pairwise disjoint and finite sets E, F, C, P, a mapping $l : C \rightarrow \{and, or, xor\}$, and a binary relation $A \subseteq (E \cup F \cup P \cup C) \times (E \cup F \cup P \cup C)$ such that*

- *An element of E is called* event. $E \neq \emptyset$.
- *An element of F is called* function. $F \neq \emptyset$.
- *An element of P is called* process interface.
- *An element of C is called* connector.
- *The mapping l specifies the type of a connector $c \in C$ as and, or, or xor.*
- *A defines the control flow as a coherent, directed graph. An element of A is called* an arc. *An element of the union $N = E \cup F \cup P \cup C$ is called a* node.

In order to allow for a more concise characterization of EPCs, notations are introduced for preset and postset nodes, incoming and outgoing arcs, paths, transitive closure, corona, and several subsets.

Definition 2.2 (Preset and Postset of Nodes). *Let N be a set of nodes and $A \subseteq N \times N$ a binary relation over N defining the arcs. For each node $n \in N$, we define $\bullet n = \{x \in N | (x, n) \in A\}$ as its* preset, *and $n\bullet = \{x \in N | (n, x) \in A\}$ as its* postset.

Definition 2.3 (Incoming and Outgoing Arcs). *Let N be a set of nodes and $A \subseteq N \times N$ a binary relation over N defining the arcs. For each node $n \in N$, we define the set of incoming arcs $n_{in} = \{(x, n) | x \in N \wedge (x, n) \in A\}$, and the set of outgoing arcs $n_{out} = \{(n, y) | y \in N \wedge (n, y) \in A\}$.*

Definition 2.4 (Paths and Connector Chains). *Let $EPC = (E, F, P, C, l, A)$ be a flat EPC and $a, b \in N$ be two of its nodes. A path $a \hookrightarrow b$ refers to the existence of a sequence of EPC nodes $n_1, \dots, n_k \in N$ with $a = n_1$ and $b = n_k$ such that for all $i \in 1, \dots, k$ holds: $(n_1, n_2), \dots, (n_i, n_{i+1}), \dots, (n_{k-1}, n_k) \in A$. This includes the empty path of length zero, i.e., for any node $a : a \hookrightarrow a$. If $a \neq b \in N$ and $n_2, \dots, n_{k-1} \in C$, the path $a \overset{c}{\hookrightarrow} b$ is called connector chain. This includes the empty connector chain, i.e., $a \overset{c}{\hookrightarrow} b$ if $(a, b) \in A$. The transitive closure A^* contains (n_1, n_2) if there is a non-empty path from n_1 to n_2, i.e., there is a a non-empty set of arcs of A leading from n_1 to n_2. For each node $n \in N$, we define its transitive preset $*n = \{x \in N | (x, n) \in A^*\}$, and its transitive postset $n* = \{x \in N | (n, x) \in A^*\}$.*

Definition 2.5 (Upper Corona, Lower Corona). *Let $EPC = (E, F, P, C, l, A)$ be a flat EPC and N its set of nodes. Then its upper corona is defined as $\overset{c}{*}n = \{v \in (E \cup F \cup P) | v \overset{c}{\hookrightarrow} n\}$ for some node $n \in N$. It includes those non-connector nodes of the transitive preset that reach n via a connector chain. In analogy, its lower corona is defined as $n\overset{c}{*} = \{w \in (E \cup F \cup P) | n \overset{c}{\hookrightarrow} w\}$.*

Definition 2.6 (Subsets). *For an $EPC = (E, F, P, C, l, A)$, we define the following subsets of its nodes and arcs:*

- *$E_s = \{e \in E \mid |\bullet e| = 0 \wedge |e\bullet| = 1\}$ being the set of start events,*
  $E_{int} = \{e \in E \mid |\bullet e| = 1 \wedge |e\bullet| = 1\}$ being the set of intermediate events, and
  $E_e = \{e \in E \mid |\bullet e| = 1 \wedge e\bullet| = 0\}$ being the set of end events.
- *$P_s = \{p \in P \mid |\bullet p| = 0 \wedge |p\bullet| = 1\}$ being the set of start process interfaces,*
  $P_e = \{p \in P \mid |\bullet p| = 1 \wedge |p\bullet| = 0\}$ being the set of end process interfaces.

- $J = \{c \in C \mid |{\bullet}c| > 1 \text{ and } |c{\bullet}| = 1\}$ *as the set of join- and*
  $S = \{c \in C \mid |{\bullet}c| = 1 \text{ and } |c{\bullet}| > 1\}$ *as the set of split-connectors.*
- $C_{and} = \{c \in C \mid l(c) = and\}$ *being the set of and-connectors,*
  $C_{xor} = \{c \in C \mid l(c) = xor\}$ *being the set of xor-connectors, and*
  $C_{or} = \{c \in C \mid l(c) = or\}$ *being the set of or-connectors.*
- $J_{and} = \{c \in J \mid l(c) = and\}$ *being the set of and-join connectors,*
  $J_{xor} = \{c \in J \mid l(c) = xor\}$ *being the set of xor-join connectors,*
  $J_{or} = \{c \in J \mid l(c) = or\}$ *being the set of or-join connectors,*
- $S_{and} = \{c \in S \mid l(c) = and\}$ *being the set of and-split connectors,*
  $S_{xor} = \{c \in S \mid l(c) = xor\}$ *being the set of xor-split connectors, and*
  $S_{or} = \{c \in S \mid l(c) = or\}$ *being the set of or-split connectors.*
- $C_{EF} = \{c \in C \mid \overset{c}{*}c \subseteq E \wedge c\overset{c}{*} \subseteq (F \cup P)\}$ *as the set of event-function connectors (ef-connectors) and*
  $C_{FE} = \{c \in C \mid \overset{c}{*}c \subseteq (F \cup P) \wedge c\overset{c}{*} \subseteq E\}$ *as the set of function-event connectors (fe-connectors).*
- $A_{EF} = A \cap ((E \cup C_{EF}) \times (F \cup P \cup C_{EF}))$ *as the set of event-function arcs,*
  $A_{FE} = A \cap ((F \cup P \cup C_{FE}) \times (E \cup C_{FE}))$ *as the set of function-event arcs.*
- $A_s = \{(x,y) \in A \mid x \in E_s\}$ *as the set of start-arcs,*
  $A_{int} = \{(x,y) \in A \mid x \notin E_s \wedge y \notin E_e\}$ *as the set of intermediate-arcs, and*
  $A_e = \{(x,y) \in A \mid y \in E_e\}$ *as the set of end-arcs.*

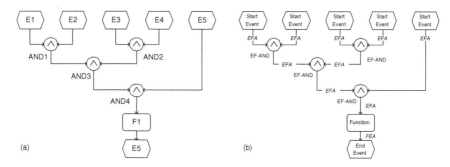

Figure 2.4. An EPC (a) with labelled nodes and (b) its nodes related to the subsets of Definition 2.6.

Figure 2.4 illustrates the different subsets of an EPC. Consider the connector $AND3$. This is an event-function connector (labelled as *EF-AND*) since its upper corona (those non-connector nodes from which there is a connector chain to $AND3$) contains only events and its lower corona only contains a function. The arc from $AND1$ to $AND3$ is an event-function arc (labelled as *EFA*) since it connects two event-function connectors. Note that arcs from events to event-function connectors and arcs from event-function connectors to functions are also event-function arcs.

We summarize the EPC syntax requirements as follows.

Definition 2.7 (Syntactically Correct EPC). *An* $EPC = (E, F, P, C, l, A)$ *is called syntactically correct, if it fulfills the requirements:*

1. *EPC is a simple, directed, coherent, and antisymmetric graph such that* $\forall n \in N : \exists e_1 \in E_s, e_2 \in E_e$ *such that* $e_1 \hookrightarrow n \hookrightarrow e_e$.
2. *There are no connector cycles, i.e.* $\forall a, b \in C : \text{if } a \neq b \text{ and } a \overset{c}{\hookrightarrow} b, \text{ then } \not\exists b \overset{c}{\hookrightarrow} a$.
3. $|E_s \cup P_s| \geq 1 \wedge |E_e \cup P_e| \geq 1$. *There is at least one start node and one end node in an EPC.*
4. $|F| \geq 1$. *There is at least one function in an EPC.*
5. *Events have at most one incoming and one outgoing arc.*
   $\forall e \in E : |\bullet e| \leq 1 \wedge |e \bullet| \leq 1$.
   This implies that E_s, E_{int}, *and* E_e *partition E.*
6. *Functions have exactly one incoming and one outgoing arc.*
   $\forall f \in F : |\bullet f| = 1 \wedge |f \bullet| = 1$.
7. *Process interfaces have one incoming or one outgoing arc, but not both.*
   $\forall p \in P : (|\bullet p| = 1 \wedge |p \bullet| = 0) \vee (|\bullet p| = 0 \wedge |p \bullet| = 1)$.
   This implies that P_s *and* P_e *partition P.*
8. *Connectors have one incoming and multiple outgoing arcs or multiple incoming and one outgoing arc.* $\forall c \in C : (|\bullet c| = 1 \wedge |c \bullet| > 1) \vee (|\bullet c| > 1 \wedge |c \bullet| = 1)$.
   This implies that J *and* S *partition C.*
9. *Events must have function, process interface, or fe-connector nodes in the preset, and function, process interface, or ef-connector nodes in the postset.*
   $\forall e \in E : \bullet e \subseteq (F \cup P \cup C_{FE}) \wedge e \bullet \subseteq (F \cup P \cup C_{EF})$.
10. *Functions must have events or ef-connectors in the preset and events or fe-connectors in the postset.*
    $\forall f \in F : \bullet f \subseteq (E \cup C_{EF}) \wedge f \bullet \subseteq (E \cup C_{FE})$.
11. *Process interfaces are connected to events only.*
    $\forall p \in P : \bullet p \subseteq E \wedge p \bullet \subseteq E$.
12. *Connectors must have either functions, process interfaces, or fe-connectors in the preset and events or fe-connectors in the postset; or events or ef-connectors in the preset and functions, process interfaces, or ef-connectors in the postset.*
    $\forall c \in C : (\bullet c \subseteq (F \cup P \cup C_{FE})) \wedge c \bullet \subseteq (E \cup C_{FE}) \vee$
    $(\bullet c \subseteq (E \cup C_{EF}) \wedge c \bullet \subseteq (F \cup P \cup C_{EF}))$.
13. *Arcs either connect events and ef-connectors with functions, process interfaces, and ef-connectors or functions, process interfaces, and fe-connectors with events and fe-connectors.*
    $\forall a \in A : (a \in (F \cup P \cup C_{FE}) \times (E \cup C_{FE})) \vee (a \in (E \cup C_{EF}) \times (F \cup P \cup C_{EF}))$.

According to this definition, the EPCs of Figures 2.1 and 2.4 are syntactically correct. In Section 3.3, we define reduction rules for EPCs with relaxed syntax requirements. Relaxed syntactical correctness removes the requirements that the EPC graph is simple and antisymmetric (1), that there are no connector cycles (2), that the set of functions is not empty (4), and that functions and events have to alternate (9 to 13). We will later define semantics for this class of EPCs.

Definition 2.8 (Relaxed Syntactically Correct EPC). *An* $EPC = (E, F, P, C, l, A)$ *is called relaxed syntactically correct if it fulfills the following requirements:*

1. *EPC is a directed and coherent graph such that* $\forall n \in N : \exists e_1 \in E_s, e_2 \in E_e$ *such that* $e_1 \hookrightarrow n \hookrightarrow e_2$.
2. $|E_s \cup P_s| \geq 1 \wedge |E_e \cup P_e| \geq 1$. *There is at least one start node and one end node in an EPC.*
3. *Events have at most one incoming and one outgoing arc.*
   $\forall e \in E : |\bullet e| \leq 1 \wedge |e\bullet| \leq 1$.
4. *Functions have exactly one incoming and one outgoing arcs.*
   $\forall f \in F : |\bullet f| = 1 \wedge |f\bullet| = 1$.
5. *Process interfaces have one incoming or one outgoing arcs.*
   $\forall p \in P : (|\bullet p| = 1 \wedge |p\bullet| = 0) \vee (|\bullet p| = 0 \wedge |p\bullet| = 1)$.
6. *Connectors have at least one incoming and one outgoing arc such that*
   $\forall c \in C : (|\bullet c| = 1 \wedge |c\bullet| \geq 1) \vee (|\bullet c| \geq 1 \wedge |c\bullet| = 1)$.

If an EPC is syntactically correct it is also syntactically correct according to a relaxed definition.

2.2.3 Formal Syntax Definition of Hierarchical EPCs

Hierarchical decomposition is a general principle of many system analysis techniques such as data-flow diagrams, object-oriented analysis, or organization charts (see [38, pp.557] or [413, Ch.7]). Hierarchical refinement is also an appropriate technique for the description of complex processes at different levels of granularity [9, p.34]. Such deposition techniques were also defined for EPCs (see [325, 284, 191]). Figure 2.5 gives the example of a return deliveries process that is included in the procurement module of the SAP Reference Model. Within this EPC the *Warehouse* function is hierarchically decomposed to another EPC that is depicted on the right-hand side of the figure. The semantics of such a decomposition mean that the subprocess is started when the hierarchical function is activated. When the subprocess is completed, control is forwarded to the event subsequent to the hierarchical function. We define hierarchical EPCs in a slightly different way compared to [325, 284] in order to achieve a clear separation of the EPC and the hierarchy concept. Still, not all requirements of [325] are met by the example in Figure 2.5 since only the start event of the subprocess matches the pre-event in the parent process and not the end events.

Definition 2.9 (Hierarchical EPC). *A hierarchical EPC $EPC_H = (Z, h)$ consists of a set of EPCs Z and a partial function $h : D \rightharpoonup Z$ on a domain D of decomposed functions and process interfaces such that*

- *Z is a set of EPCs. $N(z)$ refers to the nodes of one individual EPC $z \in Z$. Accordingly, $E(z), E_e(z), E_s(z), F(z), P(z), C(z)$, and $A(z)$ refer to the sets of events, start events, end events, functions, process interfaces, connectors, and arcs of an EPC $z \in Z$. We refer to the union of all functions and process interfaces by $F = \bigcup_{z \in Z} F(z)$ and $P = \bigcup_{z \in Z} P(z)$.*
- *The domain D is a subset of functions and process interfaces of EPCs contained in Z, i.e., $D \subseteq F \cup P$.*

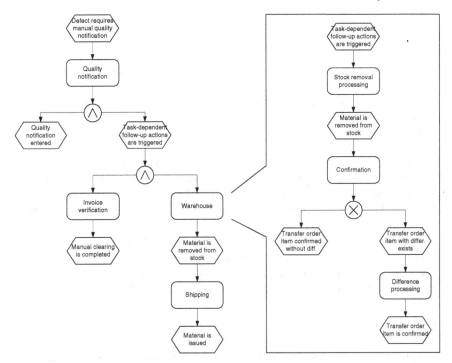

Figure 2.5. The return deliveries process from the SAP Reference Model with a hierarchical decomposition of the Warehouse function.

– *The mapping h specifies a partial function from the domain D to the set of EPCs Z. For a node $d \in D$ such that $h(d) = z$, z is called "subprocess of d" or "process referenced from d".*
– *$G \subseteq (Z \times Z)$ defines the hierarchy graph for a hierarchical EPC.*
  A pair $(z_1, z_2) \in G$ if and only if $\exists d \in (D \cap (F(z_1) \cup P(z_1))) : h(d) = z_2$.

According to [325], a syntactically correct hierarchical EPC must fulfill the following constraints.

Definition 2.10 (Syntactically Correct Hierarchical EPC). *A hierarchical EPC_H $= (Z, h)$ with the domain D of h is called syntactically correct if it fulfills the following constraints:*

1. *All EPCs of Z must be syntactical correct flat EPCs.*
2. *All functions of the domain D map to an EPC of Z.*
   $\forall f \in F : f \in D \Rightarrow h(f) \in Z$.
3. *All process interfaces map to an EPC of Z.*
   $\forall p \in P : p \in D \wedge h(p) \in Z$.
4. *If $f \in D$, then the upper corona of f is equal to the set of start events of $h(f)$, i.e.,*
   $\overset{c}{*}f = E_s(h(f))$.

5. If $f \in D$, then the lower corona of f is equal to the set of end events of $h(f)$, i.e.,
$$f \overset{c}{*} = E_e(h(f)).$$
6. For all $p \in P$ the preset event of p is a subset of the start events of $h(p)$, i.e.,
$$\bullet p \subseteq E_s(h(f)).$$
7. For all $p \in P$ the postset event of p is a subset of the end events of $h(p)$, i.e.,
$$p \bullet \subseteq E_e(h(f)).$$
8. The hierarchy graph G of EPC_H is acyclic.

While constraint 4 is fulfilled in Figure 2.5 (*task-dependent follow-up actions are triggered* precedes the hierarchical function *warehouse* and it is the start event of the subprocess), constraint 5 is not fulfilled since the post-event to *warehouse* differs from the end events of the subprocess. If the constraints are met, however, the hierarchy relation can be used to flatten the hierarchical EPC. Therefore, the event after the *warehouse* function should be renamed to *Transfer order item confirmed with or without difference*. In this case, the relationships between the corona of functions or process interfaces and the start and end events of the referenced EPC can be utilized to merge the EPC with its subprocess as defined in [151, 299].

2.2.4 Formal Syntax Definition of Standard EPCs

Throughout the remainder of this book, we will have a specific focus on a subset of EPCs that we refer to as standard EPCs.

Definition 2.11 (Standard EPC). *A flat* $EPC = (E, F, P, C, l, A)$ *that has an empty set* $P = \emptyset$ *is called standard EPC. For brevity* P *can be omitted in the definition. Accordingly,* $EPC = (E, F, C, l, A)$ *refers to a standard EPC.*

In the following sections and chapters, we will use the terms EPC and standard EPC as synonyms. We also assume EPCs to be relaxed syntactically correct.

2.3 EPC Syntax Extensions

Several variants and extensions were proposed for EPCs and some of them are listed in [375, p.106]. EPC Variants include Real-Time EPC (rEPC) [182], EPC* for workflow execution [473], Object-oriented EPC (oEPC) [383], Modified EPC (modEPC) [349], Agent-oriented EPC (xEPC) [222], Yet Another EPC (yEPC) [279, 281, 282], Nautilus EPCs [224], Semantic EPCs [424, 425], and iEPCs [298, 357]. There is also a plethora of EPCs with non control flow elements (see [378, 380, 384, 358, 387, 254, 382, 231, 61, 385, 47]) that serve as structured annotations to the process model. In the following subsections, we give an overview of EPC extensions for control flow and configurability (see Table 2.2).

Table 2.2. Overview of EPC extensions for control flow and configurability

Category	Name of Concept	Authors
Control Flow	SEQ-Connector	Priemer [341]
	ET-Connector	Rosemann [358]
	OR_1-Connector	Rosemann [358]
	OR-Connector variants	Rittgen [349, 350]
	Fuzzy-Connector	Thomas et al. [426, 21]
	Multiple-Instance-Connector	Rodenhagen [351]
	Empty-Connector	Mendling et al. [279]
	Multiple Instances	Mendling et al. [279]
	Cancellation	Mendling et al. [279]
Configurability	Configurable Function	Rosemann et al. [362]
	Configurable Connector	Rosemann et al. [362]
	Configuration Requirement	Rosemann et al. [362]
	Configuration Guideline	Rosemann et al. [362]
	Configuration Order	Rosemann et al. [362]

2.3.1 Control Flow Extensions

Control flow extensions are defined either to introduce expressive power or to provide a clarification of semantics. The *SEQ*-connector is introduced in *Priemer* [341]. It can be used to specify non-parallel, but arbitrary orders of activities. As such, a *SEQ* split-join pair captures the semantics of workflow pattern 17 (interleaved parallel routing) as described in [12]. *Rosemann* introduces an *ET*-connector that explicitly models a decision table and a so-called OR_1 connector to mark branches that are always executed [358]. The motivation of both these proposals is to offer a straightforward way to model certain behavior. In contrast, the works of *Rittgen* are motivated by semantic ambiguities of the OR-join (see [349, 350]). We will discuss his proposal for *every-time, first-come*, and *wait-for-all* OR-joins in Section 2.4.3. The aim of *Thomas et al.* [426, 21, 423] is to provide modeling support for decisions that are taken based on fuzzy information. The authors introduce a *fuzzy XOR*-connector that takes multiple inputs and triggers alternative outputs. *Rodenhagen* presents *multiple instantiation* as a missing feature of EPCs [351]. He proposes dedicated begin and end symbols to model that a branch of a process may be executed multiple times. This notation does not enforce that a begin symbol is followed by a matching end symbol.

The work by *Mendling, Neumann, and Nüttgens* on yEPCs [279, 281, 282] is a response to missing support for some of the workflow patterns identified in [12]. In order to capture the semantics of unsupported patterns, three new elements are introduced: empty connector, cancellation area and multiple instantiation. The *empty split* can be interpreted as a hyperarc from the event before the empty split to the functions subsequent to it; the *empty join* analogously as a hyperarc from multiple functions before it to its subsequent event. In this case, the split semantics match the deferred choice pattern and the join semantics match the multiple merge pattern. Interleaved parallel routing and milestones can also be represented by the help of empty connectors. *Multiple instantiation* in yEPCs is described similarly as in YAWL by giving the *min* and *max* cardinality of instances that may be created. The *required* parameter specifies an integer number of instances that must finish in order to complete the function. The *creation* parameter specifies whether further instances may be created at run-time (dynamic) or not (static). *Cancellation* areas (symbolized by a lariat) include a set of functions and events. The end of the lariat is connected to a function. When this function is completed, all functions and events in the lariat are cancelled. In [274], the authors provide a transformation from yEPCs to YAWL.

2.3.2 Configurability Extensions

A first approach towards the configurability of EPCs can be found in *Rosemann* [358, p.245] where type operators are defined to describe process alternatives. Configurable EPCs (C-EPCs) extend EPCs for specification of variation points, configuration constraints and configuration guidelines in a reference model. C-EPCs play a central role in the realization of an integrated, model-driven Enterprise Systems Configuration life cycle as proposed in [344].

Functions and connectors can be configured in a C-EPC. For a *configurable function* a decision has to be made: whether to perform it in every process instance during run time (ON), whether to exclude it permanently (OFF - it will not be executed in any process instance), or whether to defer this decision to run time (OPT - for each process instance it has to be decided whether to execute the function or not). *Configurable connectors* subsume build-time connector types that are less or equally expressive, therefore, a configurable connector can only be configured to a connector type that restricts its behavior. A configurable OR-connector may be mapped to a regular OR-, XOR-, AND-connector or to a single sequence of events and functions (indicated by SEQ_n for some process path starting with node n). A configurable AND-connector may only be mapped to a regular AND-connector. A configurable XOR-connector may be mapped to a regular XOR-connector or to a single sequence SEQ_n. Interdependencies between configurable EPC nodes can be specified via *configuration requirements* (logical expressions that define constraints for inter-related configuration nodes). *Configuration guidelines* formalize recommendations and best practices (also in the form of logical expressions) in order to support the configuration process semantically. Additional work formalizes C-EPC syntax [362], its mapping to EPCs [294] and its identification from existing systems [197]. Recently, configuration of roles and objects has been defined for an extension of EPCs called iEPCs [357].

2.4 EPC Semantics

In addition to related work on the syntax of EPCs, there are several contributions towards the formalization of EPC semantics. This section first illustrates the semantic problems related to the OR-join. We then give a historical overview of semantic definitions and provide a formalization for EPCs that is used in this book. We also present an implementation of these semantics as a ProM plug-in that generates the reachability graph for a given EPC.

2.4.1 Informal Semantics as a Starting Point

Before discussing EPC formalization problems, we need to establish an informal understanding of state representation and state changes of an EPCs. A formal definition is given later. The informal declaration of state concepts helps to discuss formalization issues in this section. The *state*, or *marking*, of an EPC is defined by assigning a number of *tokens* (or process folders) to its arcs.[1] The formal semantics of an EPC define which state changes are possible for a given marking. These state changes are formalized by a *transition relation*. A node is called *enabled* if there are enough tokens on its incoming arcs that it can fire. That is, a state change defined by a transition can be applied. This process is also called *firing*. A firing of a node n consumes tokens from its input arcs n_{in} and produces tokens at its output arcs n_{out}. The formalization of whether an OR-join is enabled is a non-trivial issue since not only the incoming arcs must be considered. The sequence $\tau = n_1 n_2 ... n_m$ is called a firing sequence if it is possible to execute a sequence of steps; i.e. after firing n_1 it is possible to fire n_2, etc. Through a sequence of firings, the EPC moves from one *reachable* state to the next. The *reachability graph* of an EPC represents how states can be reached from other states. A marking that is not a final marking but from which no other marking can be reached is called a *deadlock*. The notion of an initial and a final marking will be formally defined in Section 2.4.5.

2.4.2 EPC Formalization Problems

We have briefly stated that the OR-join synchronizes all active incoming branches. This reveals a non-trivial problem: if there is a token on one incoming arc, does the OR-join have to wait or not? Following the informal semantics of EPCs, it is only allowed to fire if it is not possible for a token to arrive on the other incoming arcs (see [325]). In the following subsection, we will show what the formal implications of these intended semantics are. Before that, we present some example EPCs, the discussion of which raises some questions that will not be answered immediately. We will revisit them later on to illustrate the characteristics of different formalization approaches.

Figure 2.6(a) shows an EPC with an OR-join on a loop. There is a token on arc $a2$ from function $f1$ to the OR-join $c1$. The question is whether $c1$ can fire. If it could fire, it would be possible for a token to arrive on arc $a9$ from $f3$ to the join. This

---

[1] This state representation based on arcs reflects the formalization of *Kindler* [216, 217, 218] and can be related to arcs between tasks in YAWL that are interpreted as implicit conditions [11]. Other approaches assign tokens to the nodes of an EPC, e.g., [366]. Later, we will make a distinction between state and marking in our formalization of EPC operational semantics.

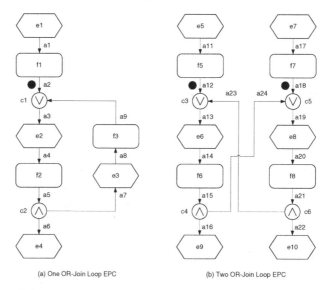

(a) One OR-Join Loop EPC   (b) Two OR-Join Loop EPC

Figure 2.6. EPCs (a) with one OR-join and (b) with two OR-joins on the loop

would imply that it should wait and not fire. On the other hand, if it must wait, it is not possible that a token might arrive at $a9$. Figure 2.6(b) depicts an EPC with two OR-joins ($c3$ and $c5$) on a loop which are both enabled (see [6]). Here the question is whether both or none of them can fire. Since the situation is symmetrical, it seems unreasonable that only one of them should be allowed to fire.

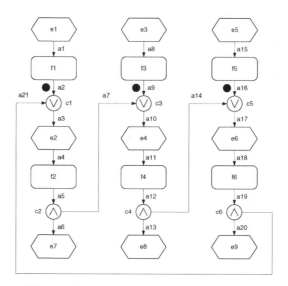

Figure 2.7. EPCs with three OR-joins on the loop

The situation might be even more complicated, as Figure 2.7 illustrates (refer to [216, 217, 218]). This EPC includes a loop with three OR-joins: $c1$, $c3$, and $c5$, all of which are enabled. Following the informal semantics, the first OR-join $c1$ is allowed to fire if it is not possible for a token to arrive on arc $a21$ from the AND-split $c6$. In other words, if $c1$ is allowed to fire, it is possible for a token to arrive on arc $a7$ that leads to the OR-join $c3$. Furthermore, the OR-join $c5$ could eventually fire. The first OR-join $c1$ would also have to wait for that token before firing. In short, if $c1$ could fire, it would have to wait. One can show that this also holds in reverse: if it could not fire, it would not have to wait. This observation is also true for the two other OR-joins. In the subsequent section, we will discuss whether this problem can be resolved.

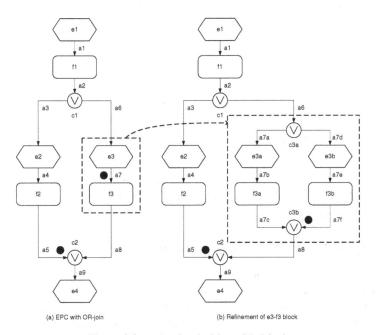

(a) EPC with OR-join   (b) Refinement of e3-f3 block

Figure 2.8. EPC refined with an OR-Block

Refinement is another issue related to OR-joins. Figure 2.8 shows two versions of an EPC process model. In Figure 2.8(a) there is a token on $a7$. The subsequent OR-join $c2$ must wait for this token and synchronize it with the second token on $a5$ before firing. In Figure 2.8(b) the sequence $e3$-$a7$-$f3$ is refined with a block of two branches between an OR-split $c3a$ and an OR-join $c3b$. The OR-join $c2$ is enabled and should wait for the token on $a7f$. The question here is whether such a refinement might change the behavior of the OR-join $c1$. Figure 2.8 is just one simple example. The answer to this question may be less obvious if the refinement is introduced in a loop that already contains an OR-join. Figure 2.9 shows a respective case of an OR-join $c1$ on a loop that is refined with an OR-Block $c3a$-$c3b$. One would expect

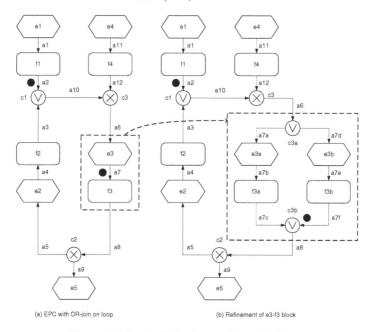

(a) EPC with OR-join on loop   (b) Refinement of e3-f3 block

Figure 2.9. Cyclic EPC refined with an OR-Block

that the EPC of Figure 2.8(a) exhibits the same behavior as the one in (b). In the following section, we will discuss these questions from the perspective of different formalization approaches.

2.4.3 Approaches to EPC Semantics Formalization

The transformation to Petri nets plays an important role in early formalizations of EPC semantics. In *Chen and Scheer* [78], the authors define a mapping to colored Petri nets and address the non-local synchronization behavior of OR-joins. This formalization builds on the assumption that an OR-split always matches a corresponding OR-join. The colored token that is propagated from the OR-split to the corresponding OR-join signals which combination of branches is enabled. The authors also describe the state space of some example EPCs by giving reachability graphs. However, this first Petri net semantics for EPCs has two obvious weaknesses: a formal algorithm to calculate the state space is missing and the approach is restricted to EPCs with matching OR-split and OR-join pairs. Therefore, this approach does not provide semantics for the EPCs shown in figures 2.6 and 2.7. Even though the approach is not formalized in all its details, it should be able to handle the refined EPC of Figure 2.8(b) and the inner OR-join $c3b$ in Figure 2.8(b).

The transformation approach by *Langner, Schneider, and Wehler* [236, 237, 238] maps EPCs to Boolean nets in order to define formal semantics. Boolean nets are a variant of colored Petri nets whose token colors are 0 (negative token) and 1 (positive token). Connectors propagate both negative and positive tokens according to their logical type. This mechanism is able to capture the non-local synchronization semantics of the OR-join similar to dead-path elimination in workflow systems (see [247, 248]). The XOR-join only fires if there is one positive token on incoming branches and a negative token on all other incoming branches, otherwise it is blocked. A drawback of this semantic definition is that the EPC syntax has to be restricted: arbitrary structures are not allowed. If there is a loop, it must have an XOR-join as entry point and an XOR-split as exit point. This pair of connectors in a cyclic structure is mapped to one place in the resulting Boolean net. As a consequence this approach does not provide semantics for the EPCs in Figures 2.6 and 2.7. Still, it can cope with any pair of matching OR-split and OR-join. The Boolean nets define the expected semantics of the refined EPC of Figure 2.8(b) and of the inner OR-Block introduced as a refinement in Figure 2.8(b).

Van der Aalst [4] presents a mapping approach to derive Petri nets from EPCs, but does not give a mapping rule for OR-connectors because of the semantic problems illustrated in Section 2.4.2. The mapping provides clear semantics for XOR and AND-connectors as well as for the OR-split, but since the OR-join is not formalized the approach does not provide semantics for the EPCs of Figures 2.6 to 2.9. *Dehnert* presents an extension of this approach by mapping the OR-join to a Petri net block [99]. Since the resulting Petri net block may or may not necessarily synchronize multiple tokens at runtime (a non-deterministic choice), its state space is larger than the actual state space with synchronization. Based on the so-called relaxed soundness criterion, it is possible to cut away undesirable paths and check whether a join should be synchronized (see [100]).

In [349, 350] *Rittgen* discusses the OR-join. He proposes to distinguish between three types of OR-joins on the syntactic level: every-time, first-come and wait-for-all. The every-time OR-join reflects XOR-join behavior, the first-come OR-join passes the first incoming token and blocks afterwards, and the wait-for-all OR-join depends on a matching split similar to the approach of *Chen and Scheer*. This proposal could provide semantics for the example EPCs of Figures 2.6 to 2.9 in the following way. If we assume every-time semantics, all OR-joins of the example EPCs could fire. While the loops would not block in this case, there would be no synchronization at all which contradicts the intended OR-join semantics. If the OR-joins behave according to the first-come semantics, all OR-joins could fire. There would also be no synchronization and the loops could be run only once. If the OR-joins had wait-for-all semantics, we would have the same problems as before with the loops. Altogether, the proposal by *Rittgen* does not provide a general solution to the formalization problem.

Building on prior work of *Rump* [473, 366], *Nüttgens and Rump* [325] define a transition relation for EPCs that also addresses the non-local semantics of the OR-join, but there is a problem: the transition relation for the OR-join refers to itself under negation. *Van der Aalst, Desel, and Kindler* [6] show that a fixed point for this transition relation does not always exist. They present an example to prove the opposite: an EPC with two OR-joins on a circle which wait for each other as depicted in Figure 2.6(b). This vicious circle is the starting point for the work of *Kindler* towards a sound mathematical framework for the definition of non-local semantics for EPCs. In a series of papers [216, 217, 218], *Kindler* elaborates on this problem in detail. The technical problem is that for the OR-join the transition relation R depends upon itself in negation. Instead of defining one transition relation, he considers a pair of transition relations (P, Q) on the state space Σ of an EPC and a monotonously decreasing function $R : 2^{\Sigma \times N \times \Sigma} \rightarrow 2^{\Sigma \times N \times \Sigma}$. A function $\varphi((P, Q)) = (R(Q), R(P))$ has a least fixed point and a greatest fixed point. P is called pessimistic transition relation and Q optimistic transition relation. An EPC is called *clean*, if $P = Q$. For most EPCs this is the case. Some EPCs, such as the vicious circle EPC, are *unclean* since the pessimistic and the optimistic semantics do not coincide. Moreover, *Cuntz* provides an example of a clean EPC which becomes unclean by refining it with another clean EPC [87, p.45]. *Kindler* shows that there are even acyclic EPCs that are unclean (see [218, p.38]). Furthermore, *Cuntz and Kindler* present optimizations for an efficient calculation of the state space of an EPC and a respective prototype implementation called EPC Tools [89, 90]. EPC Tools also offers a precise answer to the questions regarding the behavior of the example EPCs in Figures 2.6 to 2.9.

- Figure 2.6(a): For the EPC with one OR-join on a loop, there is a fixed point and the connector is allowed to fire.
- Figure 2.6(b): The EPC with two OR-joins on a loop is unclean. Therefore, it is not clear whether the optimistic or the pessimistic semantics should be considered.
- Figure 2.7: The EPC with three OR-joins is also unclean (the pessimistic deviates from the optimistic semantics).
- Figure 2.8(a): The OR-join $c2$ must wait for the second token on $a7$.
- Figure 2.8(b): The OR-join $c2$ must wait for the second token on $a7f$.
- Figure 2.9(a): The OR-join $c1$ must wait for the second token on $a7$.
- Figure 2.9(b): The OR-join $c1$ is allowed to fire: the second OR-join $c2$ in the OR-block must wait.

Even though the approach by *Kindler* provides semantics for a large subclass of EPCs (clean EPCs), there are some cases like the EPCs of Figure 2.6(b) and 2.7 that do not have semantics. The theorem by *Kindler* proves that it is not possible to calculate these EPCs semantics as long as the transition relation is defined with a self-reference under negation. Such a semantics definition may imply some unexpected results. For example, the EPC of Figure 2.9(a) behaves differently than its refinement in Figure 2.9(b).

While it is argued that unclean EPCs only have theoretical relevance, there actually are unclean EPCs in practice. Figure 2.10 shows the Test Equipment Management EPC from the Quality Management branch of the SAP Reference Model (see [211]). The marking of this EPC in the figure can be produced by firing the OR-split on the right-hand side of the EPC. Both XOR-joins are on a loop resulting in an unclean marking. This illustrates the need in theory *and* practice to also provide semantics for EPCs that are unclean, according to *Kindler's* definition [218].

Van Hee, Oanea, and Sidorova discuss a formalization of extended EPCs as they are implemented in the simulation tool of the ARIS Toolset (see [191]) based on a transition system [172]. This transition system is mapped to colored Petri nets in order to be verified with CPN Tools (see [198]). The considered EPC extension

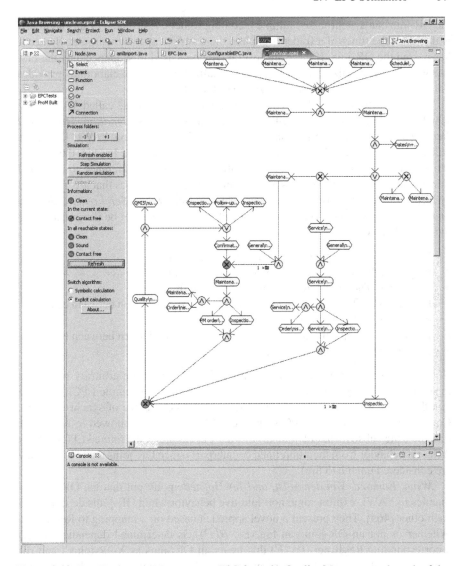

Figure 2.10. Test Equipment Management EPC from the Quality Management branch of the SAP Reference Model

includes data attributes, time and probabilities which are used for the simulation in ARIS. The essential idea of this formalization and the ARIS implementation is that process folders can have timers and that these timers are used at an OR-join for synchronization purposes.[2] If a folder arrives at an OR-join it has to wait until its timer expires. Since the timers are only reduced if there are no folders to propagate,

---

[2] Note that this general approach can be parameterized in ARIS with respect to sychronization and waiting semantics (see [172, p.194]).

the OR-join can synchronize multiple incoming folders. A problem of this approach is that once the timer of a folder is expired there is no way to synchronize it once it has passed the OR-join. If there are several OR-joins used in sequence only the first one will be synchronized. Therefore this formalization –though elaborate– provides only a partial solution to the formalization of the OR-join.

Van der Aalst and Ter Hofstede define a workflow language called YAWL [11] which also offers an OR-join with non-local semantics. As *Mendling, Moser, and Neumann* propose transformation semantics for EPCs based on YAWL [274], we will discuss how the OR-join behavior is formalized in YAWL. In [11], the authors propose a definition of the transition relation $R(P)$ with a reference to a second transition relation P that ignores all OR-joins. Similar semantics that are calculated on history-logs of the process are proposed by *Van Hee, Oanea, Serebrenik, Sidorova, and Voorhoeve* in [171]. The consequence of this definition can be illustrated using the example EPCs.

- Figure 2.6(a): The single OR-join on the loop can fire.
- Figure 2.6(b): The two OR-joins on the loop can fire.
- Figure 2.7: The three OR-joins on the loop can fire.
- Figure 2.8(a): The OR-join $c2$ must wait for the second token between e3 and f3.
- Figure 2.8(b): Both OR-joins can fire.
- Figure 2.9(a): The OR-join $c1$ must wait for the second token between e3 and f3.
- Figure 2.9(b): Both OR-joins can fire.

Kindler notes that each choice for defining P "appears to be arbitrary or ad hoc in some way" [218] and uses the pair (P, Q) instead. The example EPCs illustrate that the original YAWL semantics provide for a limited degree of synchronization. Consider the vicious circle EPC with three OR-joins: all are allowed to fire but, if one does, the subsequent OR-join has to wait. Furthermore, the refined EPCs exhibit different behavior from their unrefined counterparts since OR-joins are ignored (they are considered unable to fire).

Wynn, Edmond, Van der Aalst, and Ter Hofstede point out that the OR-join semantics in YAWL exhibit some non-intuitive behavior when OR-joins depend upon each other [465]. They present a novel approach based on a mapping to Reset nets. Whether or not an OR-join can fire (i.e. $R(P)$), is determined depending on (a) a corresponding Reset net (i.e. P) that treats all OR-joins as XOR-joins[3], and (b) a predicate called *superM* that prevents firing if an OR-join is on a directed path from another enabled OR-join. In particular, the Reset net is evaluated using backward search techniques that grant coverability to be decidable (see [245, 128]). A respective verification approach for YAWL nets is presented in [464]. Using these semantics, the example EPCs behave as follows:

---

[3] In fact, [465] proposes two alternative treatments for the "other OR-joins" when evaluating an OR-join: treat them either as XOR-joins (optimistic) or as AND-joins (pessimistic). The authors select the optimistic variant because the XOR-join treatment of other OR-joins more closely match the informal semantics of the OR-join.

- Figure 2.6(a): The single OR-join on the loop can fire since *superM* evaluates to false and no more tokens can arrive at c_1.
- Figure 2.6(b): The two OR-joins are not enabled since *superM* evaluates to true because if the respectively other OR-join is replaced by an XOR-join an additional token may arrive.
- Figure 2.7: The three OR-joins are not enabled because if one OR-join assumes the other two to be XOR-joins then this OR-join has to wait.
- Figure 2.8(a): The OR-join $c2$ must wait for the second token on $a7$.
- Figure 2.8(b): The OR-join $c2$ must wait for the second token on $a7f$.
- Figure 2.9(a): The OR-join $c1$ must wait for the token on $a7$.
- Figure 2.9(b): The OR-join $c1$ must wait because if $c3b$ is assumed to be an XOR-join a token may arrive via $a3$. The OR-join $c3b$ must also wait because if $c1$ is an XOR-join another token may move to $a7c$. Therefore, there is a deadlock.

The novel approach based on Reset nets provides interesting semantics but in some cases also leads to deadlocks.

Mendling and Van der Aalst introduce a semantics definition based on state and context [266, 268]. Both are assignments on the arcs. While the state uses similar concepts as *Langner, Schneider, and Wehler* (positive and negative tokens), the context captures whether a positive token can be expected in the future or not. Context is considered for the firing of the OR-join. This semantics definition implies that the examples of Section 2.4 behave as follows:

- Figure 2.6(a): The single OR-join on the loop produces a wait context at $a9$. Therefore, it is blocked.
- Figure 2.6(b): The two OR-joins produce a wait context at $a23$ and $a24$. Therefore, they are both blocked.
- Figure 2.7: The three OR-joins are blocked due to a wait context at $a7$, $a14$, and $a21$.
- Figure 2.8(a): The OR-join $c2$ must wait for the second token on $a7$.
- Figure 2.8(b): The OR-join $c2$ must wait for the second token on $a7f$.
- Figure 2.9(a): The OR-join $c1$ must wait for the token on $a7$.
- Figure 2.9(b): The OR-join $c1$ must wait for the token on $a7$. The OR-split $c3a$ produces a negative token on $a7c$ so that $c3b$ can fire.

It can be seen that the refined EPCs exhibit the expected behavior similar to the unrefined cases (the OR-join in the structured block does not deadlock). If there is an OR-join as an entry point to a loop it will deadlock if there is not a second XOR-entry that can propagate a token into this loop.

Table 2.3 summarizes existing work on the formalization of the OR-join. Several early approaches define syntactical restrictions, such as OR-splits to match corresponding OR-joins or models to be acyclic (see [78, 238, 349]). Newer approaches impose little or even no restrictions (see [218, 11, 464]), but exhibit unexpected behavior for OR-block refinements on loops with further OR-joins on it. The solution based on Reset nets seems to be promising from the intuition of its behavior yet it requires extensive calculation effort since it depends upon backward search to decide

Table 2.3. Overview of EPC semantics and their limitations

OR-join semantics	Limitations
[78]	OR-join must match OR-split
[238]	Joins as loop entry undefined
[349] every-time	missing synchronization
[349] first-come	OR-join can block
[349] wait-for-all	OR-join as loop entry undefined
[218]	EPC can be unclean
[172]	folders with expired timers do not synchronize
[11]	limited synchronization
[464]	OR-join may block
[266]	OR-join loop entries block

coverability. Note that reachability is undecidable for reset nets illustrating the computational complexity of the OR-join in the presence of advanced routing constructs. The state-context semantics partially resolve these problems because OR-joins cannot be used anymore as single loop entries [266]. In the following subsection, we provide further details on the state-context semantics. Since OR-join decisions can be taken with local knowledge, we will consider these semantics later for verification purposes.

2.4.4 EPC Semantics Based on State and Context

In this subsection, we introduce a novel concept for EPC semantics.[4] The formalization of this concept follows in the subsequent section. The principal idea of these semantics borrows some concepts from *Langner, Schneider, and Wehler* [238] and adapts the idea of Boolean nets with true and false tokens in an appropriate manner. The transition relations depend on the state and the context of an EPC. The *state* of an EPC is defined as an assignment of positive and negative tokens to the arcs. Positive tokens signal which functions have to be carried out in the process while negative tokens indicate which functions are to be ignored for the moment. The transition rules of AND-connector and OR-connectors are adopted from the Boolean nets formalization which facilitates synchronization of OR-joins in structured blocks. In order to allow for a more flexible utilization of XOR-connectors in a cyclic structure, we have modify and extended the approach of Boolean nets in three ways:

1. XOR-splits produce one positive token on one of their their output arcs but no negative tokens. XOR-joins fire each time there is a positive token on an incoming arc. This mechanism provides the expected behavior in both structured

---

[4] An earlier version of these semantics is described in [267]. Essentially, this version is different in two ways: (1) Dead context is propagated already if only one input is dead. Without that, XOR-loops could not be marked dead. (2) We introduce a concept to clean up negative tokens that could not be forwarded to an OR-join (see *negative upper corona* in phase 4 for positive token propagation).

XOR-loops and structured XOR-blocks where an XOR-split matches an XOR-join.

2. In order to signal to the OR-joins that it is not possible to have a positive token on an incoming branch, we define the *context* of an EPC. The context assigns a status of *wait* or *dead* to each arc of an EPC. A wait context indicates that it is still possible that a positive token might arrive and a dead context status means that either a negative token will arrive next or no positive token can arrive anymore. For example, XOR-splits produce a dead context on those output branches that are not taken and a wait context on the output branch that receives a positive token. A dead context at an input arc is then used by an OR-join to determine whether it has to synchronize with further positive tokens or not. Since dead and wait context might be conflicting and thus have to alternate, both context and state are propagated in separate phases to guarantee termination.

3. The propagation of context status and state tokens is arranged in a four phase cycle: (a) dead context, (b) wait context, (c) negative token and (d) positive token propagation.

   a) In this phase, all *dead context* information is propagated in the EPC until no new dead context can be derived.

   b) All *wait context* information is propagated until no new wait context can be derived. It is necessary to have two phases (first the dead context propagation and then the wait context propagation) in order to avoid infinite cycles of context changes (details below).

   c) All *negative tokens* are propagated until no negative token can be propagated anymore. This phase cannot run into an endless loop (details below).

   d) One of the enabled nodes is selected and propagates *positive tokens* leading to a new iteration of the four phase cycle.

We will now give an example to illustrate the behavior of the EPC semantics before defining state, context, and each transition phase in detail.

Revisiting the Cyclic EPC Refined with an OR-Block

Figure 2.11 revisits the example of the cyclic EPC refined with an OR-block that we introduced as Figure 2.9 in Section 2.4.2.

In Figure 2.11(a) an initial marking with two positive tokens on $a1$ and $a11$ is given. These positive tokens induce a wait context on all arcs which implies that all of them might potentially receive a positive token at some point in time. The context status is indicated by a letter next to the arc: w for wait and d for dead. Subsequently, the positive tokens can be propagated to the arcs $a2$ and $a12$ respectively and the context of $a1$ and $a11$ changes to dead. In this situation, the OR-join $c1$ is not allowed to fire due to the wait context on arc $a3$ but has to synchronize with positive and negative tokens that might arrive there. The XOR-join is allowed to fire without considering the second arc $a10$. In (b) the OR-split $c3a$ has fired (following the execution of $c3$) and produces a positive token on $a7a$ and a negative token on $a7d$. Accordingly, the context of $a7d$ is changed to dead. This dead context is propagated

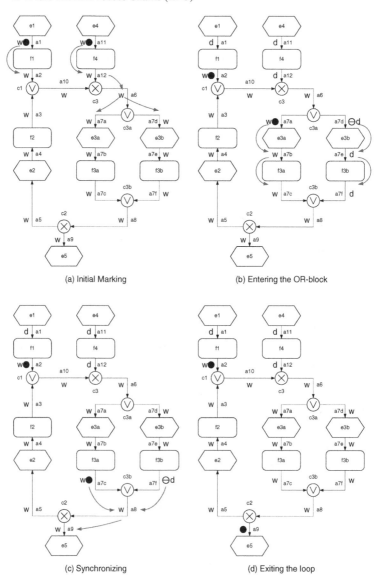

Figure 2.11. Example of EPC marking propagation

down to arc $a7f$. The rest of the context remains unchanged. The state shown in (b) is followed by (c) where the positive and the negative tokens are synchronized at the connector $c3b$ and one positive token is produced on the output arc $a8$. Please note that the OR-join $c3b$ does not synchronize with the other OR-join $c1$ that is on the loop. In the *Kindler* and the Reset nets semantics, $c3b$ would have to wait for the token from $a2$. Here, the wait context propagation is blocked by the negative token. In (d) the XOR-split $c2$ produces a positive token on $a9$ and a dead context on $a5$. This dead context is propagated via $a3$ to the rest of the loop in the dead context propagation phase. In the wait context propagation phase, the dead context of the loop is reset to wait, which is propagated from $c1$. As a consequence, the OR-join $c1$ is not enabled.

This example allows us to make two observations. First, the context propagation blocks OR-joins that are entry points to a loop in a wait position since the self-reference is not resolved, and second, the XOR-split produces a dead context but not a negative token. The disadvantage of producing negative tokens would be that the EPC is flooded with negative tokens if an XOR-split was used as an exit of a loop. These tokens would give downstream joins the wrong information about the state of the loop since it would still be live. An OR-join could then synchronize with a negative token while a positive token is still in the loop. In contrast, the XOR-split as a loop exit produces a dead context. Since there is a positive token in the loop, it overwrites the dead context at the exit in the wait context propagation phase. Downstream OR-joins then have the correct information that there are still tokens to wait for.

Definition of State, Context and Marking

We define both state and context as an assignment to the arcs. The term *marking* refers to state and context together. The EPC transition relations defines which state and/or context changes are allowed for a given marking in a given phase.

Definition 2.12 (State and Context). *Let $EPC = (E, F, C, l, A)$ be a standard EPC. Then, a mapping $\sigma : A \rightarrow \{-1, 0, +1\}$ is called a state of an EPC. The positive token captures the state as it is observed from outside the process. It is represented by a black filled circle. The negative token depicted by a white open circle with a minus on it has a similar semantics as the negative token in the Boolean nets formalization. Arcs with no state tokens on them do not depict a circle. Furthermore, a mapping $\kappa : A \rightarrow \{wait, dead\}$ is called a context of an EPC. A wait context is represented by a w and a dead context by a d next to the arc.*

In contrast to Petri nets, we distinguish the terms *marking* and *state*: the term marking refers to state σ and context κ collectively.

Definition 2.13 (Marking of an EPC). *Let $EPC = (E, F, C, l, A)$ be a EPC. Then, the set of all markings M_{EPC} of an EPC is called marking space with $M_{EPC} \subseteq A \rightarrow (\{-1, 0, +1\} \times \{wait, dead\})$. A mapping $m \in M_{EPC}$ is called a marking. Note that $m \in M_{EPC}$ defines the two mappings presented above, i.e., $m(a) =$*

$(\sigma(a), \kappa(a))$. *The projection of a given marking m to a subset of arcs $S \subseteq A$ is referred to as m_S.*

The marking m_a of an arc a can be written as $m_a = (\kappa(a), \sigma(a)) \cdot a$, for example $(w, 1)a$ for an arc with a wait context and a positive token. If we refer to the κ- or the σ-part of m, we write κ_m and σ_m, respectively, that is $m(a) = (\sigma_m(a), \kappa_m(a))$.

Phase 1: Dead Context Propagation

The transition relation for dead context propagation defines rules for deriving a dead context if one input arc of a node has a dead context status. Note that this rule might result in arcs having a dead context that could still receive a positive token. Those arcs are reset to a wait context in the subsequent phase of wait context propagation (Phase 2).

Figure 2.12 gives an illustration of the transition relation. *Please note that the figure does not depict the fact that the rules for dead context propagation can only be applied if the respective output arc does not hold a positive or a negative token.* Concrete tokens override context information. For instance, an arc with a positive token will always have a wait context. Rules (a) and (b) indicate that if an input arc of a function or an event is dead then the output also arc has to have a dead context status. Rule (c) means that each split-connector propagates a dead context to its output arcs. These transition relations formalize the observation that if an input arc cannot receive a token anymore, this also holds true for its output arcs (unless they already hold positive or negative tokens). The join-connectors require only one dead context status at their input arcs for reproducing it at their output arc (see (d)). It is important to note that a dead context is propagated until there is an end arc or an arc that carries a token.

Phase 2: Wait Context Propagation

The transition relation for wait context propagation defines rules for deriving a wait context if one or more input arcs of a node have a wait context status. Figure 2.12 gives an illustration of the transition relation. *All transitions can only be applied if the respective output arc does not hold a positive or a negative token.* Concrete tokens override context information (an arc with a positive token will always have a wait context). Rules (a) and (b) show that if an input arc of a function or an event has a wait context, then the output arc also has to have a wait context status. Rule (c) means that each split-connector propagates a wait context to its output arcs. The AND-join requires all inputs to have a wait context status in order to reproduce it at its output arc (see (d)). XOR- and OR-joins propagate a wait context if one of their input arcs has a wait context (see (e) and (f)). Similar to the dead context propagation, the wait context is propagated until an end node is received or until an arc holds a token. The wait context is propagated by an AND-join where all of the inputs have a wait context.

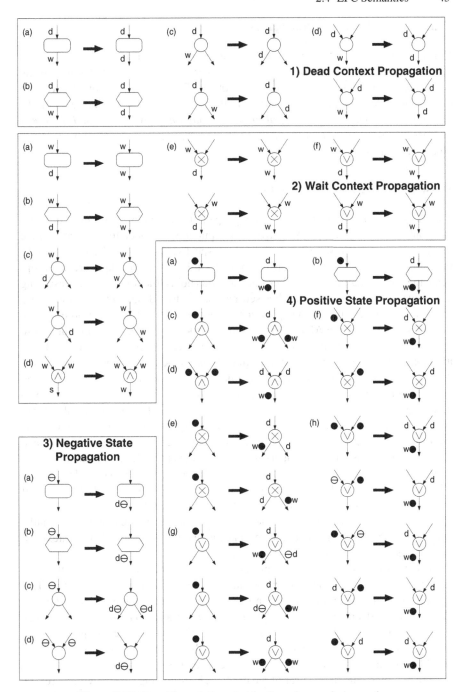

Figure 2.12. Transition relations for the four phases of propagation

Phase 3: Negative Token Propagation

Negative tokens can result from branches that are not executed after OR-joins or start events. The transition relation for negative token propagation includes four firing rules that consume and produce negative tokens. Furthermore, the output arcs are set to a dead context. Figure 2.12 gives an illustration of the transition relation. *All transitions can only be applied if all input arcs hold negative tokens and if there is no positive token on the output arc.* In the following section, we will show that this phase terminates.

Phase 4: Positive Token Propagation

The transition relation for positive token propagation specifies firing rules that consume negative and positive tokens from the input arcs of a node to produce positive tokens on its output arcs. Figure 2.12 gives a respective illustration. Rules (a) and (b) show that functions and events consume positive tokens from the input arc and propagate them to the output arc. Furthermore, and this holds true for all rules, consuming a positive token from an arc implies setting this arc to a dead context status. Rules (c) and (d) illustrate that AND-splits consume one positive token and produce one on each output arc while AND-joins synchronize positive tokens on all input arcs to produce one on the output arc. Rule (e) depicts the fact that XOR-splits forward positive tokens to one of their output arcs. In contrast to the Boolean net formalization, they do not produce negative tokens but a dead context on the output arcs which do not receive the token. Correspondingly, XOR-joins (f) propagate each incoming positive token to the output arc, no matter what the context or the state of the other input arcs is. If there are negative tokens on the incoming arcs, they are consumed. The OR-split (g) produces positive tokens on those output arcs that have to be executed and negative tokens on those that are ignored. Note that the OR-join is the only construct that may introduce negative tokens (apart from start events that hold a negative token in the initial marking). Rule (h) shows that on OR-join can only fire either if it has full information about the state of its input arcs (each input has a positive or a negative token) or all arcs that do not hold a token are in a dead context. Finally, in all rules each output arc that receives a negative token is set to a dead context and each that gets a positive token is set to a wait context.

The transition relations of state propagation permit the observation that the EPC semantics are *safe*: it is not possible to have more than one token on an arc. This property is enforced by the definition of state since it is a mapping from the arcs to the set of -1,0, and +1. The state propagation rules also guarantee safeness since a node can fire only if all its outputs are empty. Due to the safeness property, we already know that the state space is finite since also the number of arcs is finite for an EPC. Another observation is that there are several state and context propagations that are not interesting to the user of the model. The following section will, therefore, make a distinction between the *transition relation* of an EPC that covers all state and context changes and the *reachability graph* that only covers the propagation of positive tokens and hides context and negative token propagation.

2.4.5 Reachability Graph of EPCs

In this section, we formalize the concepts that were introduced in the previous section. In particular, we define the reachability graph of EPCs based on markings (state and context mappings σ and κ collectively). The reachability graph hides the transitions of the context propagation and negative token propagation phases. These are defined in the Appendix A. We first provide definitions for marking, initial marking and final marking. We then define the reachability graph RG based on the transition relations and an algorithm to calculate RG. *Please note that all definitions are applicable for relaxed syntactically correct EPCs* (see Definition 2.8 on page 25).

Definition of Initial and Final Marking

In this paragraph, we define the sets of the initial and the final markings of an EPC similar to the definition in *Rump* [366]. An initial marking is an assignment of positive or negative tokens to all start arcs while all other arcs have no token. Only end arcs may hold positive tokens in a final marking.

Definition 2.14 (Initial Marking of an EPC). *Let $EPC = (E, F, C, l, A)$ be a relaxed syntactically correct EPC and M_{EPC} its marking space. $I_{EPC} \subseteq M_{EPC}$ is defined as the set of all possible initial markings, i.e. $m \in I_{EPC}$ if and only if[5]:*

- $\exists a_s \in A_s : \sigma_m(a_s) = +1$,
- $\forall a_s \in A_s: \sigma_m(a_s) \in \{-1, +1\}$,
- $\forall a_s \in A_s: \kappa_m(a_s) = wait$ if $\sigma_m(a_s) = +1$ and $\kappa_m(a_s) = dead$ if $\sigma_m(a_s) = -1$, and
- $\forall a \in A_{int} \cup A_e : \kappa_m(a) = wait$ and $\sigma_m(a) = 0$.

While this definition contains enough information for verification purposes (by the bundling of start and end events with OR-connectors as proposed in [274], for example) it does not provide executable semantics according to the original definition of EPCs. As pointed out in [349], it is not possible to equate the triggering of a single start event with the instantiation of a new process. This is because EPC start events do not only capture the creation of a process instance but also external events that influence the execution of a running EPC (see [78]). This observation suggests an interactive validation approach as presented by [109] where the user makes explicit assumptions about potential combinations of start events. Here we assume that in the initial marking all start arcs $a_s \in A_s$ have either a positive or a negative token with the matching context[6].

---

[5] Note that the marking is given in terms of arcs. Intuitively, one can think of start events holding positive or negative tokens. However, the corresponding arc will formally represent this token.

[6] The context of non-start arcs is derived when the four propagation phases are entered the first time. We choose to initialize all non-start arcs with a wait context (cf. Figure 2.11). Note that this context might be changed in the dead context propagation phase before any token is moved.

Definition 2.15 (Final Marking of an EPC). *Let $EPC = (E, F, C, l, A)$ be a relaxed syntactically correct EPC and M_{EPC} its marking space. $O_{EPC} \subseteq M_{EPC}$ is defined as the set of all possible final markings, i.e. $m \in O_{EPC}$ if and only if:*

- $\exists a_e \in A_e: \sigma_m(a_e) = +1$ *and* $\kappa_m(a_e) = wait$ *and*
- $\forall a \in A_s \cup A_{int} : \sigma_m(a) \leq 0$ *and* $\kappa_m(a) = dead.$

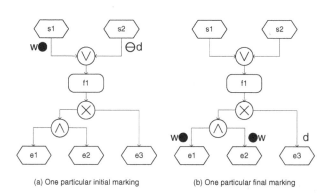

(a) One particular initial marking   (b) One particular final marking

Figure 2.13. Initial and final marking of an EPC

Initial and final markings are the start and end points for calculating the transition relation of an EPC. Figure 2.13(a) illustrates one particular initial marking $i \in I$ which assigns a positive token to the left start arc and a negative token to the right start arc. The OR-join synchronizes both these tokens and may produce (after some steps) the marking that is depicted in Figure 2.13(b). There the left branch of the XOR-split has been taken which results in positive tokens on the end arcs after the AND-split and a dead context on the right end arc.

Calculating the Reachability Graph for EPCs

In this section, we define the reachability graph of an EPC and present an algorithm to calculate it. This algorithm builds on the transition relations R^d, R^w, R^{-1}, and R^{+1} for each of the four phases. For a marking m, we refer to the resulting markings after completing the propagations of each of the first three phases as $m \overset{max}{\underset{d}{\to}} m_d \overset{max}{\underset{w}{\to}} m_w \overset{max}{\underset{-1}{\to}} m_{-1}$, respectively. Furthermore, if a marking m_{+1} can be produced from m by applying the propagations of the fourth phase we write $m \overset{n}{\underset{+1}{\to}} m_{+1}$. The corresponding definitions A.1 to A.8 are included in the Appendix A. Using these transition relations, we formalize the concept of reachability related to an EPC.

Definition 2.16 (Reachability related to an EPC). *Let $EPC = (E, F, C, l, A)$ be a relaxed syntactically correct EPC, $N = E \cup F \cup C$ its set of nodes, and M_{EPC} its marking space. Then, a marking $m' \in M_{EPC}$ is called reachable from another*

marking m if and only if $\exists n \in N \wedge m_d, m_w, m_{-1} \in M_{EPC} : m \stackrel{max}{\underset{d}{\to}} m_d \stackrel{max}{\underset{w}{\to}}$
$m_w \stackrel{max}{\underset{-1}{\to}} m_{-1} \stackrel{n}{\underset{+1}{\to}} m$. *Furthermore, we define the following notations:*

- $m \stackrel{n}{\to} m'$ *if and only if m' is reachable from m.*
- $m \to m' \Leftrightarrow \exists n \in N : m \stackrel{n}{\to} m'$.
- $m \stackrel{\tau}{\to} m'$ *if and only if $\exists_{n_1,...,n_q,m_1,...,m_{q+1}} : \tau = n_1 n_2 ... n_q \in N * \wedge$*
  $m_1 = m \wedge m_{q+1} = m' \wedge m_1 \stackrel{n_1}{\to} m_2, m_2 \stackrel{n_2}{\to} ... \stackrel{n_q}{\to} m_{q+1}$.
- $m_1 \stackrel{*}{\to} m_q \Leftrightarrow \exists \tau : m_1 \stackrel{\tau}{\to} m_q$.

Definition 2.17 (Reachability Graph of an EPC). *Let $EPC = (E, F, C, l, A)$ be a relaxed syntactically correct EPC, $N = E \cup F \cup C$ its set of nodes, $\stackrel{n}{\to}$ the one-step reachability relation, M_{EPC} its marking space, and $I_{EPC} \subseteq M_{EPC}$ the set of all possible initial markings. The reachability graph of EPC is the graph $RG = (V, W)$ consisting of a set of vertices $V = I_{EPC} \cup \{m' \in M_{EPC} \mid \exists_{m \in I_{EPC}} : m \stackrel{*}{\to} m'\}$ and labeled edges $W = \{(m, n, m') \in V \times N \times V \mid m \stackrel{n}{\to} m'\}$.*

The calculation of RG requires an EPC as input and a set of initial markings $I \subseteq I_{EPC}$. For several EPCs from practice, such a set of initial markings will not be available. In this case, one can easily calculate the set of all possible initial markings. Algorithm 1 uses an object-oriented pseudo code notation to define the calculation. In particular, we assume that RG is an instance of the class *ReachabilityGraph*, *propagated* an instance of class *Set*, and *toBePropagated* an instance of class *Stack* that provides the methods *pop()* and *push()*. Furthermore, *currentMarking*, *oldMarking* and *newMarking* are instances of class *Marking* that provides the methods *clone()* to return a new, but equivalent marking, *propagateDeadContext(EPC)*, *propagateWaitContext(EPC)* and *propagateNegativeTokens(EPC)* to change the marking according to the transitions of the respective phase (to determine max_d, max_w, and max_{-1} of the current marking). Finally, the method *propagatePositiveTokens(EPC)* returns a set of (node,marking) pairs including the node that can fire and the marking that is reached after the firing.

In lines 1-3, the sets RG and *propagated* are initialized with the empty set and the stack object *toBePropagated* is filled with all initial markings of the set I_{EPC}. The while loop between lines 4-18 calculates new markings for the marking that is on top of the stack *toBePropagated*. In particular, *currentMarking* receives the top marking from the stack (line 5) and it is cloned into the *oldMarking* object (line 6). In lines 7-9, the propagations of dead and wait context and of negative tokens are applied on *currentMarking*. In line 10, the pairs of nodes and new markings that can be reached from the old marking are stored in the set *nodeNewMarking*. After that the old marking is added to the *propagated* set (line 11). In lines 12-17, a new transition *(oldMarking, node, newMarking)* is added to RG for each pair of node and new marking. If a new marking has not yet been propagated, it is pushed on top of the *toBePropagated* stack (lines 14-16). Using a stack, the reachability graph is calculated in a depth-first manner. Finally in line 19, RG is returned.

Algorithm 1 Pseudo code for calculating the reachability graph of an EPC

Require: $EPC = (E, F, C, l, A), I \subseteq M$
1: $RG \leftarrow \emptyset$
2: $toBePropagated \leftarrow I_{EPC}$
3: $propagated \leftarrow \emptyset$
4: **while** $toBePropagated \neq \emptyset$ **do**
5:     $currentMarking \leftarrow toBePropagated.pop()$
6:     $oldMarking \leftarrow currentMarking.clone()$
7:     $currentMarking.propagateDeadContext(EPC)$
8:     $currentMarking.propagateWaitContext(EPC)$
9:     $currentMarking.propagateNegativeTokens(EPC)$
10:    $nodeNewMarking \leftarrow currentMarking.propagatePositiveTokens(EPC)$
11:    $propagated.add(oldMarking)$
12:    **for all** $(node, newMarking) \in nodeNewMarkings$ **do**
13:        $RG.add(oldMarking, node, newMarking)$
14:        **if** $newMarking \notin propagated$ **then**
15:            $toBePropagated.push(newMarking)$
16:        **end if**
17:    **end for**
18: **end while**
19: **return** RG

2.4.6 Tool Support for EPC Semantics

There is some tool support for different versions of EPC semantics: most notably EPC Tools [90] and ARIS Simulator [191, 172]. Based on the previous algorithm, we have implemented the EPC semantics based on state and context as a conversion plug-in for the *ProM* (Process Mining) framework [111, 444, 41]. ProM was originally developed as a tool for *process mining*, a domain that aims at extracting information from event logs to capture the business process as it is being executed (see [8, 19, 83, 144, 179]). In the meantime, the functionality of ProM was extended to include other types of analysis, model conversions, model comparison, etc. This was enabled by the plug-able architecture of ProM, which allows to add new functionality without changing the framework itself and the fact that ProM supports multiple modeling languages. Since ProM can interact with a variety of existing systems, e.g. *workflow management systems* such as Staffware, Oracle BPEL, Eastman Workflow, WebSphere, InConcert, FLOWer, Caramba and YAWL, *simulation tools* such as ARIS, EPC Tools, Yasper and CPN Tools, *ERP systems* like PeopleSoft and SAP, *analysis tools* such as AGNA, NetMiner, Viscovery, AlphaMiner and ARIS PPM (see [41]), the plug-in for the new EPC semantics can easily be used for the analysis of existing models. There are currently more than 150 plug-ins in release 4.1. ProM basically supports five kinds of plug-ins:

Mining plug-ins to take a log and produce a model,
Import plug-ins to import a model from file and possibly use a log to identify the relevant objects in the model,

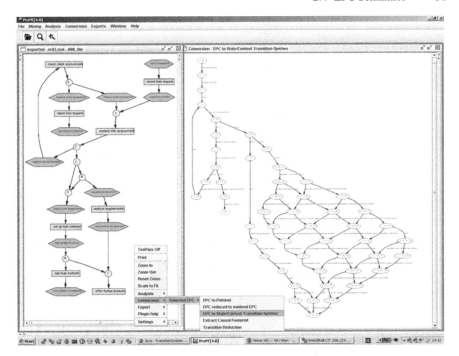

Figure 2.14. Calculating the reachability graph in ProM

Export plug-ins to export a model to file.

Conversion plug-ins to convert one model into another.

Analysis plug-ins to analyze a model, potentially in combination with a log.

The conversion plug-in maps an EPC to the transition systems package (see [18, 365]) that was developed for an implementation of the incremental workflow mining approach by *Kindler, Rubin, and Schäfer* [219, 220, 221]. Figure 2.14 illustrates how the conversion plug-in works. First, one has to load an EPC business process model into ProM (by using the import plug-in for the ARIS XML format [192] or for the EPC Markup Language [291], for instance). In the figure, the EPC example model for a loan request process that we introduced in the beginning of this chapter is loaded. Since ProM generates a new layout automatically, the model looks different compared to the previous figure. Once the EPC is displayed in ProM, one can click on it, trigger the conversion plug-in "EPC to State/Context Transition System" and the reachability graph is calculated and shown in a new ProM window. The dense network of states and transitions on the right-hand side stems from the concurrent execution if there is both a positive risk assessment for the loan request and the requester is a new customer. There are two markings that do not serve as a source for another transition in case if the request is rejected or accepted. Both these markings are displayed with a green border since they are proper final markings. If they were deadlocks they would be drawn with a red border.

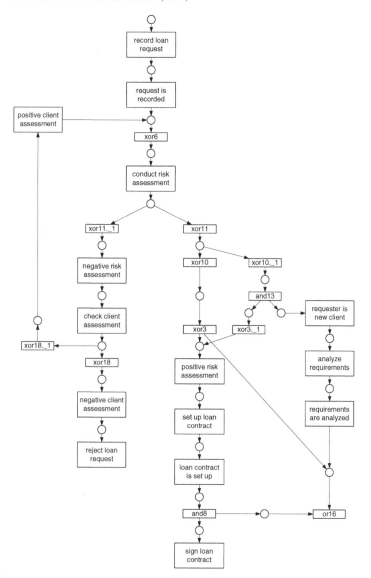

Figure 2.15. A Petri net that is bisimilar to the Loan Request EPC

One of the nice features of the transition system package is that it provides an export to the file format of Petrify. *Petrify* is a software tool developed by *Cortadella, Kishinevsky, Lavagno, and Yakovlev* [86, 85] that can not only generate the state space for a Petri net but also a Petri net from a transition system. The concepts of this Petri net synthesis builds on the theory of regions by *Ehrenfeucht and Rozenberg* [116, 36]. Running Petrify with the reachability graph of the Loan Request example EPC of Figure 2.1 generates a free-choice Petri net as shown in Figure 2.15. It is interesting to see how the OR-join *or*16 is treated in the Petri net synthesis as it requires a token at each of the two input places before it can fire. If both the *positive risk assessment* and the *requester is new client* branch are executed, the OR-join synchronizes these paths via its two input places. If only the *positive risk assessment* branch is executed, the required tokens are produced by *xor*3. The decision point *xor*11 is the same as in the EPC model. It can be seen that each alternative of an XOR-split becomes a transition of its own (see *xor*10 and *xor*10.$_1$ or *xor*11 and *xor*11.$_1$) while the AND-split *and*13 remains one transition in the Petri net. The generation of a reachability graph for an EPC and the synthesis of a Petri net could be an important step to bring EPCs and Petri nets closer together. Such a procedure could be a way to get rid of OR-joins for a Petri net implementation that has been modelled with EPCs in the design phase.

Another useful application related to the ProM plug-in is the possibility to export to the FSM format via the Petri net analysis plug-in in ProM. This format can be loaded into the visualization tool FSMTool by *Groote and Van Ham* [163, 149, 150]. FSMTool provides sophisticated interactive and customizable visualization of large state transition systems. The general visualization principle of FSMTool is to project

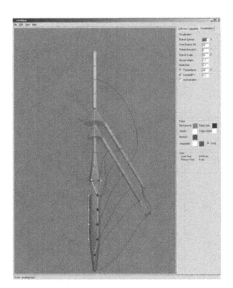

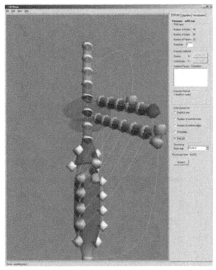

Figure 2.16. A visualization of the state space of the Loan Request Petri net

Figure 2.17. Another visualization of the Loan Request state space

the state space on levels of a backbone in such a way that structural symmetry can easily be seen. The Figures 2.16 and 2.17 visualize the state space of the Loan Request Petri net that was generated by Petrify as a three-dimensional backbone. The two decision points of this process are represented as cones in the upper part of the backbone. Each of these decision points splits off a new branch of execution that is visualized as a separate arm. On the first arm for negative risk assessment there is a green line in Figure 2.16 (in Figure 2.17 it is blue) that represents an iteration of the loop. The other green lines highlight the activation of a node that is closer to the start node than the node that had control before. The thick pillar of the backbone represents the parallel execution after the AND-split. Overall, the FSMTool is a useful addition to the ProM plug-ins for understanding the complexity of the state space. Certain information about function labels is not present, however, and there is no direct connection to the process model.

This shortcoming is the motivation of the work by *Verbeek, Pretorius, Van der Aalst, and Van Wijk* [445] on a two-dimensional projection of state spaces as an extension to the Diagraphica tool of *Pretorius and Van Wijk* [339, 340]. Diagraphica can also load FSM files and in addition the diagram of a Petri net. Figure 2.18 shows that Diagraphica uses an attribute clustering technique where, in this case, the attributes are related to the places of the Petri net. As Figure 2.19 shows, there may be multiple places in a cluster depending on the selections of the user. Transitions are represented as arcs. This figure permits an interesting observation. Below the diagonal line of yellow clusters, the clustering hierarchy does not branch anymore. This means that in the selected places, only one can be marked simultaneously (see [445, p.16]). Further interpretations of different clustering patterns are discussed in [445].

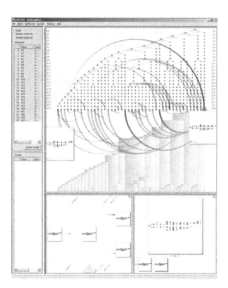 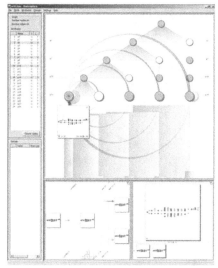

Figure 2.18. Visualization of the Petri net and the state space in DiaGraphica

Figure 2.19. Clustering of places for the same state space in DiaGraphica

Based on the implementation of the reachability graph calculation in ProM, we can relate the novel EPC semantics to several other tools and approaches for analysis, synthesis, and visualization of process models and state spaces. In this way, researchers can easily benefit from the EPC semantics and analyze its relationship to other formalisms.

2.5 EPCs and Other Process Modeling Languages

In this section, we provide a comparison of EPCs with other business process modeling languages. The selection includes Workflow nets [2], UML Activity Diagrams (UML AD) [330], BPMN [328] and YAWL [11] and is meant to illustrate differences and commonalities without going into mapping details. We first discuss whether these other process modeling languages offer elements similar to the different EPC connectors. After that, we utilize the workflow patterns documented in [12] to compare the languages. BPEL [91, 26, 24], which is also receiving increasing attention as a standard, is not included here since it addresses the execution rather than the conceptual modeling of processes. For further details on the relationship between EPCs and BPEL refer to [302, 470, 303, 271, 273, 272]. For a workflow pattern analysis of BPEL see [458]. The XPDL standard [462, 463] has also gained some support in the industry for the definition of executable workflow process. A workflow pattern analysis of XPDL is reported in [1]. Other approaches for comparing process modeling languages are reported in [411, 364, 53, 310, 252].

2.5.1 Comparison Based on Routing Elements

The six different connectors of EPCs (XOR-split and XOR-join, AND-split and AND-join, OR-split and OR-join) provide the means to model complex routing and ordering between activities of a business process. Table 2.4 uses these routing elements as a benchmark to compare EPCs with other business process modeling languages. It shows that the behavioral semantics of XOR-connectors and AND-connectors, as well as OR-split connectors, can be represented in most of the considered languages. In *Workflow nets* XOR-connectors and AND-connectors are captured by places and transitions with multiple input and output arcs, respectively. OR-split behavior can be specified as a complex subnet that determines each possible combination of inputs. OR-join behavior cannot be modelled directly but a relaxed soundness analysis is possible. In *UML AD* the XOR-split maps to a Decision, the XOR-join to a Merge, the AND-split to a Fork, the AND-Join to a Join and the OR-split to a Fork with guards on its output arcs. OR-joins cannot be represented in UML AD directly. In *BPMN* routing elements are called gateways, and each EPC connector can be transformed to a respective gateway. In *YAWL*, there are also similar splits and joins matching the behavior of the EPC connectors.

Table 2.4. EPC routing elements and equivalent elements in other business process modeling languages

EPC	Workflow nets	UML AD	BPMN	YAWL
XOR-split	multi-out place	Decision	XOR-gateway	XOR-split task
XOR-join	multi-in place	Merge	XOR-gateway	XOR-join task
AND-split	multi-out transition	Fork	AND-gateway	AND-split task
AND-join	multi-in transition	Join	AND-gateway	AND-join task
OR-split	complex subnet	Fork	OR-gateway	OR-split task
OR-join	-	-	OR-gateway	OR-join task

2.5.2 Comparison Based on Workflow Patterns

Motivated by the heterogeneity of workflow languages and products, *Van der Aalst, Ter Hofstede, Kiepuszewski and Barros* have gathered a set of 20 workflow patterns [12]. These patterns can be utilized to clarify semantics or to serve as a benchmark. Table 2.5 illustrates the result of several workflow pattern analyses of EPCs [279], Workflow nets [11], UML AD [459], BPMN [460] and YAWL [11]. It can be seen that EPCs support the basic control flow patterns *multiple choice* and *synchronizing merge*. These patterns can be directly represented with the different EPC connectors. EPCs also permit *arbitrary cycles* and offer *implicit termination*. *Multiple instances with apriori design time knowledge* can be modelled by an AND-block with as many instances as required of the same activity in parallel. The yEPC extension provides support for all patterns.

In contrast to EPCs, *Workflow nets* support the state-based patterns but perform weak when it comes to *advanced branching and synchronization* patterns. *UML AD* cover several patterns missing only the *synchronizing merge, multiple instances without apriori runtime knowledge* and two state-based patterns. *BPMN* performs even better since it supports the *synchronizing merge*, but only in a structured block. As *YAWL* was defined to provide a straight-forward support for the workflow patterns, it is no surprise that it has the best score. The *implicit termination* pattern is not supported in order to force the designer to make the completion condition explicit. The comparison reveals that the patterns supported by EPCs are, in most cases, also supported by the other languages. Because of this large overlap several of the findings that are elaborated throughout the remainder of this book can be more or less directly applied to the other languages, YAWL in particular.

2.6 Summary

In this chapter, we gathered state of the art work on EPCs. Building on the foundations of prior work, we established a syntax definition and a semantics definition for EPCs. In particular, we focused on transition relations that are defined based on both state and context changes. We presented an algorithm to calculate the reachability graph of an EPC that builds on the the transition relations described in Appendix A

Table 2.5. Workflow pattern support of EPCs and other business process modeling languages

Workflow Pattern	EPC	Wf. nets	UML AD	BPMN	YAWL
Basic Control Flow Patterns					
1. Sequence	+	+	+	+	+
2. Parallel Split	+	+	+	+	+
3. Synchronization	+	+	+	+	+
4. Exclusive Choice	+	+	+	+	+
5. Simple Merge	+	+	+	+	+
Advanced Branching and					
Synchronization Patterns					
6. Multiple Choice	+	+	+	+	+
7. Synchronizing Merge	+	-	-	+/-	+
8. Multi Merge	-	+	+	+	+
9. Discriminator	-	-	+	+/-	+
Structural Patterns					
10. Arbitrary Cycles	+	+	+	+	+
11. Implicit Termination	+	-	+	+	-
Patterns involving					
Multiple Instantiation (MI)					
12. MI without Synchronization	-	+	+	+	+
13. MI with apriori Design Time Knowledge	+	+	+	+	+
14. MI with apriori Runtime Knowledge	-	-	+	+	+
15. MI without apriori Runtime Knowledge	-	-	-	-	+
State-based Patterns					
16. Deferred Choice	-	+	+	+	+
17. Interl. Parallel Routing	-	+	-	+/-	+
18. Milestone	-	+	-	-	+
Cancellation Patterns					
19. Cancel Activity	-	+/-	+	+	+
20. Cancel Case	-	-	+	+	+

and a respective implementation as a plug-in for ProM. The major motivations for using the state-context semantics are semantic gaps and non-intuitive behavior of existing formalizations. The comparison to other business process modeling languages revealed that EPCs share their routing elements with several other process modeling languages. The findings that are elaborated throughout the remainder of this book can, therefore, be adapted to these languages in future research.

3

Verification of EPC Soundness

The aim of this book is to evaluate the power of metrics for predicting errors in business process models. In order to do so, we need to establish a clear and unambiguous understanding of which EPC business process model is correct and how it can be verify. This chapter presents verification techniques that can be applied to identify errors in EPCs with a focus on reachability graph analysis and reduction rules. Other verification techniques such as calculating invariants (see [313, 440]), reasoning (see [337, 112]) or model integration (see [403]) will not be considered.

In this chapter we will define a notion of EPC soundness for business process models (Section 3.1) and demonstrate how an analysis of the reachability graph can be applied to verify soundness of an EPC (Section 3.2). We then present a method of implementing the analysis as an extension of the EPC to Transition System plug-in for ProM. Since this verification approach suffers from the "state explosion" problem, we turn to an optimization based on a set of reduction rules (Section 3.3). For this approach we present the implementation as a batch program called *xoEPC* and show the results of reducing the SAP Reference model. Section 3.4 summarizes the chapter.

3.1 Soundness of EPCs

This section discusses existing correctness criteria for business process models (Section 3.1.1) and proposes a novel soundness notion that directly relates to multiple start and end events of EPCs (Section 3.1.2). Section 3.2 shows how the reachability graph can be utilized for the verification of EPC soundness.

3.1.1 Correctness Criteria for Business Process Models

Soundness, first introduced by *Van der Aalst* in [2], is an important correctness criterion for business process models. The original soundness property is defined for a Workflow net: a Petri net with one source and one sink that must satisfy the following requirements: (i) for every state reachable from the source, there must exist a firing

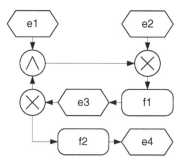

Figure 3.1. A relaxed sound EPC with structural problems

sequence to the sink (option to complete); (ii) the state with a token in the sink is the only state reachable from the initial state with at least one token in it (proper completion); and (iii) there are no dead transitions [2]. *Van der Aalst* shows that soundness of a Workflow net is equivalent to liveness and boundedness of the corresponding short-circuited Petri net.[1] Several liveness and boundedness analysis techniques are, therefore, directly applicable to the verification of soundness. Soundness can be verified with Petri net analysis tools such as Woflan [442, 443, 441].

Research on soundness of workflow models has resulted in the specification of several soundness derivatives due to certain aspects which proved to be too restrictive in certain application domains. *Dehnert and Rittgen* argue that business processes are often conceptually modelled in such a way that only the desired behavior results in a proper completion. Since such models are not used for workflow execution, non-normative behavior is resolved by the people working in the process in a cooperative and ad-hoc fashion. Processes are accordingly labelled *relaxed sound* if every transition in a Petri net representation of the process model is included in at least one proper execution sequence [101]. As already mentioned in Section 2.4.3, relaxed soundness can be used to analyze EPCs. If OR-joins are mapped to a Petri net block (see [99]), the Petri net state space is larger than the actual state space with synchronization. Based on the relaxed soundness criterion, it is possible to check whether a join should synchronize (see [100]).

Figure 3.1 illustrates a subtle implication of the relaxed soundness definition. Consider an initial marking that includes both start arcs after $e1$ and $e2$. Entering the loop at the XOR-join, the right token can be propagated via the XOR-split to synchronize with the left token at the AND-join. If the loop is exited at the XOR-split the process can complete properly. Since this execution sequence covers all nodes, the model is relaxed sound. There is, however, a structural problem: the loop can never be executed another time without running into a deadlock. The right token

---

[1] "A Petri net is said to be *k-bounded* or simply *bounded* if the number of tokens in each place does not exceed a finite number k for any marking that is reachable from the initial marking" [313, p.547]. "A Petri net is said to be *live* if, no matter what marking has been reached from the initial marking, it is possible to ultimately fire *any* transition of the net by progressing through some further firing sequence" [313, p.548].

must also never leave the loop without synchronizing with the left token at the AND-join. The relaxed soundness criterion is, therefore, too weak in some cases. The fact that relaxed soundness process models can still include livelocks and deadlocks was a motivation for *Puhlmann and Weske* to define a notion of *lazy soundness* [342]. A lazy sound process is deadlock and livelock free as long as the final node has not been reached. Clean-up activities, such as cancelling parts of the process, are therefore still permitted. Since such cleaning-up is needed for some of the workflow patterns, the authors also reject *weak soundness* as defined by *Martens* [259] because it does not provide this feature. Both weak and lazy soundness still allow dead activities.

Soundness was also extended towards *k-soundness* in order to study processes with shared resources [42]. $k > 1$ refers, in this case, to the number of tokens that are allowed on the initial and final place. A related term, *generalized soundness* [175], means that a process is k-sound for all $k > 1$. *Structural soundness* is fulfilled if there exists a $k > 1$ such that the process is k-sound. Both generalized and structural soundness are decidable (see [428, 175]) and a verification approach for generalized soundness is reported in [173]. Relationships between the different soundness notions are discussed in [431].

Beyond the soundness property, *structuredness* (or well-structuredness) is also discussed as a correctness criterion (see [3]). In essence, a structured process can be constructed by nesting simple building blocks like split and join of the same connector type. We used such a structured OR-block in Section 2.4.2 to illustrate how refinement can affect the behavior in some EPC formalizations. Structuredness of a process model guarantees soundness if the model is live (see [102]). Some process modeling languages, like BPEL and several workflow systems [214], enforce the definition of a structured model by imposing syntactical restrictions[2] in order to provide correctness by design (see [248, 91, 26, 24]. Finding a structured model with behavior equivalent to an originally unstructured model is also used as a verification technique (see [215, 15, 16, 253, 469, 169]). Structuredness as a correctness criterion has been criticized for being too strict (see [102]) since some sound process models are discarded right from the start. Nesting of structured blocks, however, neither meets the way people comprehend processes nor does every process easily fit into this scheme. Structuredness should, therefore, be regarded as a general guideline from which one can deviate if necessary.

Figure 3.2 summarizes the correctness criteria of soundness, relaxed soundness, structuredness and their relations [102]. It also links the Petri net classes of free-choice nets and state machines.[3] Importantly, it highlights that a sound process model is also relaxed sound and that a model that is both relaxed sound and structured is also sound. In the following section, we aim to analyze EPCs with respect to a strict

---

[2] BPEL relaxes structured modeling by allowing synchronization links between parallel activities.

[3] A *free-choice net* is a Petri net in which a place that is in the preset of multiple transitions is the only place in all these presets (see [105]). Therefore, the choice is "free" in a sense that it can be made without considering other places. A *state machine* is a subclass of free-choice nets in which each transition has exactly one pre- and one postcondition (cf. e.g. [104]). Therefore, there is no concurrency in a state machine.

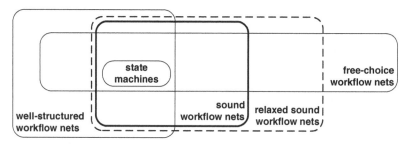

Figure 3.2. Relations between different Petri net-properties (see [102, p.389])

correctness criterion that guarantees that the models can be utilized in subsequent phases of the BPM life cycle as defined in Section 1.2. While the soundness definition would be a candidate for analysis, it is not directly applicable for EPCs: workflow nets have one unique start and one unique end node but EPCs may have multiple start and end events. Accordingly, we will have to consider several initial and several final markings related to an EPC-specific soundness criterion.

3.1.2 Definition of EPC Soundness

The definition of soundness for workflow nets cannot be used directly for EPCs as they may have multiple start and end events. Based on the definitions of the initial and final states of an EPC, we define EPC soundness as analogous to soundness of Workflow nets [2]. According to *Rump* [366], there must be a set of initial markings for an EPC such that there exists at least one initial marking in which a particular start arc holds a positive token. We, therefore, require that a definition of soundness includes such a set of initial markings and that proper completion is guaranteed for each initial marking. Accordingly, we demand that there exists a set of final markings that is reachable from some of these initial markings such that at least one final marking in which a particular end arc holds a positive token exists. If this requirement is fulfilled every arc contributes to properly completing the behavior of the EPC. The requirement that the EPC has to be relaxed syntactically correct excludes those pathological EPCs for which no semantics can be determined: if there are multiple input arcs of a function or if there are loops without an entry or exit connector, for example.

Definition 3.1 (Soundness of an EPC). *Let* $EPC = (E, F, C, l, A)$ *be a relaxed syntactically correct EPC,* $N = E \cup F \cup C$ *its set of nodes,* M_{EPC} *its marking space, and* I_{EPC} *and* O_{EPC} *the set of possible initial and final markings. An EPC is sound if there exists a non-empty set of initial markings* $I \subseteq I_{EPC}$ *and a set of final markings* $O \subseteq O_{EPC}$ *such that:*

(i) For each start-arc a_s *there exists an initial marking* $i \in I$ *where the arc (and hence the corresponding start event) holds a positive token. Formally:*
$$\forall a_s \in A_s : \exists i \in I : \sigma_i(a_s) = +1$$

(ii) For every marking m reachable from an initial state $i \in I$, there exists a firing sequence leading from marking m to a final marking $o \in O$. Formally:
$$\forall i \in I : \forall m \in M : (i \xrightarrow{*} m) \Rightarrow \exists o \in O \ (m \xrightarrow{*} o)$$
(iii)The final markings $o \in O$ are the only markings reachable from a marking $i \in I$ such that there is no node that can fire. Formally:
$$\forall m \in M : ((i \to m) \wedge \nexists m'(m \to m')) \Rightarrow m \in O$$

This soundness definition deserves some comment with respect to dead nodes, live-locks and contact situations. The original soundness definition requires that a work-flow net must not include *dead transitions* (property iii). In Definition 3.1 it is not ex-plicitly demanded that there are no dead arcs. Still, this property is implicitly granted due to the fact that the EPC is relaxed syntactically correct and that all decisions of an EPC are free-choice. Together with EPC soundness (i) it follows that an arc can either be reached by some token from a start arc that carries a positive token in some initial marking or there must be a deadlock on the path between the start arcs and the respective arc. If the latter is the case, the EPC is not sound because (iii) is violated. We summarize this property in the following observation without a proof.

Observation 3.1 (No dead nodes in sound EPCs) *Let $EPC = (E, F, C, l, A)$ be a relaxed syntactically correct EPC, $N = E \cup F \cup C$ its set of nodes, and M_{EPC} its marking space. If an EPC is sound according to Definition 3.1, all arcs are reachable from some initial marking $i \in I$.*

It is not possible to construct a *livelock* for an EPC. Since we consider relaxed syn-tactically correct EPCs, each loop must have a split-connector as an exit. If there is a loop in the EPC that has an AND-split as an exit (similar to a token machine in Petri net terms), a token t_1 can either reach an end arc from the AND-split or it must previ-ously deadlock. In either case, the token t_2 that is produced in the second iteration of the loop can only be propagated to the input arcs of the node that has t_1 on one of its output arcs. Since the number of arcs between the AND-split and the end arc is finite, the loop will eventually be deadlocked when a token t_i cannot be propagated further from its output arc outside the loop. The consequence of this fact is twofold. First, due to the relaxed syntactical correctness of the EPC and its free-choice behavior, all start arcs which can produce a marking that includes the loop with an AND-split exit must run into a deadlock and are, therefore, not sound. Second, due to the safeness of the EPC we only have to look for deadlocks in the reachability graph for verifying soundness: looking for livelocks is not required. We also summarize this property in the following observation without a proof.

Observation 3.2 (Loops with AND-split exit are not sound) *If there is a loop with an AND-split exit in a relaxed syntactically correct EPC, it is not sound no matter which set of initial markings is considered.*

So-called *contact situations* refer to a marking where there is a token on at least one of the input arcs (token t_2) and another one (token t_1) on at least one of the output arcs of a node n. Due to the safeness property of the EPC (see Section 2.4.4) n cannot fire (see [218]). Because of the free-choice property of EPCs, token t_2 on the input arc has the option to follow the other token t_1 in all its firings. t_2 will either be in a deadlock when t_1 is on an end arc and t_2 on the input arc of the node which is blocked by t_1 on its output arc. Alternately, there is a join that does not receive the required tokens on other input arcs in order to propagate t_2 to its output. This is also a deadlock. Accordingly, a contact situation implies the option to deadlock. The following observation formulates this fact the other way round.

Observation 3.3 (Contact situation is not sound) *If an $EPC = (E, F, C, l, A)$ is sound, there is no marking reachable that is a contact situation.*

Given the soundness definition, the example EPCs of Figures 2.6 and Figure 2.7 are not sound as the OR-joins block each other. Both EPCs of Figure 2.8 are sound. Both EPCs of Figure 2.9 are not sound because if the token at $a7$ or $a7f$ exits the loop the OR-join $c1$ is blocked. In the subsequent section, we show how soundness can be verified based on the reachability graph of an EPC.

3.2 Reachability Graph Verification of Soundness

In this section, we present an approach to verifying soundness based on the reachability graph of an EPC. Since the reachability graph of an EPC is finite and there are no livelocks in an EPCs, we have to consider deadlocks as the starting point of the analysis. In the reachability graph, deadlocks are leaf vertices that are not a final marking.

Definition 3.2 (Deadlock of an EPC). Let $m \in M$ be a marking of an EPC. The marking m is called a deadlock if:

(i) There is no node that can fire in m. Formally:
   $\nexists m' \in M : m \rightarrow m'$
(ii) m is not a final marking. Formally:
   $m \notin O$

The verification of soundness requires the reachability graph as input. Algorithm 2 shows an object-oriented pseudo code doing the calculation. We assume that RG is an instance of the class $ReachabilityGraph$ that provides the methods $getLeaves()$ and $getRoots()$. We then define the objects $BadLeaves$, $GoodLeaves$ and $Good-Roots$ as instances of a class $MarkingList$ that offers the methods $add(marking)$, $remove(marking)$ and $missing()$. The first two methods change the markings that are included in the list while the latter method returns a list of nodes that do not have a positive token in any marking of the $MarkingList$. This method initializes a list with all start and end arcs and iterates over the markings of the list. For each marking arcs with a positive token are deleted. After the iteration, the list includes only the missing arcs. Using this method we can determine whether I and O cover all start and end arcs. The objects $current, pre,$ and $post$ are instances of class $Marking$ that provides the methods $isLeaf()$, $getPredecessors()$ and $getSuccessors()$. The objects $predecessorStack$ and $successorStack$ are instances of $Stack$ that provides a $pop()$ and a $push(element)$ method, and $GoodRootSuccessors$ and $BadLeavesPredecessors$ are sets.

The algorithm covers three different phases. In the first phase, the deadlocks are determined and stored in the $BadLeaves$ list of markings (lines 2-6). If there are no deadlocks ($BadLeaves$ is empty), the EPC is sound and the algorithm returns all roots and all leaves of the reachability graph and two empty sets indicate that there are no start arcs and no end arcs missing in the set of initial markings and final markings. In the second phase (lines 10-23), all predecessor markings of deadlocks are determined. If there is an initial marking found via the $isRoot()$ method, this marking is removed from the $GoodRoots$ list. If the marking is not a root, all those predecessors are added to the stack which have not yet been visited as indicated by the $BadLeavesPredecessors$ list. As a result of this phase, $GoodRoots$ now includes only those initial markings that never result in a deadlock. If $GoodRoots$ was empty, we could stop after line 23 and return two empty lists for good root and leaf elements plus two lists of all start and end arcs. Due to the limited size of the page, we omitted a respective if statement. In the third phase (lines 24-37), we determine those leaves of the reachability graph that can be reached from good roots. The calculation is performed in reference to the second phase. Finally, line 38 returns the list of good roots and of good leaves as well as a list of start arcs that are not covered by initial markings and end arcs that are not included in final markings. The EPC is sound if both arc lists are empty.

We implemented Algorithm 2 as an extension to the EPC to Transition System plug-in for ProM (see Section 2.4.6). Figure 3.3 shows the refined EPC of Figure 2.9 on page 34 as it is modelled in Visio. Loading this model in ProM results in a new layout that is displayed in Figure 3.4. If we now use the conversion plug-in to create a transition system, we get a pop-up window that reports the result of the soundness check.[4] For the refinement EPC there is only one initial marking (positive token after $e4$ and negative token after $e1$) that does not result in a deadlock. The start arc after $e1$ does not have a positive token in any initial marking. The EPC is, therefore, not sound.

Figure 3.6 shows the transition system that is generated for the EPC. Two of the three initial markings are painted with a red border to indicate that they may run into a deadlock. One initial marking has a green border to highlight that it never runs into a deadlock. The initial marking on the top right of the graph immediately produces a deadlock and though the other red initial marking can complete properly, it may also deadlock.

The verification of soundness based on the reachability graph and its implementation in ProM is a powerful tool to identify behavioral problems of EPCs. The potential number of markings, however, grows exponentially with the number of arcs. The reachability graph of a model with 17 arcs like the refinement example depicted in Figure 3.3 can have up to $|V| = 3^{|A|} = 3^{17} = 129,140,163$ markings as vertices and $|V| \times (|V| - 1) = 16,677,181,570,526,406$ transitions in the worst case. This problem is called the state explosion problem in the Petri nets community (see [436]).

---

[4] The result is also written to the message panel at the bottom of ProM.

Algorithm 2 Pseudo code for verification of soundness

Require: RG
1: $BadLeaves \leftarrow \emptyset, GoodLeaves \leftarrow \emptyset, GoodRoots \leftarrow RG.getRoots()$
2: **for all** $leaf \in RG.getLeaves()$ **do**
3:      **if** $\neg leaf.isFinalMarking()$ **then**
4:          $BadLeaves.add(leaf)$
5:      **end if**
6: **end for**
7: **if** $|BadLeaves| = 0$ **then**
8:      **return** $RG.getLeaves(), RG.getRoots(), \emptyset, \emptyset$
9: **end if**
10: $BadLeavesPredecessors \leftarrow \emptyset, predecessorStack \leftarrow BadLeaves$
11: **while** $predecessorStack \neq \emptyset$ **do**
12:     $current \leftarrow predecessorStack.pop()$
13:     **if** $current.isRoot$ **then**
14:         $GoodRoots.remove(current)$
15:     **else**
16:         **for all** $pre \in current.getPrecessors()$ **do**
17:             **if** $pre \notin BadLeavesPredecessors$ **then**
18:                 $predecessorStack.push(pre)$
19:             **end if**
20:         **end for**
21:         $BadLeavesPredecessors.add(current)$
22:     **end if**
23: **end while**
24: $GoodRootSuccessors \leftarrow \emptyset, successorStack \leftarrow GoodRoots$
25: **while** $successorStack \neq \emptyset$ **do**
26:     $current \leftarrow successorStack.pop()$
27:     **if** $current.isLeaf()$ **then**
28:         $GoodLeaves.add(current)$
29:     **else**
30:         **for all** $post \in current.getSuccessors()$ **do**
31:             **if** $post \notin GoodRootSuccessors$ **then**
32:                 $successorStack.push(post)$
33:             **end if**
34:         **end for**
35:         $GoodRootSuccessors.add(current)$
36:     **end if**
37: **end while**
38: **return** $GoodLeaves, GoodRoots, GoodLeaves.missing(), GoodRoots.missing()$

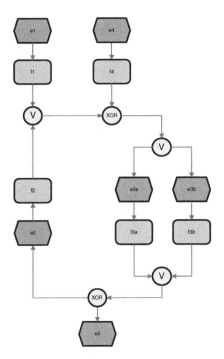

Figure 3.3. The second refinement example EPC in Visio

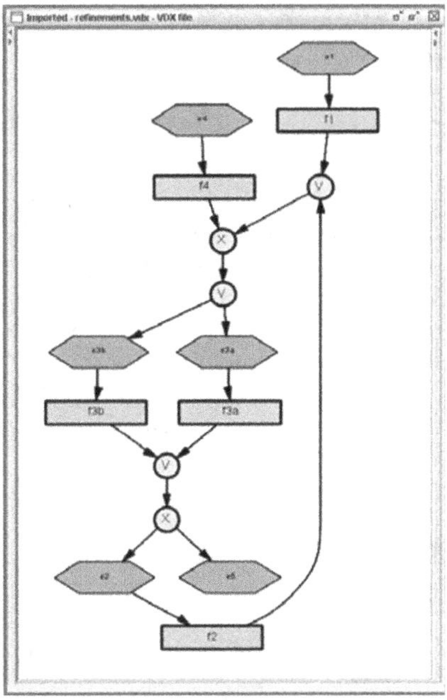

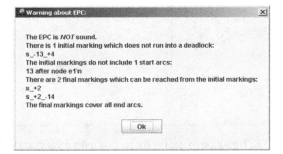

Figure 3.4. The second refinement example EPC loaded in ProM

Figure 3.5. Feedback about EPC soundness

One approach to cope with this problem is to apply reduction rules that preserve the property under consideration (see [313]), i.e. EPC soundness. In the following section, we will investigate in how far reduction rules can be applied for EPCs.

3.3 Verification by Reduction Rules

In the previous section, we presented a verification approach for EPC soundness based on the reachability graph. Similar to Petri nets, the concurrency of functions

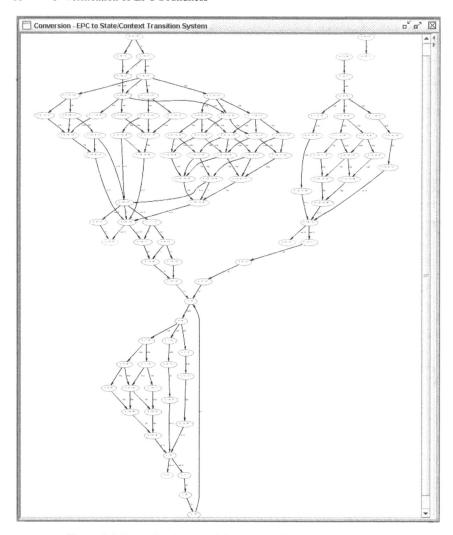

Figure 3.6. Transition System of the second refinement example EPC

and events can lead to a performance problem due to the state explosion. In this section, we focus on an approach based on reduction rules to increase the performance of the verification process. First, we revisit related work on reduction rules for business process models (Section 3.3.1). We then present a set of reduction rules for EPCs that extends existing rule sets and that is easy to apply for a given model (Section 3.3.2). In the following pages, we use the term *reduction kit* to refer to a set of reduction rules (see [120]). It must be noted that our EPC reduction kit is sound but not complete: the fact that an EPC is not completely reduced does not provide an answer to the verification question. There is still a possibility of unknown errors. Even if the model is not completely reduced, however, the reachability graph verification is more efficient for the unreduced EPC. If the EPC is reduced to the trivial model and no errors are recorded, it is sound. In Section 3.3.3 we present a reduction algorithm and a respective implementation in the *xoEPC* program. Section 3.3.4 illustrates the application of *xoEPC* in the analysis of the SAP Reference model. In particular, we present which rules are used how often, how many EPCs could be reduced and how many errors were found.

3.3.1 Related Work on Reduction Rules

The state explosion problem is one of the motivations for considering reduction rules for Petri nets. A set of six reduction rules that preserve liveness, safeness and boundedness of a Petri net is introduced in *Berthelot* [55, 56] and summarized in *Murata* [313, p.553]. Unfortunately, this set of rules is not complete. There are live, safe and bounded Petri nets that cannot be reduced to the trivial model by these rules. Figure 3.7 shows an illustration of the six reduction rules including (a) *fusion of series places*, (b) *fusion of series transitions*, (c) *fusion of parallel places*, (d) *fusion of parallel transitions*, (e) *elimination of self-loop places*, and (f) *elimination of self-loop transitions*. For the Petri net class of free choice nets, *Esparza* shows that there exists a complete reduction kit including rules for fusion of places and transitions similar to (a) and (b) of *Murata* and two linear dependency rules to eliminate nonnegative linearly dependent places and transitions [120, 105]. By showing that soundness corresponds to liveness and boundedness of the short-circuited net, *Van der Aalst* makes the reduction kit of *Murata* applicable to the analysis of workflow nets [2].

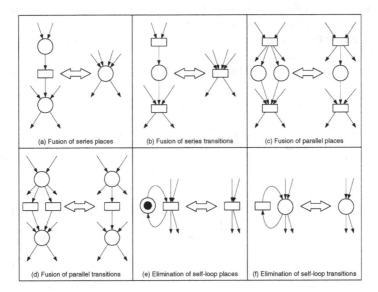

(a) Fusion of series places	(b) Fusion of series transitions	(c) Fusion of parallel places
(d) Fusion of parallel transitions	(e) Elimination of self-loop places	(f) Elimination of self-loop transitions

Figure 3.7. Six reduction rules to preserve liveness, safeness, and boundedness [313]

Sadiq & Orlowska discuss the applicability of reduction rules for business process models that are defined in a language called workflow graphs [372, 373, 374]. They provide a kit including (a) the *adjacent reduction rule* to merge parallel splits and joins, (b) the *closed reduction rule* to eliminate redundant synchronization arcs and (c) the *overlapped reduction rule* that eliminates a proper block with one XOR-split, multiple AND-splits, multiple XOR-joins and one AND-join. *Lin et al.* show that the reduction kit of *Sadiq & Orlowska* is not complete by giving a counter example [249]. They propose a new reduction kit including seven rules: (a) the *terminal reduction rule* to eliminate sequential start and end nodes, (b) the *sequential reduction rule* to eliminate sequences, (c) the *adjacent reduction rule* of *Sadiq & Orlowska*, (d) the *closed reduction rule* of *Sadiq & Orlowska*, (e) the *choice-convergence reduction rule* to move a choice out of a parallel structure, (f) the *sychronizer-convergence reduction rule* that moves a sychronization out of a choice structure and (g) the *merge-fork reduction rule* which actually replaces a simple structure with a complicated one. *Van der Aalst, Hirnschall and Verbeek* showed that the original reduction kit is not complete and question approaches to continue adding rules for counter examples [10]. They use a completely different approach building on well-known Petri net results. By providing a mapping to Petri nets they show that the resulting net is free choice [10]. This makes the complete reduction kit of *Esparza* applicable and basic Petri net analysis techniques and tools can be applied and soundness can be checked in polynomial time.

A set of reduction rules for flat EPCs was first mentioned in *Van Dongen, Van der Aalst and Verbeek* in [109]. The idea is to eliminate those structures of an EPC that are trivially correct for any semantics formalization. Rule (a) deletes sequential elements from the EPC, i.e. elements with one input and one output arc. Rule (b) merges multiple parallel arcs between connectors of the same type. This might result in connectors with one-one cardinality so that rule (a) can be applied. Rules (c) and (d) merge consecutive join and split connectors of the same type. Rule (e) eliminates the backward arc of a simple XOR-loop. Finally, rule (f) reduces OR-loops based on

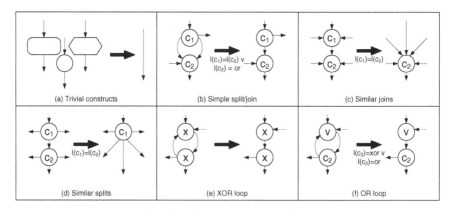

Figure 3.8. Six reduction rules of [109]

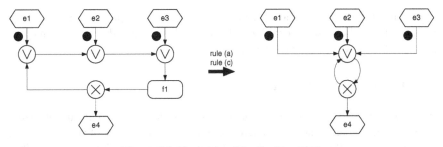

Figure 3.9. Unclean and deadlocking EPC

the assumption that only arcs from outside the loop are synchronized (see [108]). The authors use this reduction kit to derive a more compact EPC for further analysis. The domain expert then has to specify the set of allowed initial markings for the reduced EPC. This information is used in a coverability analysis of a Petri net representation of the EPC to identify structural problems. The approach has been implemented as an analysis plug-in which is shipped with the standard distribution of ProM.

While the rules by *Van Dongen et al.* are indeed helpful to reduce the complexity of the verification problem, it is possible to reduce erroneous models (assuming the semantics of this book) with the combination of rule (c) and (f). Figure 3.9 shows an EPC that is unclean under the semantics of *Kindler* [218] and in deadlock under the semantics of *Wynn et al.* [464] as well as under the semantics presented in Section 2.4.4. This EPC can still be easily reduced by first merging the three OR-joins with rule (c) and then eliminating the OR-loop with rule (f). The further application of rule (a) yields a trivial EPC consisting only of three start events, one OR-join and one end event. Since loops without XOR-entries deadlock following our novel semantics, we have to consider structured loops with OR-entries as error cases.

In [466], *Wynn, Verbeek, Van der Aalst, Ter Hofstede and Edmond* discuss reduction rules for Reset nets, a Petri net class that offers so-called reset arcs which clean tokens from the net. Their reduction kit of seven reduction rules is mainly inspired by rules for Petri nets by *Murata* [313] and for free-choice nets by *Esparza* [120, 105]. The rules 1 to 4 (*fusion of series places* and of *series transitions* as well as *fusion of parallel places* and *parallel transitions*) can be directly related to the rules of *Murata* and *Esparza*. Rule 5 (*abstraction rule*) removes a sequence of a place s and a transition t where s is the only input of t and t the only output of s and there is no direct connection between the inputs of s and the outputs of t. Rule 6 for *self-loop transitions* matches the self-loop rule of *Murata*. Rule 7 (*fusion of equivalent subnets*) allows identical parts of the net to be merged.

Based on a Reset net formalization, *Wynn, Verbeek, Van der Aalst, Ter Hofstede and Edmond* define a reduction kit for YAWL [467]. They also prove that it preserves soundness by constructing respective Reset net reductions. Several rules are defined for YAWL nets including *fusion of series, parallel, and alternative conditions*; *fusion of series, parallel, and alternative tasks*; *elimination of self-loop tasks, fusion of AND-split and AND-join tasks*; *fusion of XOR-split and XOR-join tasks*; *fusion of an OR-join and another task* and *fusion of incoming edges to an OR-join*. The last two rules differ from the other rules since they are not explicitly proved based on Reset net rules. This is because the enabling rule of an OR-join depends on the reachability analysis of the YAWL net (see [464]).

3.3.2 A Reduction Kit for EPCs

In this section, we take the work of *Van Dongen et al.* as a starting point and introduce novel reduction rules. Since we want to increase the performance of verification, we are interested in rules which involve as few directly connected nodes as possible. We are not interested, however, in the completeness of the rules. For each reduction rule, we have to show that it does not introduce a deadlock into the EPC that affects property (ii) of EPC soundness. For rules that reduce the set of initial or final markings we have to show that properties (i) to (iii) of EPC soundness are not violated. Additionally, both the source and the target EPC have to fulfill the requirements of relaxed syntactically correctness.

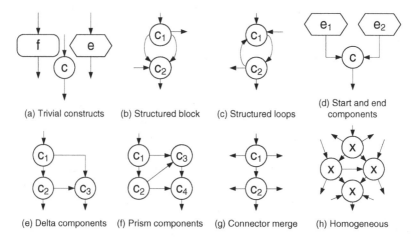

Figure 3.10. Overview of patterns that are addressed by EPC reduction rules

In this context, a *reduction rule T* is a binary relation that transforms a source EPC_1 to a simpler target EPC_2 that has less nodes and/or arcs (see [120]). We associate an index function f_A with an EPC for keeping track of multiple arcs that might be derived in the reduction process. A reduction rule is bound to a *condition* that defines for which arcs and nodes it is applicable. We define the *construction* of the target EPC and *error cases* for several of the rules. Our strategy is to record errors while applying the reduction and continue with the reduced model to potentially find further errors. Figure 3.10 gives an overview of the reduction rules that we discuss on the following pages.

Some of the reduction rules we will define might introduce pre-existing arcs to the reduced EPC. Consider the EPC on the left hand side of Figure 3.11. The

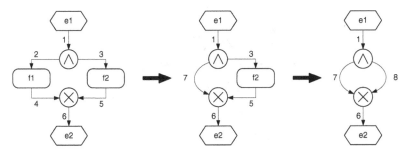

Figure 3.11. Reduction producing arcs that already exist

reduction of trivial constructs that we will introduce afterwards first replaces the function $f1$ and its input and output arcs (2 and 4) by a single arc (7). The same procedure is then applied for function $f2$. The problem in this case is that an arc between the AND-split and the XOR-join already exists. We use the index set I_A, the index function f_A and the count function ξ to keep track of added arcs that already exist. While the EPC on the right-hand side has only one arc between the two connectors, there are two indices 7 and 8 in the index set I_A pointing at it. Without indices we lose the information indicating that the two connectors are problematic. The indexing mechanism allows us to define several rules in a more simple way as opposed to parameterizing each rule to deal with potentially multiple arcs. Note that the EPC semantics can be easily adapted to deal with the index set extension.

Definition 3.3 (Index Set and Index Function for Arcs). Let $EPC = (E, F, C, l, A)$ be a relaxed syntactically correct EPC. Then $I_A \subset I\!N$ is an index set such that $f_A : I_A \rightarrow A$ is a totally surjective function mapping all elements of I_A onto the set of arcs. Furthermore, we define the function $\xi : I_A \times A \rightarrow I\!N$ such that for $a \in A, I_A : \xi(a, I_A) = |\{x \in I_A \mid f_A(x) = a\}|$.

In the following pages, we define the different reduction rules. These definitions build on reduction relations T_x, where $x \in \{a, b, c, d, d1a, d1b, d2a, d2b, e, f, g, h\}$ refers to the different rule types as depicted in Figure 3.10.

Trivial Constructs

The reduction of trivial constructs allows for eliminating sequential nodes from EPCs that have one input and one output arc. These nodes do not cause deadlock problems and neither does their removal. The rule is similar to the fusion of series places and transitions for Petri nets by *Murata* [313] and previously defined by *Van Dongen et al.* [109]. Figure 3.12 illustrates the rule.

Definition 3.4 (Reduction of Trivial Constructs). Let EPC_1 and EPC_2 be two relaxed syntactically correct EPCs with the respective index sets I_{A_1} and I_{A_2}, index and count functions f_{A_1}, f_{A_2}, ξ_1, and ξ_2. The pair $((EPC_1, I_{A_1}), (EPC_2, I_{A_2})) \in T_a$ if the following conditions hold for a node $n \in N_1$ of EPC_1, and if EPC_2 can

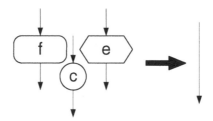

Figure 3.12. Reduction of trivial constructs

be constructed from EPC_1 as follows:

Condition:

1) there exists $n \in N_1$ such that
$$|n_{in}| = |n_{out}| = 1 \wedge$$
$$n_{in} = \{(v,n)\} \wedge \xi_1((v,n), I_{A_1}) = 1 \wedge$$
$$n_{out} = \{(n,w)\} \wedge \xi_1((n,w), I_{A_1}) = 1.$$

Construction:

2) $E_2 = E_1 \setminus \{n\}$
3) $F_2 = F_1 \setminus \{n\}$
4) $C_2 = C_1 \setminus \{n\}$
5) $A_2 = (A_1 \cup \{(v,w)\}) \setminus \{(v,n),(n,w)\}$
6) Introduce i_{vw} such that $i_{vw} \in \mathbb{N} \setminus I_{A_1} \wedge$
$$I_{A_2} = (I_{A_1} \cup \{i_{vw}\}) \setminus \{i \in I_{A_1} \mid f_{A_1}(i) = (v,n) \vee f_{A_1}(i) = (n,w)\} \wedge$$
$$\forall i \in I_{A_2} \setminus \{i_{vw}\} : f_{A_2}(i) = f_{A_1}(i) \wedge$$
$$f_{A_2}(i_{vw}) = (v,w)$$

There are no error cases.

It can be shown that the rule preserves relaxed syntactical correctness. If all nodes of EPC_1 were on a path from a start to an end node, this must obviously still hold for EPC_2 after reduction. The cardinality restrictions still hold since there is no node beyond the deleted node that has a different cardinality after reduction. Finally, the only case where the rule can produce self-arcs is if an undesirable structure exists such that not every node is on a path from a start to an end node (cf. Figure 2.3 on page 22). According to relaxed syntactical correctness, however, such a structure is not allowed.

Structured Blocks

Structured blocks include a split and a join connector with multiple arcs from the split to the join (see Figure 3.13). To be concise, the multiple arcs are an illustration of the fact that there are multiple indices in I_{A_1} pointing at the arc from c_1 to c_2. Such structured blocks usually appear when parallel or alternative sequences are reduced by other rules. If the type of both connectors is equivalent, the rule matches the parallel place and transition reduction rules of *Murata* [313] and the structured component rule of *Van Dongen et al.* [109]. In these cases, it is safe to fuse the parallel arcs: the multiple indices are replaced by a single index. There are four problematic cases: if c_1 is an XOR or an OR and c_2 is an AND, the process can run into a deadlock which implies that it is not sound. If c_2 is an XOR and c_1 is an AND or an OR, there is a lack of synchronization which can result in contact situations. The process is again not sound. We record the error in these cases and continue searching for further errors in the reduced model.

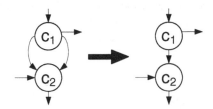

Figure 3.13. Reduction of structured blocks

Definition 3.5 (Reduction of Structured Block). Let EPC_1 and EPC_2 be two relaxed syntactically correct EPCs with the respective index sets I_{A_1} and I_{A_2}, index and count functions f_{A_1}, f_{A_2}, ξ_1, and ξ_2. The pair $((EPC_1, I_{A_1}), (EPC_2, I_{A_2})) \in T_b$ if the following conditions hold for a pair of connectors $c_1, c_2 \in C_1$ of EPC_1, and if EPC_2 can be constructed from EPC_1 as follows:

Condition:
1) there exists $c_1, c_2 \in C_1$ such that
   $$c_1 \neq c_2 \wedge (c_1, c_2) \in A_1 \wedge \xi((c_1, c_2), I_{A_1}) > 1$$
Construction:
2) $E_2 = E_1$
3) $F_2 = F_1$
4) $C_2 = C_1$
5) $A_2 = A_1$
6) Introduce i_{cc} such that $i_{cc} \in I\!N \setminus I_{A_1} \wedge$
   $$I_{A_2} = I_{A_1} \cup \{i_{cc}\} \setminus \{i \in I_{A_1} \mid f_{A_1}(i) = (c_1, c_2)\} \wedge$$
   $$\forall i \in I_{A_2} \setminus \{i_{cc}\} : f_{A_2}(i) = f_{A_1}(i) \wedge$$
   $$f_{A_2}(i_{cc}) = (c_1, c_2)$$
Error Cases:
7) $l(c_1) = xor \wedge l(c_2) = and$ (Deadlock)
8) $l(c_1) = or \wedge l(c_2) = and$ (Potential Deadlock)
9) $l(c_1) = and \wedge l(c_2) = xor$ (Lack of Synchronization)
10) $l(c_1) = or \wedge l(c_2) = xor$ (Potential Lack of Synchronization)

Obviously the rule preserves the cardinality restrictions of all nodes and the coherence restriction of relaxed syntactical correctness.

Structured Loops

Structured loops include a join as an entry to the loop and a split as exit, with one arc from the join to the split and one in the opposite direction (see Figure 3.14). If the type of both connectors is XOR, the rule is similar to the loop elimination rules by *Murata* [313] and the XOR-loop rule of *Van Dongen et al.* [109]. In these cases, it is safe to delete the back arc. There are also problematic cases: if c_1 is not an XOR, the loop cannot be entered because the entry-join deadlocks. If c_2 is not an XOR, the process can run into a contact situation (see Observation 3.2). In both cases, the process is not sound and an error is recorded before applying the reduction rule.

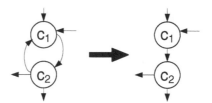

Figure 3.14. Reduction of structured loops

Definition 3.6 (Reduction of Structured Loop). Let EPC_1 and EPC_2 be two relaxed syntactically correct EPCs with the respective index sets I_{A_1} and I_{A_2}, index and count functions f_{A_1}, f_{A_2}, ξ_1, and ξ_2. The pair $((EPC_1, I_{A_1}), (EPC_2, I_{A_2})) \in T_c$ if the following conditions hold for a pair of connectors $c_1, c_2 \in C_1$ of EPC_1, and if EPC_2 can be constructed from EPC_1 as follows:
Condition:
1) there exists $c_1, c_2 \in C_1$ such that
    $c_1 \neq c_2 \land (c_1, c_2) \in A_1 \land (c_2, c_1) \in A_1 \land$
    $\xi((c_1, c_2), I_{A_1}) = 1 \land \xi((c_2, c_1), I_{A_1}) = 1$
Construction:
2) $E_2 = E_1$
3) $F_2 = F_1$
4) $C_2 = C_1$
5) $A_2 = A_1 \setminus \{(c_2, c_1)\}$
6) $I_{A_2} = I_{A_1} \setminus \{i \in I_{A_1} \mid f_{A_1}(i) = (c_2, c_1)\} \land$
    $\forall i \in I_{A_2} : f_{A_2}(i) = f_{A_1}(i)$
Error Cases:
7) $l(c_1) \neq xor$ (Loop cannot be entered)
8) $l(c_2) \neq xor$ (Potential contact situation)

The rule again preserves the cardinality restrictions of all nodes and the coherence restriction of relaxed syntactical correctness.

Figure 3.15 shows an example from the SAP Reference Model of the Personnel Appraisal process from the Personal Development branch. It includes two problems

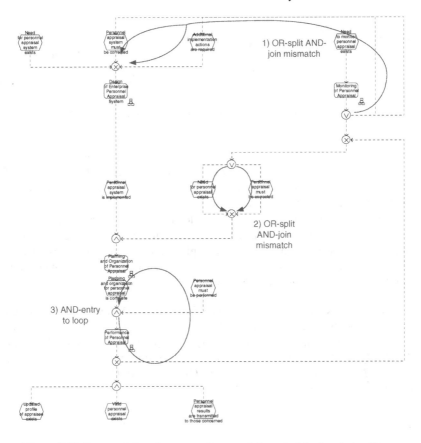

Figure 3.15. Personnel Development – Personnel Appraisal (reduced size 8)

with structured blocks. The first error at the top involves an OR-split and an AND-join. With this mismatch, it is possible that the OR-split activates only one branch. As a consequence, the AND-join can deadlock. The second problem is caused by another mismatch of an OR-split and an AND-join in the center of the figure. The third error relates to an AND-join that is an entry point to a loop. Since we have two loop-entries (there is an XOR-join entry at the left top of the model) this problem cannot be detected by the structured loop rule. It is a particular type of a start and end component that we discuss in the following.

Start and End Components

A specific verification problem of EPCs, in contrast to workflow nets, is that they may have multiple start and end nodes. Real-world models sometimes have more than 20 start events (i.e. $|I_{EPC}| = 2^{20} - 1$ initial markings). In this case, the reduction of these nodes becomes a critical issue to make verification feasible regarding the complexity (see [440, 276]). In this section we introduce reduction rules for so-called

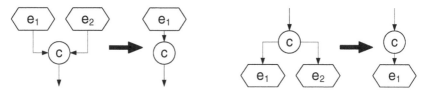

Figure 3.16. Reduction of structured start and end components

structured and unstructured start and end components. Both these rule sets aim to reduce the number of start and end events without affecting the soundness of the EPC. For unstructured start and end components, we distinguish a set for connectors not on a cycle and connectors on a cycle.

Figure 3.16 illustrates the reduction rules for *structured start and end components*. A structured start component contains two start events and one join connector, while a structured end component has one split connector and two end events. In both cases, the second event and the respective arc can be eliminated without affecting the overall soundness. Furthermore, there are no error cases.

Definition 3.7 (Reduction of Structured Start and End Components). Let EPC_1 and EPC_2 be two relaxed syntactically correct EPCs with the respective index sets I_{A_1} and I_{A_2}, index and count functions f_{A_1}, f_{A_2}, ξ_1, and ξ_2. The pair $((EPC_1, I_{A_1}), (EPC_2, I_{A_2})) \in T_d$ if the following conditions hold for two start or two end events $e_1, e_2 \in E_1$ and a connector $c \in C_1$ of EPC_1, and if EPC_2 can be constructed from EPC_1 as follows:

Condition:
1) there exists $c \in C_1, e_1, e_2 \in E_1$ and $a_1, a_2 \in A_1$ such that
$$e_1 \neq e_2 \wedge$$
$$a_1 = (e_1, c), a_2 = (e_2, c) \in A_1 \vee a_1 = (c, e_1), a_2 = (c, e_2) \in A_1 \wedge$$
$$\xi(a_1, I_{A_1}) = 1 \wedge \xi(a_2, I_{A_1}) = 1$$
Construction:
2) $E_2 = E_1 \setminus \{e_2\}$
3) $F_2 = F_1$
4) $C_2 = C_1$
5) $A_2 = A_1 \setminus \{a_2\}$
6) $I_{A_2} = I_{A_1} \setminus \{i \in I_{A_1} \mid f_{A_1}(i) = a_2\} \wedge$
$\quad \forall i \in I_{A_2} : f_{A_2}(i) = f_{A_1}(i)$
There are no error cases.

The rule preserves the cardinality restrictions of all nodes and the restriction that all nodes must be on a path from a start to an end node. The reduced model is, therefore, relaxed syntactically correct.

Figure 3.17 shows an EPC from the SAP Reference Model that illustrates the correctness of the reduction rule and two observations can be made. The two start events on the top left-hand side can be merged in such a way that afterwards the subsequent AND-join is deleted. In this case, a token on the start arc in the reduced EPC

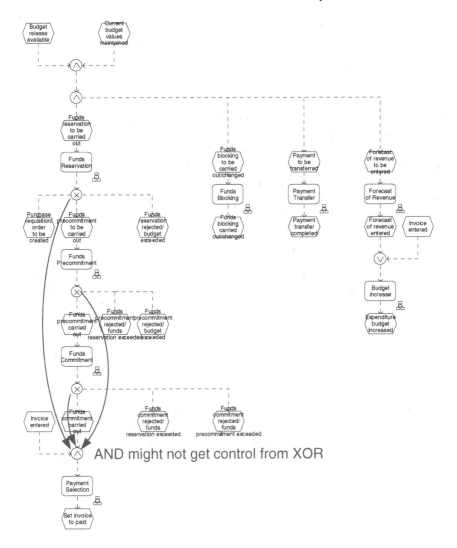

Figure 3.17. Financial Accounting – Funds Management – Budget Execution

represents the case where there are tokens on each of the two start arcs in the unreduced model. Both cases lead to the same behavior once the subsequent AND-split connector is reached. Additionally, the red arrows highlight three errors of the EPC, implying that the model is not sound. In each of these cases, end events are connected to one XOR-split while there is an AND-join that may later need a token to continue processing. The reduction rule merges the two end events into one in each case. For example, the *Purchase requisition/order to be created* and the *Funds reservation rejected/budget exceeded* end events after the first problematic XOR-split. This way, the erroneous behavior is preserved since it is not important *how many* XOR-jumps out of the process exist, but only *if* there exists one. The identification of such problematic jumps is subject of the next reduction rule for unstructured start and end components.

Figure 3.18 shows the reduction rules for *unstructured start and end components* that are applicable for connectors that are *not on a cycle*. In case (a) there is an AND-split connector c_1 followed by an end event. Since this end event is reachable if the connector is reachable, we can delete e_1 and only consider the input arc of c_1. The output arc not pointing to e_1 will always receive control via c_1 no matter whether there is an arc to e_1 or not. If c_1 is not an AND-split but an OR- or an XOR-split, we can consider case (b) where the structure is extended with a join-connector c_2 and a start event e_2. If c_2 is an AND-join it might not get control from the (X)OR-split c_1 which implies that the structure is not sound. In this case, an error is recorded and the branch to e_1 as the reason is deleted. This pattern appears three times in Figure 3.17.

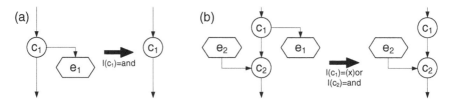

Figure 3.18. Reduction of unstructured start and end components, not on cycle

Definition 3.8 (Reduction of Unstructured Acyclic Start and End Components (a)). Let EPC_1 and EPC_2 be two relaxed syntactically correct EPCs with the respective index sets I_{A_1} and I_{A_2}, index and count functions f_{A_1}, f_{A_2}, ξ_1, and ξ_2. The pair $((EPC_1, I_{A_1}), (EPC_2, I_{A_2})) \in T_{d1a}$ if the following conditions hold for one end event $e_1 \in E_1$ and a connector $c_1 \in C_1$ of EPC_1, and if EPC_2 can be constructed from EPC_1 as follows:

Condition:
1) there exists $c_1 \in C_1, e_1 \in E_1$ and $a_1 \in A_1$ such that
$e_1 \bullet = \emptyset \wedge$
$a_1 = (c_1, e_1,) \in A_1 \wedge l(c_1) = and \wedge$
$\xi(a_1, I_{A_1}) = 1 \wedge$
$\nexists n \in N \setminus \{c_1\} : c_1 \hookrightarrow n \hookrightarrow c_1$

Construction:
2) $E_2 = E_1 \setminus \{e_1\}$
3) $F_2 = F_1$
4) $C_2 = C_1$
5) $A_2 = A_1 \setminus \{a_1\}$
6) $I_{A_2} = \{i \in I_{A_1} \mid f_{A_1}(i) \neq a_1\} \wedge$
$\forall i \in I_{A_2} : f_{A_2}(i) = f_{A_1}(i)$

There are no error cases.

Definition 3.9 (Reduction of Unstructured Acyclic Start and End Components (b)). Let EPC_1 and EPC_2 be two relaxed syntactically correct EPCs with the respective index sets I_{A_1} and I_{A_2}, index and count functions f_{A_1}, f_{A_2}, ξ_1, and ξ_2. The pair $((EPC_1, I_{A_1}), (EPC_2, I_{A_2})) \in T_{d1b}$ if the following conditions hold for one start or one end event $e_1, e_2 \in E_1$ and a connector $c_1, c_2 \in C_1$ of EPC_1, and if EPC_2 can be constructed from EPC_1 as follows:

Condition:

1) there exists $c_1, c_2 \in C_1, e_1, e_2 \in E_1$ and $a_1, a_2, a_3 \in A_1$ such that
$$e_1 \neq e_2 \wedge c_1 \neq c_2 \wedge$$
$$e_1 \bullet = \emptyset \wedge \bullet e_2 = \emptyset$$
$$l(c_1) \neq and \wedge l(c_2) = and \wedge$$
$$a_1 = (c_1, e_1,), a_2 = (e_2, c_2), a_3 = (c_1, c_2) \in A_1 \wedge (c_2, c_1) \notin A_1 \wedge$$
$$\xi(a_1, I_{A_1}) = 1 \wedge \xi(a_2, I_{A_1}) = 1 \wedge \xi(a_3, I_{A_1}) = 1 \wedge$$
$$\nexists n \in N \setminus \{c_1, c_2\} : c_1 \hookrightarrow n \hookrightarrow c_1 \vee c_2 \hookrightarrow n \hookrightarrow c_2$$

Construction:

2) $E_2 = E_1 \setminus \{e_1\}$
3) $F_2 = F_1$
4) $C_2 = C_1$
5) $A_2 = A_1 \setminus \{a_1\}$
6) $I_{A_2} = I_{A_1} \setminus \{i \in I_{A_1} \mid f_{A_1}(i) = a_1\} \wedge$
$\quad \forall i \in I_{A_2} : f_{A_2}(i) = f_{A_1}(i)$

Error Cases:

7) The reduction rule always yields an error since c_2 might not get control from c_1.

Both these rules for unstructured acyclic start and end components preserve the cardinality restrictions of all nodes and the coherence restriction of relaxed syntactical correctness.

Figure 3.19 shows the reduction rules for *unstructured start and end components* that are applicable for connectors that are *on a cycle*. By considering two connectors, we make sure that the reduction does not delete the last exit or the last entry point of a loop. Such a reduction would violate the relaxed syntactical correctness of the reduced EPC. In case (a) there are two exit-connectors $c_1, c_2 \in C_1$ to a cyclic part of the EPC and at least one of them, i.e. $c_{nonxor} \in \{c_1, c_2\}$, is not of type XOR. This implies that if the loop is executed multiple times the non-XOR-connector c_{nonxor} will repeatedly create tokens at the same exit of the loop. According to our definition of safe semantics, this leads to contact situations and unsound behavior of the EPC. Therefore, the reduction rule eliminates the reason for this error (the end-event from the non-XOR-connector c_{nonxor}). In case (b) there are two entry connectors to a loop. If there is an AND-join among them (c_{and}) the EPC is not sound since there will be a token missing on the start arc in the second execution of the loop. The start-event leading to the AND-join c_{and} is, therefore, deleted and an error is recorded.

Definition 3.10 (Reduction of Unstructured Cyclic Start and End Components (a)). Let EPC_1 and EPC_2 be two relaxed syntactically correct EPCs with the respective index sets I_{A_1} and I_{A_2}, index and count functions f_{A_1}, f_{A_2}, ξ_1, and ξ_2. The pair $((EPC_1, I_{A_1}), (EPC_2, I_{A_2})) \in T_{d2a}$ if the following conditions hold for one

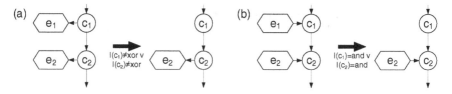

Figure 3.19. Reduction of unstructured start and end components, not on cycle

start or one end event $e_1, e_2 \in E_1$ and a connector $c_1, c_2 \in C_1$ of EPC_1, and if EPC_2 can be constructed from EPC_1 as follows:

Condition:

1) there exists $c_1, c_2 \in C_1, e_1, e_2 \in E_1$ and $a_1, a_2, a_3 \in A_1$ such that
$$e_1 \neq e_2 \wedge c_1 \neq c_2 \wedge$$
$$e_1 \bullet = \emptyset \wedge e_2 \bullet = \emptyset$$
$$a_1 = (c_1, e_1,), a_2 = (c_2, e_2), a_3 = (c_1, c_2) \in A_1 \wedge (c_2, c_1) \notin A_1 \wedge$$
$$\xi(a_1, I_{A_1}) = 1 \wedge \xi(a_2, I_{A_1}) = 1 \wedge \xi(a_3, I_{A_1}) = 1 \wedge$$
$$\exists n_1 \in N \setminus \{c_1\} : c_1 \hookrightarrow n_1 \hookrightarrow c_1 \wedge$$
$$\exists n_2 \in N \setminus \{c_2\} : c_2 \hookrightarrow n_2 \hookrightarrow c_2 \wedge$$
there exists $c_{nonxor} \in \{c_1, c_2\}, e_{nonxor} \in \{e_1, e_2\}$:
$$l(c_{nonxor}) \neq xor \wedge a_{nonxor} = (c_{nonxor}, e_{nonxor})$$

Construction:

2) $E_2 = E_1 \setminus \{e_{nonxor}\}$
3) $F_2 = F_1$
4) $C_2 = C_1$
5) $A_2 = A_1 \setminus \{a_{nonxor}\}$
6) $I_{A_2} = I_{A_1} \setminus \{i \in I_{A_1} \mid f_{A_1}(i) = a_{nonxor}\} \wedge$
$\forall i \in I_{A_2} : f_{A_2}(i) = f_{A_1}(i)$

Error Cases:

7) The reduction rule always reports an error since c_{nonxor} produces repeatedly tokens on a_{nonxor}.

Definition 3.11 (Reduction of Unstructured Cyclic Start and End Components (b)). Let EPC_1 and EPC_2 be two relaxed syntactically correct EPCs with the respective index sets I_{A_1} and I_{A_2}, index and count functions $f_{A_1}, f_{A_2}, \xi_1,$ and ξ_2. The pair $((EPC_1, I_{A_1}), (EPC_2, I_{A_2})) \in T_{d2b}$ if the following conditions hold for one start or one end event $e_1, e_2 \in E_1$ and a connector $c_1, c_2 \in C_1$ of EPC_1, and if EPC_2 can be constructed from EPC_1 as follows:

Condition:

1) there exists $c_1, c_2 \in C_1, e_1, e_2 \in E_1$ and $a_1, a_2, a_3 \in A_1$ such that
$$e_1 \neq e_2 \wedge c_1 \neq c_2 \wedge$$
$$\bullet e_1 = \emptyset \wedge \bullet e_2 = \emptyset \wedge$$
$$a_1 = (e_1, c_1,), a_2 = (e_2, c_2), a_3 = (c_1, c_2) \in A_1 \wedge (c_2, c_1) \notin A_1 \wedge$$
$$\xi(a_1, I_{A_1}) = 1 \wedge \xi(a_2, I_{A_1}) = 1 \wedge \xi(a_3, I_{A_1}) = 1 \wedge$$
$$\exists n_1 \in N \setminus \{c_1\} : c_1 \hookrightarrow n_1 \hookrightarrow c_1 \wedge$$
$$\exists n_2 \in N \setminus \{c_2\} : c_2 \hookrightarrow n_2 \hookrightarrow c_2 \wedge$$

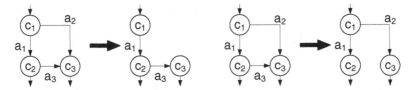

Figure 3.20. Reduction of Delta Components

there exists $c_{and} \in \{c_1, c_2\}, e_{nonxor} \in \{e_1, e_2\}$:
$l(c_{and}) = and \wedge a_{and} = (e_{and}, c_{and})$
Construction:
2) $E_2 = E_1 \setminus \{e_{and}\}$
3) $F_2 = F_1$
4) $C_2 = C_1$
5) $A_2 = A_1 \setminus \{a_{and}\}$
6) $I_{A_2} = I_{A_1} \setminus \{i \in I_{A_1} \mid f_{A_1}(i) = a_{and}\} \wedge$
$\forall i \in I_{A_2} : f_{A_2}(i) = f_{A_1}(i)$
Error Cases:
7) The reduction rule always reports an error since c_{and} will not have a token on its input arc a_{and} in the second execution of the cyclic part.

Both these rules for unstructured cyclic start and end components preserve the cardinality restrictions of all nodes and the coherence restriction of relaxed syntactical correctness. If we had considered only a single pair of a connector and an event, we would not be able to guarantee that every node would still be on a path from a start to an end node.

Delta Components

In this section, we will discuss a subpart of an EPC built from three connectors that we call delta component. A delta component contains one input arc to a first split which is followed by another split and a join in the postset. The preset of the join connector also only includes the two splits. There are two output arcs from a delta component: one from the second split and one from the join. Accordingly, there are 3^3 types of delta components for each combination of three connector labels (see Figure 3.20). For some of the delta components it is possible to eliminate the arc from the first split to the join or from the second split to the join. In some cases no reduction is possible. Some delta components produce a deadlock or a contact situation at the join connector. If there is an error case, an empty circle represents a missing token and a filled circle a token that is potentially too much (see Figures 3.21–3.23).

Figure 3.21 illustrates delta components where the first split is an XOR. If both split connectors are XORs (see first column) the join should also be an XOR. In this case, the arc between the first split and the join can be deleted and the same combination of outputs can still be produced. This also holds if the second split is an OR. If the split is an AND, either both outputs or the right one only is activated.

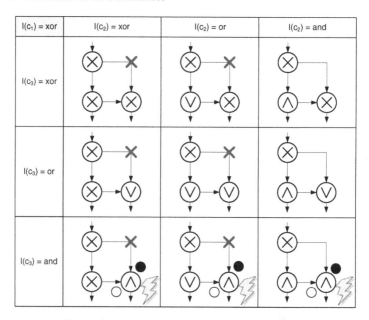

Figure 3.21. Reduction of XOR Delta Components

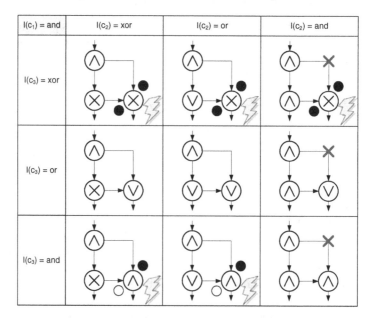

Figure 3.22. Reduction of AND Delta Components

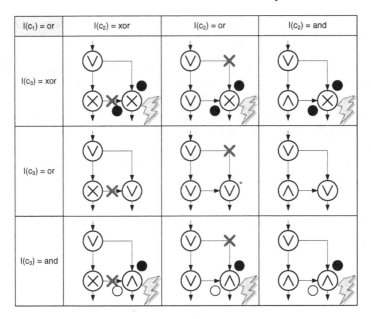

$l(c_1)$ = or	$l(c_2)$ = xor	$l(c_2)$ = or	$l(c_2)$ = and

Figure 3.23. Reduction of OR Delta Components

Therefore, no arc can be deleted. The XOR delta component runs into a deadlock if the join is an AND, but should be an XOR or an OR. We record the error and apply the reduction rule as if the connector had the appropriate label accordingly.

Figure 3.22 depicts delta components with an AND as the first split. In this case, a reduction is only possible if the second split is also an AND. The join should be an AND or an OR in order to avoid a lack of synchronization such as in the first row where the join is an XOR. This lack of synchronization results in contact situations in the reachability graph. If the join is an AND but the second split is an XOR or an OR (third row), there is a potential deadlock since the arc between second split and join might not get a positive token. For both the first and the second column, no reduction can be applied. In this case, the left output is optional while the right output is always covered.

Figure 3.23 shows those delta components that have an OR as first split connector. If the join is an XOR, there is a potential lack of synchronization with subsequent contact situations (first row). If the join is an AND, there might be tokens missing to fire (third row). The second row shows the well-behaving cases where the first OR-split is matched by an OR-join. In these cases, either one or both of the output arcs are taken. The arc between the XOR-split and the OR-join (first column)[5] and the arc between the first OR-split and OR-join (second column) can accordingly be deleted without restricting the output combinations. If the second split is an AND,

---

[5] Please note that this changes the behavior since the OR-join does not have to wait for the XOR-split. Still, the combination of tokens that can be produced on the remaining output arcs of the second and the third connector are the same as in the unreduced case.

the left output is optional and the right is always covered. Therefore, no reduction can be applied.

Definition 3.12 (Reduction of Delta Components). Let EPC_1 and EPC_2 be two relaxed syntactically correct EPCs with the respective index sets I_{A_1} and I_{A_2}, index and count functions f_{A_1}, f_{A_2}, ξ_1, and ξ_2. The pair $((EPC_1, I_{A_1}), (EPC_2, I_{A_2})) \in T_e$ if the following conditions hold for three connectors $c_1, c_2, c_3 \in C_1$, and if EPC_2 can be constructed from EPC_1 as follows:

Condition:

1) there exists $c_1, c_2, c_3 \in C_1, a_1, a_2, a_3 \in A_1$ such that
$c_1 \neq c_2 \wedge c_1 \neq c_3 \wedge c_2 \neq c_3 \wedge$
$a_1 = (c_1, c_2), a_2 = (c_1, c_3), a_3 = (c_2, c_3) \wedge$
$c_1 \bullet = \{c_2, c_3\} \wedge \bullet c_2 = \{c_1\} \wedge \bullet c_3 = \{c_1\} \wedge$
$\xi(a_1, I_{A_1}) = 1 \wedge \xi(a_2, I_{A_1}) = 1 \wedge \xi(a_3, I_{A_1}) = 1 \wedge$

Construction for $l(c_1) = l(c_2) \vee (l(c_1) = xor \wedge l(c_2) = or)$:

2) $E_2 = E_1$
3) $F_2 = F_1$
4) $C_2 = C_1$
5) $A_2 = A_1 \setminus \{a_2\}$
6) $I_{A_2} = I_{A_1} \setminus \{i \in I_{A_1} \mid f_{A_1}(i) = a_2\}$
7) $\forall i \in I_{A_2} : f_{A_2}(i) = f_{A_1}(i)$

Construction for $l(c_1) = or \wedge l(c_2) = xor$:

8) $E_2 = E_1$
9) $F_2 = F_1$
10) $C_2 = C_1$
11) $A_2 = A_1 \setminus \{a_3\}$
12) $I_{A_2} = I_{A_1} \setminus \{i \in I_{A_1} \mid f_{A_1}(i) = a_3\} \wedge$
$i \in I_{A_2} : f_{A_2}(i) = f_{A_1}(i)$

Error cases:

13) $l(c_1) = xor \wedge l(c_3) = and$
14) $l(c_1) = and \wedge l(c_3) = xor$
15) $l(c_1) = and \wedge l(c_2) \neq and \wedge l(c_3) = and$
16) $l(c_1) = or \wedge l(c_3) = xor$
17) $l(c_1) = or \wedge l(c_3) = and$

The rule preserves both the cardinality restrictions of all nodes and the coherence restriction of relaxed syntactical correctness.

Figure 3.24 is another example from the SAP Reference Model. It describes the Quality Inspection for the Technical Object process. In this process, there are two Delta components that contain errors. Both have the structure OR-split, OR-split, XOR-join. In this component, the XOR-join can receive control twice from the first OR-split. This leads to execution problems due to a lack of synchronization. The problem could be fixed by replacing the XOR-join with an OR-join.

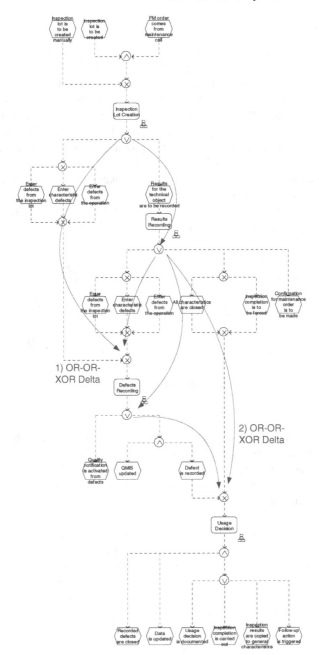

Figure 3.24. Quality Management – Test Equipment Management – Quality Inspection for the Technical Object

Prism Components

In the previous section, we saw four cases of delta components that could not be reduced: (1) c_1 is an XOR and c_2 is an AND, (2) c_1 is an AND and c_2 is an XOR, (3) c_1 is again an AND and c_2 an OR, and (4) c_1 is an OR and c_2 an AND. In all of these cases one output arc is activated optionally, while the other always receives a positive token. Figure 3.25 shows that these delta components can be extended with a fourth connector c_4 to become a prism component. The four cases must always have an OR-join as a fourth connector in order to provide proper synchronization of the mandatory and the optional branch. If the fourth is not an OR, the model is not sound due to a potential deadlock (AND) or a contact situation (XOR). The prism can be reduced by deleting the arc a_3 between the second and the third connector. The type of the third connector is not considered here since the delta rule already contributes reduction and error reports concerning the interplay of connectors c_1 to c_3.

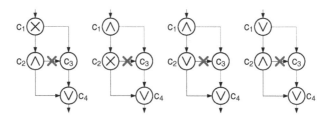

Figure 3.25. Reduction of Prism Components

Definition 3.13 (Reduction of Prism Components). Let EPC_1 and EPC_2 be two relaxed syntactically correct EPCs with the respective index sets I_{A_1} and I_{A_2}, index and count functions f_{A_1}, f_{A_2}, ξ_1, and ξ_2. The pair $((EPC_1, I_{A_1}), (EPC_2, I_{A_2})) \in T_f$ if the following conditions hold for three connectors $c_1, c_2, c_3, c_4 \in C_1$, and if EPC_2 can be constructed from EPC_1 as follows:

Condition:
1) there exists $c_1, c_2, c_3, c_4 \in C_1, a_1, a_2, a_3, a_4, a_5 \in A_1$ such that
$c_1 \neq c_2 \wedge c_1 \neq c_3 \wedge c_1 \neq c_4 \wedge c_2 \neq c_3 \wedge c_2 \neq c_4 \wedge c_3 \neq c_4 \wedge$
$((l(c_1) = xor \wedge l(c_2) = and) \vee (l(c_1) = and \wedge l(c_2) = xor) \vee$
$(l(c_1) = and \wedge l(c_2) = or) \vee (l(c_1) = or \wedge l(c_2) = and)) \wedge$
$a_1 = (c_1, c_2), a_2 = (c_1, c_3), a_3 = (c_2, c_3), a_4 = (c_2, c_4), a_5 = (c_3, c_4) \wedge$
$c_1 \bullet = \{c_2, c_3\} \wedge \bullet c_2 = \{c_1\} \wedge \bullet c_3 = \{c_1\} \wedge$
$c_2 \bullet = \{c_3, c_4\} \wedge c_3 \bullet = \{c_4\} \wedge \bullet c_4 = \{c_2, c_3\} \wedge$
$\xi(a_1, I_{A_1}) = 1 \wedge \ldots \wedge \xi(a_5, I_{A_1}) = 1$

Construction:
2) $E_2 = E_1$
3) $F_2 = F_1$
4) $C_2 = C_1$
5) $A_2 = A_1 \setminus \{a_3\}$

6) $I_{A_2} = I_{A_1} \setminus \{i \in I_{A_1} \mid f_{A_1}(i) = a_3\} \wedge$
   $\forall i \in I_{A_2} : f_{A_2}(i) = f_{A_1}(i)$
Error cases:
7) $l(c_4) \neq$ or

The rule preserves both the cardinality restrictions of all nodes and the coherence restriction of relaxed syntactical correctness.

Connector Merge

Van Dongen et al. point to the fact that two consecutive joins or splits of the same connector type provide the same behavior as if both were merged. Figure 3.26 illustrates the respective reduction rules. One consequence of such a merger is that the identity of the individual connectors is lost. This might be a problem for errors that are found by further rules since it is not clear which of the merged connectors is responsible for the error.

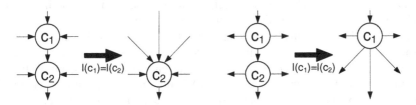

Figure 3.26. Connector Merge

Definition 3.14 (Connector Merge). Let EPC_1 and EPC_2 be two EPCs. The pair $(EPC_1, EPC_2) \in T_g$ if the following conditions hold for two connectors $c_1, c_2 \in C_1$, and if EPC_2 can be constructed from EPC_1 as follows:
Condition:
1) there exists $(c_1, c_2 \in J_1 \wedge (c_1, c_2) \in A_1) \vee (c_1, c_2 \in S_1 \wedge (c_1, c_2) \in A_1)$ such that
   $c_1 \neq c_2 \wedge$
   $(c_2, c_1) \notin A_1 \wedge$
   $l(c_1) = l(c_2) \wedge$
   $\xi((c_1, c_2), I_{A_1}) = 1$
Construction for $c_1, c_2 \in J_1$:
2) $E_2 = E_1$
3) $F_2 = F_1$
4) $C_2 = C_1 \setminus \{c_1\}$
5) $A_2 = \{(x, y) \in A_1 \mid x \neq c_1 \wedge y \neq c_1\} \cup \{(x, y) \mid x \in \bullet c_1 \wedge y = c_2\}$
6) $I_{A_2} = \{i \in I_{A_1} \mid f_{A_1}(i) \neq (c_1, c_2)\} \wedge$

   $\forall \{i \in I_{A_2} \wedge (x, y) = f_{A_1}(i)\} : f_{A_2}(i) = \begin{cases} (x, y) \text{ if and only if } x \neq c_1 \wedge y \neq c_1 \\ (x, c_2) \text{ if and only if } y = c_1 \end{cases}$

Construction for $c_1, c_2 \in S_1$:
6) $E_2 = E_1$
7) $F_2 = F_1$
8) $C_2 = C_1 \setminus \{c_2\}$
5) $A_2 = \{(x, y) \in A_1 \mid x \neq c_2 \wedge y \neq c_2\} \cup \{(x, y) \mid x = c_1 \wedge y \in c_2\bullet\}$
6) $I_{A_2} = \{i \in I_{A_1} \mid f_{A_1}(i) \neq (c_1, c_2)\} \wedge$

$$\forall \{i \in I_{A_2} \wedge (x, y) = f_{A_1}(i)\} : f_{A_2}(i) = \begin{cases} (x, y) & \text{if and only if } x \neq c_1 \wedge y \neq c_1 \\ (c_1, y) & \text{if and only if } x = c_2 \end{cases}$$

There are no error cases.

The rule preserves both the cardinality restrictions of all nodes and the coherence restriction of relaxed syntactical correctness. No self-arcs can be created since $(c_2, c_1) \notin A_1$.

Homogeneous

Similar to the Petri net class of state machines (see [104, p.172]), EPCs with no other than XOR-connectors are trivially correct. Consider the set of initial markings, which includes for each start arc an initial marking, where it is the only arc having a positive token. Since there are only XOR-connectors, there is no deadlock and the sum of positive tokens is one in all markings. Due to the relaxed syntactical correctness of the EPC, every node is on a path from a start to an end node. This also means that all end arcs are reached from the described set of initial markings. An EPC only with XOR-connectors is, therefore, sound. Acyclic EPCs are also correct if either there are only OR-connectors or if there are only AND-connectors and OR-joins. These cases are similar to the flow activity in BPEL which is correct by design (see [440]).

Definition 3.15 (Reduction of Homogeneous EPCs). Let EPC_1 and EPC_2 be two EPCs. The pair $(EPC_1, EPC_2) \in T_h$ if the following conditions hold for C_1, and if EPC_2 can be constructed from EPC_1 as follows:
Condition:
1) $\forall c \in C_1 : l(c) = xor \vee$
$\quad (\nexists n \in N : n \hookrightarrow n \wedge \forall c \in C_1 : l(c) = or) \vee$
$\quad (\nexists n \in N : n \hookrightarrow n \wedge \forall c \in S_1 : l(c) = and \wedge c \in J_1 : l(c) \neq xor)$
Construction:
2) $E_2 = \{e_1, e_2\}$
3) $F_2 = \emptyset$
4) $C_2 = \emptyset$
5) $A_2 = \{(e_1, e_2)\}$
6) $I_{A_2} = \{1, 2\}$
7) $f_{A_2}(1) = e_1, f_{A_2}(2) = e_2$
There are no error cases.

The homogeneous rule is the desirable last reduction. It obviously preserves relaxed syntactical correctness and it yields the trivial EPC which implies that there are not more errors in the source EPC_1. After applying this rule it is easy to determine whether the original EPC was sound. If there are errors recorded in the reduction process, the EPC is not sound. Otherwise, it is sound.

3.3.3 A Reduction Algorithm for EPCs

In the previous section, we defined a set of reduction rules for the verification of EPC soundness. Algorithm 3 illustrates through object-oriented pseudo code how the rules can be prioritized. Each invocation of a rule that has error cases takes the error list to append further errors (lines 7-11). The algorithm tries to minimize the utilization of the connector merge rule, since losing the identity of a connector poses problems in finding the connector that is responsible for an error. The inner while-loop (lines 3-13) accordingly calls all reduction rules except the connector merge as long as the EPC can be reduced. If that is no longer possible, i.e. the new numbers of arcs and nodes equal the old values, the loop is exited and the algorithm tries to merge one connector as part of the outer while-loop. If that succeeds, the inner loop is re-entered again. Otherwise, the reduction terminates. The size of the reduced EPC and a list of errors is returned as a result.

Algorithm 3 Pseudo code for reduction of an EPC

Require: EPC

1: $nodes \leftarrow |N|, arcs \leftarrow |A|, nodesnew \leftarrow 0, arcsnew \leftarrow 0, ErrorList \leftarrow \emptyset$
2: **while** $nodes \neq nodesnew \vee arcs \neq arcsnew$ **do**
3:     **while** $nodes \neq nodesnew \vee arcs \neq arcsnew$ **do**
4:         $nodes \leftarrow |N|, arcs \leftarrow |A|$
5:         $reduceHomogeneous(EPC)$
6:         $reduceTrivialConstructs(EPC)$
7:         $reduceStructuredBlocks(EPC, ErrorList)$
8:         $reduceStructuredLoop(EPC, ErrorList)$
9:         $reduceStartEndComponents(EPC, ErrorList)$
10:         $reduceDeltaComponent(EPC, ErrorList)$
11:         $reducePrismComponent(EPC, ErrorList)$
12:         $nodesnew \leftarrow |N|, arcsnew \leftarrow |A|$
13:     **end while**
14:     $mergeConnector(EPC)$
15:     $nodesnew \leftarrow |N|, arcsnew \leftarrow |A|$
16: **end while**
17: **return** $|N|, ErrorList$

Figure 3.27 illustrates how the reduction algorithm works on the Loan Request EPC from page 19. Deleting the *trivial constructs* yields the EPC that is shown in (b). It consists of eight connectors, one start event, two end events and an end process interface. Applying the *end component reduction* and the trivial construct reduction results in the EPC depicted in (c). On the right-hand side, there is a delta component that cannot be reduced but, together with the OR-join as a fourth connector, yields a well-behaving prism component. The *prism component reduction* then results in

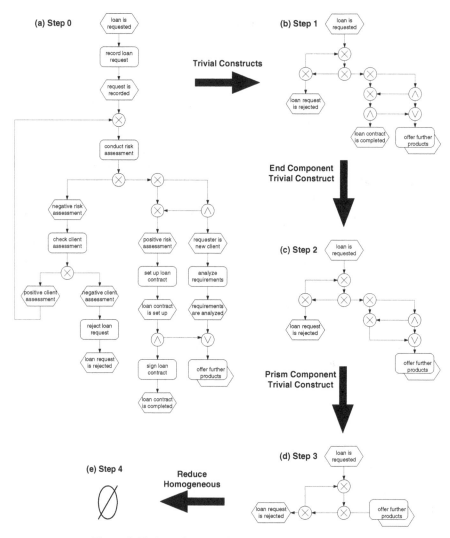

Figure 3.27. Stepwise reduction of the Loan Request EPC

the EPC given in (d). Since there are only XOR-connectors left the Homogeneous Reduction can be applied to reduce the EPC to the trivial EPC.

Algorithm 3 was implemented in a batch program called *xoEPC*.[6] *xoEPC* is written in the object-oriented scripting language XOTcl [316], which is an extension of Tcl (see [452]). Figure 3.28 gives an overview of input files that are read by *xoEPC* and the output files generated by it. *xoEPC* loads all *.xml files from the current directory and checks whether they are ARIS XML files [190, 192]. If this is the case,

---

[6] Some of the functionality of *xoEPC* is available via a web interface at http://wi.wu-wien.ac.at/epc.

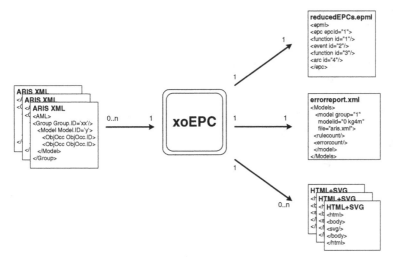

Figure 3.28. ./verif/xoEPC inputs and outputs

the XML is processed with the tDOM package [255], a Tcl implementation of the DOM specification[7]. For each EPC model that has at least one event and one function, *xoEPC* checks relaxed syntactical correctness and applies the reduction algorithm. The internal data structure of xoEPC uses an adjacency matrix representation of the EPC and the reduction methods work on this data structure. All EPCs that cannot be reduced completely are written to the reducedEPCs.epml file.[8] These EPCs can be further analyzed by loading them into ProM via the EPML import. If errors are encountered they are recorded in the errorresults.xml file. This file also records the processing time of the reduction, metadata of the model, as well as the size of the original and the size of the reduced EPC. Finally, an XHTML file with an embedded SVG graphic[9] is generated for each EPC based on the position information in the ARIS XML file. This projects the errors back to the model by highlighting the involved connectors. Figure 3.29 shows an example of an XHTML+SVG file generated by *xoEPC*. The different colors refer to the errors that are listed at the top of the screen. We discuss the errors in detail on page 101. Using this visual information, the modeler can easily fix the problems.

---

[7] For an overview of the various DOM specifications of the World Wide Web Consortium refer to http://www.w3.org/DOM/DOMTR.

[8] The reason for using EPML as an output format and not the ARIS file format is that the EPML representation is more compact and easier to generate. For details refer to [288, 41]. The ARIS format is chosen as an input format since many EPCs such as those of the SAP Reference Model are available in ARIS.

[9] For the respective specifications, see XHTML [334] and SVG [125].

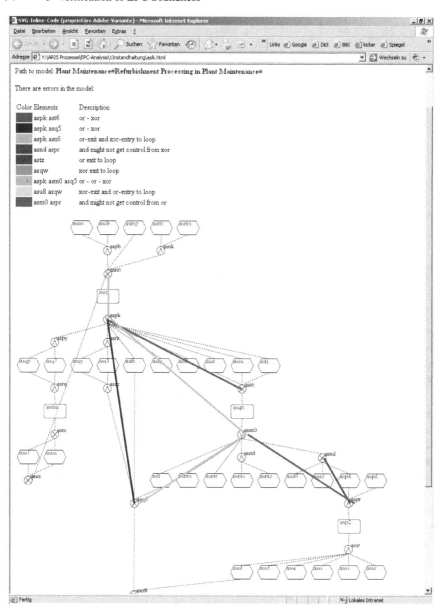

Figure 3.29. Snapshot of an SVG generated by xoEPC for the Plant Maintenance – Refurbishment Processing in Plant Maintenance EPC

3.3.4 Reduction of the SAP Reference Model

In order to test the performance of the reduction kit, we turn back to the SAP Reference Model [211] that was mentioned before. This extensive model collection includes almost 10,000 individual models. 604 of them are EPCs that have at least one event and one function and 600 of them are interpretable: they do not include functions and events with more that one input or output arc. In the following pages, we discuss the reduction performance from four perspectives: (1) Processing time of reduction, (2) Extent of reduction, (3) Applicability of reduction rules, and (4) Number of errors found.

Processing Time of Reduction

The processing of the whole SAP Reference Model took about 18 minutes on a desktop computer with a 3.2 GHz processor. Figure 3.30 shows how the processing time is distributed over different models. Each EPC model is represented by a number on the horizontal axis ordered by the processing time: the EPC that was processed the fastest is on the very left position and the most time-consuming EPC is found on the very right-hand side of the spectrum. Each EPC is assigned its processing time as the ordinate. Please note that the ordinate is given in a logarithmic scale. In Figure 3.30 it can be seen that about 320 models are processed in less than one second. We also see that only some EPCs (16) take more than 10 seconds. It is interesting to note that the 13 largest models with more than 80 nodes are also the 13 models that require the most processing time. The number of nodes and the processing time are correlated with a Pearson's coefficient of correlation of 0.592, showing that the performance very much depends on the size of the EPC. The maximum processing time was two minutes and 22 seconds for an EPC with 111 nodes, 136 arcs, and 32 connectors. The performance of the analysis is much better than the performance of the relaxed soundness analysis reported in [275, 276], which took about seven hours and 45 minutes on the same computer, in contrast to less than 30 minutes with reduction rules.

Extent of Reduction

In this section we will discuss the extent of the reduction by comparing the number of nodes from before and after the reduction. All original EPCs together include 12,529 nodes while the reduced EPCs have only 1,118 altogether. The average per model is about 21 nodes before and 1.85 nodes after the reduction. This means that 91% of the nodes are deleted in the various reduction steps. Figure 3.31 shows the EPCs ordered by size of the reduced model related to the reduced size. Two things can be gathered from this figure. 103 of 604 EPCs could not be reduced completely and these have less than 29 nodes (slightly more than the average for the unreduced models). Only 15 of them have more than 15 nodes.

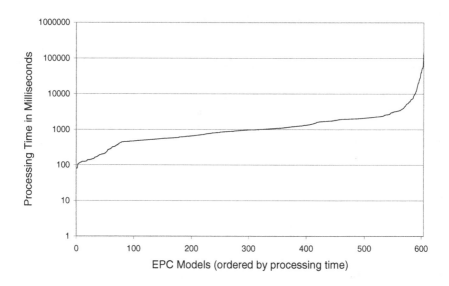

Figure 3.30. Processing time for reducing an EPC

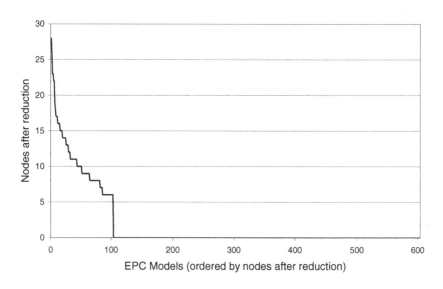

Figure 3.31. Size of reduced EPCs

Applicability of Reduction Rules

Figure 3.32 shows how often the eight reduction rules can be applied for the verification for the SAP Reference Model. Not surprisingly, the reduction of trivial constructs is used most often (about 6,600 times). It is followed by the start and end component reduction with about 2,400 applications. This is a good result considering that large sets of start and end events have been a major verification problem in previous studies (see [440, 276]). The structured block rule is the fourth best regarding the frequency of application with 345 reductions. The homogeneous rule is still applied quite often (460 times) since this rule can only be applied once for an EPC. The remaining four rules are applied less frequently. They still play an important role for the reduction approach as a whole. Running the reduction without the structured loop, delta, prism and merge rule causes 13 additional models to not be reduced completely and 53 errors would be missed.

Some of the reduced EPCs yield a specific pattern that could be used for designing additional reduction rules. The Figures 3.33–3.36 show four patterns that were found multiple times in the set of reduced EPCs. The reachability graph analysis with ProM can be used to verify them. While the EPCs of Figures 3.33, 3.34 and 3.36 are not sound, the Figure 3.35 is correct. Analyzing such reduced EPCs systematically is subject of future research.

Number of Errors Found

Prior research on the verification of the EPCs of the SAP Reference Model has shown that there are several formal errors in the models (see [473, 109, 110, 275]). In [275] the authors identify a lower bound for the number of errors of 34 (5.6%) using the relaxed soundness criterion. The reduction based on *xoEPC* identifies 90 models for which altogether 178 error patterns were found (see Figure 3.37). This is almost three times as many models as in an earlier study which used the relaxed soundness criterion (see [275]). Furthermore, there are 103 models that are not completely reduced and for 57 of them no error was found in the reduction phase. We analyzed these models using the reachability graph approach. 68 of the 103 unreduced EPCs were not sound and 36 unsound EPCs were not detected by the reduction rules. This yields 126 EPCs with errors in total for the SAP Reference Model.

Comparing the application of a rule to the error cases, as depicted in Figure 3.37, offers some first inside regarding the question why errors are introduced in models. While 44 errors in structured blocks is often in absolute terms, it is little compared to the 345 times a structured block was reduced. This is different for structured loops and delta components: the relation of errors to no-error cases is about 1:2 (11 to 21 for loops and 21 to 37 for deltas). It seems as if modelers have more problems with these sophisticated building blocks than with the structured blocks. The start and end components may be regarded as the extreme opposite, with 102 error cases compared to 2,400 applications. This is still the highest value in absolute terms and points to a problem with using unstructured start and end events. Surprisingly, the prism is applied six times, and even though it is the reduction pattern with the most nodes, it

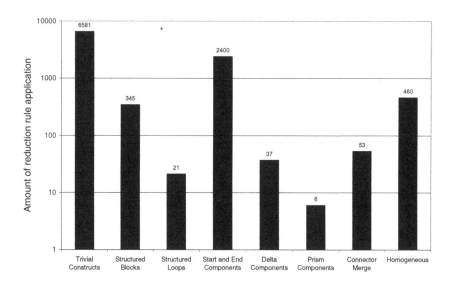

Figure 3.32. Number of Reduction Rule Applications (on logarithm scale)

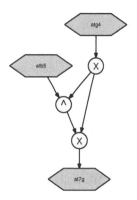

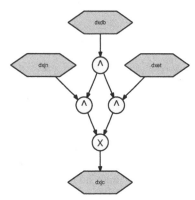

Figure 3.33. Two input component (not sound)

Figure 3.34. Three input component (not sound)

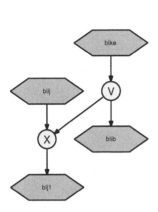

Figure 3.35. Acyclic two input two output component (sound)

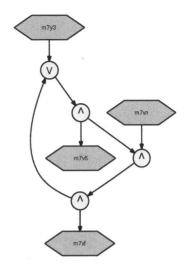

Figure 3.36. Cyclic two input two output component (not sound)

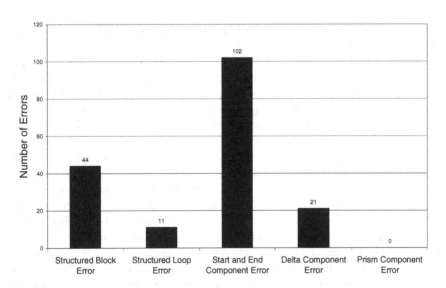

Figure 3.37. Number of Errors per Type

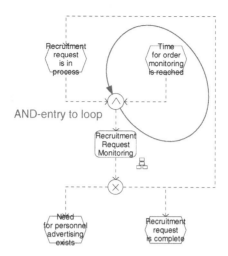

Figure 3.38. Recruitment – Recruitment – Recruitment Request Monitoring

causes no errors. One explanation could be that modelers are aware that non-trivial components are best joined with an OR.

Figure 3.38 depicts one of the small EPCs from the SAP Reference Model that was identified to be unsound by the reduction algorithm. *xoEPC* reports that there is a loop with an AND-join as entry and an XOR-split as exit. Obviously, the only possible initial marking including *Time for order monitoring is reached* cannot lead to a proper execution of the process since the AND-join cannot receive a token on its second input arc. Figure 3.39 shows another example EPC for which nine errors were found by *xoEPC*. Errors 1 and 2 are mismatches of an OR-split with XOR-join connectors. These components might potentially create more than one token on subsequent arcs. The third error is an OR-exit to a loop. If this loop is executed multiple times, it is possible that multiple tokens are created at the exit. Error 4 relates to an AND-join that might not get control from a previous XOR-split. This implies that there is no initial marking in which a positive token on the start arc pointing to the AND-join is guaranteed to run into a proper completion. The same holds true for error 9. Errors 5,6 and 8 relate to the loop at the bottom with its OR-entry and AND-exits and OR-exits. Error 7 is a delta component with two OR-splits and one XOR-join. There is again a potential lack of synchronization at the XOR-join. The reduction rules could also not reduce the EPC completely. An analysis with ProM reveals that the AND-join with the start arc involved in error 4 and 9 might also not get control from the OR-split behind the first function *Order*. All unsound models that were detected by *xoEPC* are listed in the Appendix A of [266]. EPCs that were not completely reduced and checked with the ProM plug-in are depicted in Appendix B of [266].

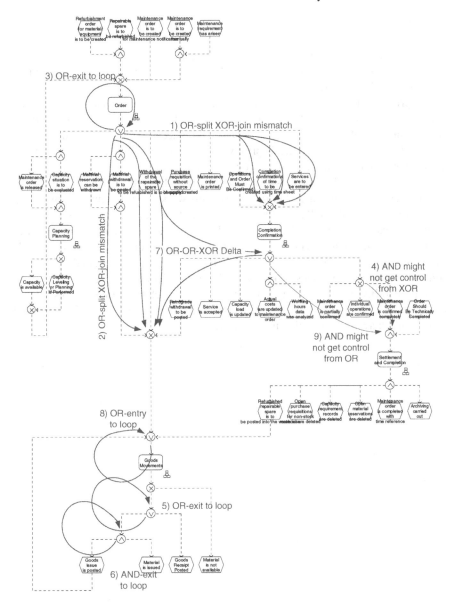

Figure 3.39. Plant Maintenance – Refurbishment Processing in Plant Maintenance

3.4 Summary

In this section, we presented an EPC-specific version of soundness as a correctness criterion for EPCs. We proposed two different approaches for soundness verification, one based on the reachability graph and a second based on reduction rules. While the first approach explicitly considers all markings and transitions of an EPC, there is a state explosion problem as the maximum number of markings grows exponentially with the number of arcs. In order to avoid a performance problem, we introduced a set of reduction rules. This set extends prior work with new reductions for start and end components, delta components, prism components and homogeneous EPCs. Both approaches were implemented as a proof-of-concept: the reachability graph verification approach as a plug-in within the ProM framework and the reduction rules as a batch program called *xoEPC* written in XOTcl. We tested the performance of *xoEPC* in the verification of the SAP Reference model which showed that the reduction rules approach is *fast*, that it provides a *precise* result for almost all models and that it finds *three times as many errors* as other approaches based on relaxed soundness. In the following chapter, we discuss which model attributes could have an impact on the error probability from a theoretical point of view. The elaboration provides a foundation for answering the question whether errors are introduced randomly in a model or whether there are factors that influence error probability.

4

Metrics for Business Process Models

Up until now, there has been little research on why people introduce errors in real-world business process models. In a more general context, Simon [404] points to the limitations of cognitive capabilities and concludes that humans act rationally only to a certain extent. Concerning modeling errors, this argument would imply that human modelers lose track of the interrelations of large and complex models due to their limited cognitive capabilities and introduce errors that they would not insert in a small model. A recent study by *Mendling et al.* [275] explores in how far certain complexity metrics of business process models have the potential to serve as error determinants. The authors conclude that complexity indeed appears to have an impact on error probability. Before we can test such a hypothesis in a more general setting, we have to establish an understanding of how we can define determinants that drive error probability and how we can measure them.

In this instance, measurement refers to a process that assigns numbers or symbols to attributes of entities in the real world [124] in order to represent the amount or degree of those attributes possessed by the entities [432, p.19]. This way, measurement opens abstract concepts to an empirical evaluation and is, therefore, a cornerstone of natural, social and engineering sciences. In this definition, an attribute refers to a property or a feature of an entity while an entity may be an object or an event in the real world. Measurement at least serves the following three purposes: understanding, control and improvement. The classical statement attributed to *Galilei*, "What is not measurable make measurable", stresses the ability of a measurement to deliver *understanding*. The principle idea behind this phrase is that measurement makes concepts more visible. In effect, entities and their relationships can be tracked more precisely bringing forth a better understanding. In an emerging discipline like complexity of business process models, it might not be clear what to measure in the first place. Proposing and discussing measures opens a debate that ultimately leads to a greater understanding [124, p.7]. Measurement then enables *control* in order to meet goals. According to *DeMarco* "you cannot control what you cannot measure" [103]. Based on an understanding of relationships between different attributes, one can make predictions such as whether goals will be met and what actions need to be taken. For business process modeling projects, it is important to establish suitable measurements since, as *Gilb* points out, projects without clear goals will not achieve their goals clearly [141]. The lack of measurements that can be automatically calculated from a given process model is a central problem of several quality frameworks. Examples include the Guidelines of Modeling (GoM) [50, 388, 51], SE-QUAL [250, 307, 228] or the work of *Güceglioglu and Demirörs* [157, 156]. While various empirical research has been conducted on quality aspects of data models (see [304, 135, 305, 136, 137]), such work is mostly missing for business process models [306]. Defining quality concepts in a measurable way would be a major step towards understanding bad process design in general. Measurement is also crucial for the *improvement* of both business process models as products and business process modeling processes. In business science, it is an agreed upon insight, from *Taylor's* scientific management [421] to *Kaplan and Norton's* balanced scorecard [205, 206], that measurement directs human behavior towards a goal. In organizational theory, this phenomenon was first recognized in the Hawthorne plant of Western Electric and is referred to as the Hawthorne Effect: what you measure will be improved (see [234, p.21]). Business process modeling has not yet established a general suite of measurements that is commonly accepted. The potential for improvements in current modeling practices is, therefore, difficult to assess. This chapter aims to contribute to a more quantitatively oriented approach to business process modeling by proposing a set of potential error determinants for EPC business process models. This is also a step towards establishing business process modeling as an engineering discipline since "to predict and control effectively you must be able to measure. To understand and evaluate quality, you must be able to measure." [234, p.4].

The remainder of this chapter is structured as follows: Section 4.1 presents the theoretical background of measurement with a focus on scale types and issues related to validity and reliability. Section 4.2 discusses which concepts are measured in the neighboring discipline of network analysis. We focus on degree, density, centrality and connectivity metrics since they seem to be promising for business process models. Section 4.3 gives an overview of complexity metrics in software engineering. We highlight the most prominent metrics and discuss their relationship to more abstract quality concepts for software products. In Section 4.4, we present related work on metrics for business process models. In Section 4.5, we identify the complexity of a process model's structure and its state space as the key determinants for error probability. Related to these two aspects we define a set of metrics and discuss their impact on error probability. Section 4.7 gives a summary before the metrics are tested in the subsequent chapter.

4.1 Measurement Theory

The representational theory of measurement (or measurement theory) explains how empirical phenomena can be captured in terms of a measurement (see [474, 124, 409]). A measurement can be formally defined as a mapping (also called *scale*) from the domain of the empirical world to the range of mathematical concepts (see [124]). In software engineering, the terms metric and measurement are often used interchangeably. There seems to be a certain reluctance to make a clear distinction between both terms, partially to avoid confusion with the term metric in a mathematical sense (see [124, p.103]). Several software engineering books only give vague characteristics of a metric (see [140, p.368], [413, p.567] or [234, p.9]). Throughout the remainder of this book we will use the term *metric* in order to refer to the *type* of a measurement that quantifies a certain attribute of an entity in the real world by following a predefined way of quantification. An implication of this definition is that entities of the real world can be compared by comparing the measurement for a certain metric. The term *statistic* is related to such an understanding of a metric since it refers to a sample as a specific entity of the real world [20, p.212]. A sample can be defined as a subset of measurements selected from a population while a population consists of the set of all measurements in which an investigator is interested [20, p.17].

Three problems related to measurement have to be considered (see [439]). First, the *representation problem* relates to the condition that the mapping should preserve relations that exist in the real world. Second, the *uniqueness problem* refers to invariance of a measurement under certain transformations. Third, the *meaningfulness problem* is concerned with drawing conclusions about the truth of statements based on comparison of assigned scale values. While the third aspect is subject to ongoing research, the first and the second problem are addressed by the scale hierarchy proposed by *Stevens* [416]. It distinguishes nominal, ordinal, interval and ratio scales. *Stevens* assumes that a scale maps an empirical relation to the real numbers and discusses how the scale values can be interpreted.

- *Nominal:* The values of this scale can only be interpreted as unique identifiers. Consider, for example, two business process models that have the unique IDs 1 and 7. The only conclusion that can be drawn from this data is that the models are not the same. Any transformation of the scale values can, therefore, be performed if the uniqueness of the identifiers is not affected.
- *Ordinal:* The ordinal scale preserves an order relation that exists in the domain of the empirical relation. For a questionnaire asking in how far several business process models are complex, the responses could be mapped to the scale values 1 for trivial, 2 for rather simple, 3 for rather complex and 4 for incomprehensible. This representation of the responses is as good as any other that does not change the order of the values. Any monotone transformation like taking logs or square roots can be applied.
- *Interval:* The interval scale is invariant to linear transformations that preserve relative distance. Consider two business process models and the point in time when they were designed. We could encode the values as days after the start of the modeling project (01 September 2000 for example) or as years AD in the range of real numbers. We could then use a linear transformation to calculate from one scale to the other.
- *Ratio:* In contrast to the interval scale, the ratio scale has a zero element that represents absence of a certain property. Consider the number of connectors a certain business process model has. The values can accordingly be multiplied by a constant as this preserves the relative ratio of the values.

There is a hierarchy between the scale types, since the classes of meaningful transformations narrow from nominal to ratio scale. *Stevens* recommends using certain statistics only for specific scale types: the mean only for interval scale data, for example [417]. Criticism of such a clerical restriction and the scale type hierarchy itself is presented in [439]. In [309], an alternative list of categories including names, ordered grades, ranks, counted fractions, counts, amounts and balances is proposed. Beyond this, *Guttman* argues that instead of restricting data analysis to permissive statistics for a scale, one should rather consider the loss function to be minimized [160]. This argument points to the problem of measurement involving validity and reliability issues.

In essence, *validity* refers to the question whether conclusions based on a measure are actually accurate and whether measurement captures what is intended to be measured. Since abstract concepts have to be translated into a measurable operational definition or a metric, there is plenty of room for mismatch (see [204, 234]). Validity can be judged in terms of freedom from systematic error. While the true scores are often not available, validity is, in general, difficult to assess. Establishing the validity of a measurement involves the three issues of content validity, criterion validity and construct validity (see [409, 258]). If a measurement is not valid it is also not possible to draw valid conclusions from it.

- *Content Validity:* This type of validity refers to the ability of a measurement scale to represent the full range of meanings associated with the empirical phenomenon. Assuming we want to find out which one of two process models is perceived to be more complex: If a questionnaire only were to offer two answers like "model A seems more complex" and "model B seems more complex", we would have a problem with content validity since the phenomenon of indifference ("both models seem equally complex") could not be represented.
- *Criterion Validity:* This type of validity points to the pragmatic value of a measurement, i.e. how closely measurement values and real phenomena are connected. Assume we are interested again in the complexity of a process model as it is perceived by modelers. If we choose to consider the number of arcs as a measurement for it, we might encounter the problem that models with the same number of arcs. For example, a sequential model and a model with arbitrary cycles are perceived as having totally different complexity. The number of arcs might, therefore, have a problem with criterion validity related to complexity since the measurement and the real phenomenon might not be closely connected.
- *Construct Validity:* This type of validity refers to theoretical considerations related to the question why a certain construct is appropriate. Consider again the perceived complexity of process models and assume that the randomly assigned ID number of the model exhibits the capability to rank a sample of process models with respect to complexity. Though we might have a certain degree of criterion validity due to the pragmatic ranking capability, we have a problem with construct validity since there is no theoretical explanation available for the connection between ID and perceived complexity.

An alternative classification of measurement validity is proposed in [433].

Reliability refers to the consistency of measurements over entities and time. While a scale can be reliable and not valid, an unreliable measurement cannot be valid. In this way, reliability establishes an upper bound on validity (see [409, p.364]). In the following sections, we will discuss metrics that can be calculated from graphs, software artifacts and business process models. Reliability essentially relates to the question of whether our calculation algorithm works correctly and deterministically. There are hardly content validity problems since all metrics are based on counts related to the models. We will, however, discuss construct validity from a theoretical point of view for each of the metrics that we identify. We will test criterion validity in the following chapter, but first we present results from the neighboring disciplines network analysis and software measurement.

4.2 Metrics in Network Analysis

Network analysis refers to structure theory and related methods in the area of applied graph theory [63, p.1]. It has a long tradition in social sciences as social network analysis (SNA) dating back to the 1930s (see [389, pp.7]), but there are also applications in engineering related to electrical circuits or in natural sciences like epidemiology. Since EPC business process models are a special class of graphs, it is worth investigating whether network analysis techniques might be applicable.

Network analysis deals with three subareas with a focus on either elements, groups or the overall network [63]. *Element-level* analysis deals with quantifying the position of an element within a network. The Google PageRank is an example that assigns an individual web page a rank based on its connections within a network of web pages. *Group-level* analysis refers to sets of elements of a network and their relationships. An application example is the case of describing political decision making with concurrent groups of interest. *Network-level* analysis considers properties of the overall network. Some properties have been studied related to the International Movie Database (IMDb) about what the average distance between any two actors is. For business process models, we are particularly interested in network-level analysis metrics. In this section, we focus on degree, density, distance, centrality and connectivity metrics. For further details on network analysis refer to [389, 64].

A graph $G = (V, E)$ defined by a set of vertices V and edges $E \subseteq V \times V$ is the starting point of network analysis. EPCs as defined in Definition 2.1 are a specific kind of graph with the sets of functions, events and connectors being the vertices (or nodes) and directed edges called arcs. A basic set of network analysis techniques is related to the degree of the vertices of a graph. The *degree d(v)* of a vertex is the number of edges that are connected to it. For a directed graph the degree of a vertex is the sum of its in-degree (the number of incoming arcs) and its out-degree (the number of outgoing arcs). The average degree

$$\overline{d}(G) = \frac{1}{|V|} \sum_{v \in V} d(v)$$

summarizes whether vertices are connected to many or to few other vertices. Since the sum of degrees equals twice the number of arcs, the average degree can also be calculated as

$$\overline{d}(G) = \frac{2 \cdot |E|}{|V|}$$

A frequently used metric in network analysis is *density* (see [389, pp.69]). Density gives the ratio of edges divided by the maximum number of possible edges. The density Δ of a directed graph is calculated as

$$\Delta(G) = \frac{|E|}{|V| \cdot (|V| - 1)}$$

ranging from 0 for an empty graph to 1 for a complete graph (assuming no self-edges from a vertex to itself). Despite its popularity the results of this metric have to be handled with care. This is due to the fact that complete graphs are rare in practice [389, p.70]. For a random graph, it can be expected that the degrees of the vertices are binomially distributed: only every other potential edge would be included yielding a Δ of 0.5. Several researchers observed that natural graphs do not follow such a binomial, but a distribution that can be expressed as a *power law* (see [65] for an overview). This power law defines the distribution over degrees using two parameters $c > 0$ and $\gamma > 0$ such that the expected amount of vertices with degree k is $ck^{-\gamma}$. The constant c is used for scaling in such a way that the sum over k yields either 1 or the number of vertices. An implication of such a power law distribution is that nodes with a small degree are more likely than nodes with a high degree. In some example graphs, γ values are estimated as for the actor collaboration graph ($\gamma \approx 2.3$) and the power grid of the United States of America ($\gamma \approx 4$) [40]. The implication of this finding is twofold. First, if such a power law is present then graphs become less dense with increasing size. Second, and due to the previous fact, density might be only applicable for a comparison of graphs of the same size. For business process models, it can be expected that nodes with a high degree value are scarce. The implications of the power law distribution must, therefore, be kept in mind when interpreting the density metric of process models.

While density captures the overall cohesion of a graph, *centrality* metrics describe to which extent the cohesion is organized around a central point [389, p.89]. Several centrality metrics are based on the distance matrix $\delta(u, v)$ of a graph in which each entry gives the shortest path between vertices u and v, also called geodesic distance. If the graph does not include cycles with negative weight, the distance matrix can be calculated in polynomial time (see [65] for an overview of algorithms). Based on the distances it is easy to determine the average distance

$$\overline{\delta}(G) = \frac{1}{|V| \cdot (|V| - 1)} \sum_{\substack{u,v \in V \\ u \neq v}} \delta(u, v)$$

and the diameter

$$diam(G) = max\{\delta(u, v) \mid u, v \in V\}$$

of a connected graph[1]. The centrality of a graph depends upon the sum of differences between the score of the most central point and any other point. It is the ratio between this sum of differences and the maximum possible sum of differences (see [133]). Centrality scores can be calculated based on degree sum, closeness and betweenness. While the *sum of degrees* of a vertex only uses information of its local importance in a graph, *closeness* considers the sum of distances between vertices. The closeness centrality of a graph is defined as the inverse of the average distance that a vertex has to all other vertices. Given the maximum sum of these differences, one can calculate the closeness centrality for the overall graph (see [133]). *Betweenness* is based on the idea that certain vertices are more important since they connect subparts of the graph. The betweenness proportion of a vertex y for a pair x and z describes the proportion of shortest paths that connect x and z via y. The pair dependency of x and y is the sum of betweenness proportions of y that involves all pairs containing x. The betweenness score of a vertex is ,therefore, half the sum of all dependency scores of that vertex. The most central point of a graph can be identified using either degree sums, closeness or betweenness scores. For further details and formulas see [133, 225]. While the diameter appears to be interesting for measuring the length of an EPC process model, the centrality concept is rather difficult to relate to business process modeling concepts. We will ,therefore, disregard centrality metrics for measuring complexity of an EPC.

Connectivity is related to questions about how many vertices have to be removed from the graph to make it unconnected. An interesting concept in this context is that of a cut-vertex. A cut-vertex (also called articulation point or separation vertex) is a vertex which, when removed, increases the number of connected components of a graph. The *number of cut-vertices* can be calculated in $O(|V|+|E|)$ based on a depth-first search tree of the graph (see [84, Ch.22] or [62]). It gives important information about how easily the overall graph can be split into its components. For an EPC, the number of cut-vertices might reveal information in how far the model could be understandable in a divide-and-conquer way, i.e. considering components that are connected via cut-vertices in isolation. Depth-first search trees can also be used to decide whether a graph is planar, i.e. if it can be drawn in such a way that edges do not cross [186]. Since process models are frequently drawn as planar graphs we assume that the planarity property has little selective power and, therefore, disregard it for process models.

In summary, degree, density, distance and connectivity metrics seem to be interesting not only in terms of graphs in general, but also for business process models in particular. We will adapt these metrics to EPCs in Section 4.5. For further network and graph analysis techniques we refer to [389, 84, 64].

---

[1] For a disconnected graph, the calculation has to be restricted to those pairs that do not have an infinite distance.

4.3 Metrics in the Software Engineering Process

In the software engineering process, several metrics are used to provide input for quality assurance (see [59, 413]). The challenge is to establish a relationship between metrics for internal attributes that are easy to measure and external ones. While internal product attributes can be directly calculated for software artifacts, this does not hold for external attributes like maintainability or reliability as well as unknown parameters like total effort and number of defects. Instead of the term error, software engineering used the generic term defect comprising faults and failures (see [193, 124]). Faults are defects that result from human errors that are encoded in the software. The terms fault and error are often used synonymously. Failures are departures of a software system from its required behavior. Several failures might potentially be tracked back to the same fault as a source. Software measurement approaches typically follow a top down design. The classical Goal-Question-Metric (GQM) approach by *Basili et al.* [45, 44] advocates a clear definition of the overall goal for a software design project. Based on this goal, several questions can be derived related to how the goal can be achieved. Respective metrics offer a quantitative answer to the questions. A similar approach is proposed by *Kan* [204] who suggests first to identify a concept of interest and to define it. In a second step an operational definition has to be found that serves as the basis for a measurement related to the concept. This measurement must be checked for validity and reliability with respect to the concept. In the remainder of this section, we will present several metrics for internal attributes related to the structure of a program like size and complexity which are frequently used in software engineering. These metrics essentially capture control flow, data flow and/or data structure. We will then discuss external quality attributes. External quality attributes model aspects like reliability, usability and maintainability that relate them to internal attributes. We also report on empirical results related to validating these metrics.

Before presenting individual metrics, we must discuss the association between a software program and its control flow graph. Since we aim to investigate the potential analogy between software measurement and business process model measurement we consider software programs to be represented as control flow graphs. A control flow graph $G = (V, E)$ can be derived from a program by mapping blocks of sequential code to vertices with one input and one output arc and branching statements like if or while to vertices with multiple input and output arcs (see [261]). Metrics defined for control flow graphs can be easily adapted to process models.

The *lines of code* metric is the traditional metric for measuring the size of software. While the idea of counting the lines of a software program is rather simple, there have been several discussions regarding whether comments should be included. *Jones* states that depending on the way lines are counted, the results might differ by the factor of five [201]. Standardization efforts such as the 242 pages long report of the Software Engineering Institute of Carnegie Mellon University illustrate the extent of choices in this area [391]. Given the control flow graph $G = (V, E)$ of a program, the lines of code can be identified with the number of vertices:

$$LoC(G) = |V|$$

One problem with lines of code is that code from different programming languages is not directly comparable. Research on language productivity has established so-called gearing factors that capture the effort of writing an arbitrary program in a certain language. For example, programming in SQL requires an average effort of 39 compared to 172 in Assembler [234, p.38]. An increase in lines of code does not necessarily imply an increase in functionality. Function Point Analysis, originally proposed in [22], addresses this problem by assigning a score to each input, output, interface, data file and inquiries based on their individual difficulty. While function points can be compared for programs written in different languages, there is the problem that function point analysis requires human interpretation of program difficulty. It can, therefore, be only partially automated. This is a major disadvantage compared to lines of code that can be counted automatically.

The *cyclomatic number CC* proposed in [260, 261, 262] is an early complexity metric. It is based on the control flow graph $G = (V, E)$ of a program and captures the number of paths through a program that are needed to visit all vertices. More precisely, it matches the maximum number of linearly independent paths through a program. The cyclomatic number is of particular importance for test theory since it defines the number of test cases required for unit tests. It can either be calculated based on the number of vertices and edges as

$$CC(G) = |E| - |V| + 1$$

or alternatively by counting the number of choices weighted with the number of alternatives. Since CC is not biased towards a specific programming language, it can be used to compare the complexity of programs written in different languages. The cyclomatic complexity density CCD is an CC extension for predicting maintenance productivity [142]. CCD is calculated as CC divided by the lines of code LoC. A second extension called essential cyclomatic complexity ECC is a measure of unstructuredness of the program [260]. It is calculated as the cyclomatic number of the code after removing all structured constructs like if and while statements. A totally structured program, therefore, has an essential cyclomatic complexity of zero. The cyclomatic number can be calculated for EPC business process models that do not include concurrency (see Figure 4.1).

Halstead's metrics provide measurable definitions for the length, vocabulary, volume, difficulty and effort of a software program based on the number of operators and operands [162]. Operators comprise commands and structuring elements like parentheses. Operands basically refer to elements that have a value like variables and constants. The operator parameters n_1 and N_1 refer to the number of distinct operators and the total occurrences of operators, respectively. The operand parameters n_2 and N_2 describe the number of distinct operands and the total occurrences of operands, respectively. *Halstead* then defines the following metrics:

Length $N = N_1 + N_2$
Vocabulary $n = n_1 + n_2$
Volume $V = N \cdot log_2(n)$
Difficulty $D = n_1/2 \cdot N_2/n_2$
Effort $E = D \cdot V$

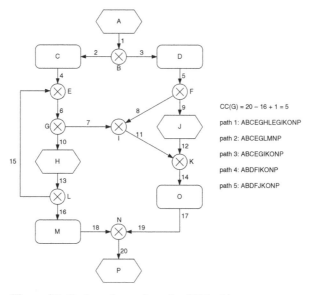

Figure 4.1. Cyclomatic number of an EPC without concurrency

The formula of volume is motivated by the number of binary mental comparisons needed to write a program of length N. The formula for difficulty is a postulate of *Halstead*'s theory. *Halstead* claims with reference to the psychologist *Stroud* that the required programming time T can be calculated as $T = E/18sec$. Although the work by *Halstead* had a lasting impact on software metrics research, it has been criticized repeatedly as "an example of confused and inadequate measurement" [124].

The *information flow metric* proposed by *Henry and Kafura* [177] is based on the data flow between different modules of a program. Information can be passed between modules in three ways: by a module invoking another one; by returning a result from the invoked module to the caller; and by exchanging information via a global data structure. The *fan-in* of a module M refers to the number of calls to the module plus the number of reads to global data structures. The *fan-out* captures calls to other modules and write operations to global data structures. Based on these parameters, the information flow complexity is calculated as

$$IFC(M) = LoC(M) \cdot (fan_{in} \cdot fan_{out})^2$$

The IFC metric can be used at design-time to predict which modules are likely to contain errors. The multiplication of fan-in and fan-out has been criticized in [124]. If a module has either no fan-in or fan-out the metric yields zero which is misleading.

The lines of code, cyclomatic complexity, *Halstead* complexity and information flow complexity metrics were developed for procedural programming languages. In [81], a set of metrics for object-oriented development is proposed. In this context, coupling and cohesion are important concepts. Coupling describes the degree of interdependence between a pair of modules and cohesion describes the degree to which the elements of a module are functional related (see [468, 413]). The proposal is based on ontological work of *Bunge, Wand* and *Weber* [66, 448] and includes six metrics.

- *Weighted methods per class:* This metric is calculated as the sum of complexity weights over all methods.
- *Depth of inheritance tree:* The inheritance tree defines a hierarchy of classes from which an individual class inherits properties and methods. The metric gives the depth of such inheritance for a class in order to describe how many ancestors potentially affect it.
- *Number of children:* This metric gives the number of successors in the inheritance tree for a particular class.
- *Coupling between object classes:* This measure states to how many other classes a class is coupled.
- *Response for class:* This metric gives the size of the set of methods that a class might use to respond to a message. It is calculated as the sum of local methods plus methods called by these local methods.
- *Lack of cohesion metric:* This is the number of disjoint sets identified by comparing each pair of methods and the instance variables they relate to. A high value for this metric would suggest a split up of the class.

A generic framework for classifying further object-oriented metrics is proposed and validated against 350 metrics in [435].

The previously presented metrics related to internal attributes of a software artifact were tested in various empirical studies for their criterion validity with respect to predicting defects or project effort. *Fenton and Ohlsson* test several hypotheses on faults and failures that LoC is a useful predictor for defects and that complexity metrics perform better [123]. They find that LoC is indeed suited to rank modules according to their absolute number of faults. They also confirm the finding of *Basili and Perricone* [43] that fault density seems to decrease with module size. Cyclomatic complexity CC does not seem to outperform LoC as a predictor for errors. *Fenton and Ohlsson* propose to rather consider CC as a predictor for comprehensibility and maintainability.

An overview of effort estimation is given in [234, pp.79]. Benchmark data is useful to assess productivity in particular. For example, in one staff month, code produced for data processing applications appear to range between 165 and 500 lines [234, p.86]. Measurements are also used to predict the dynamics of effort and defects throughout the development process. Given a record of found defects and a typical distribution of defects over time, one can estimate defects to be found in future. A typical distribution in this context is the Rayleigh curve that sharply steepens to a maximum and then decreasing falls towards zero. Such an estimation is particularly helpful for determining a suitable release date (see [234]). Regression-based prediction can also be applied in terms of effort. *Boehm's* constructive cost model (COCOMO) assumes that effort $E = aS^b F$ with S measuring size, F an adjustment factor, and a and b depending on the type of software being constructed [60]. The ISO/IEC 9126 Software Product Quality Model [195] provides an overall classification scheme for quality-related product attributes on four levels. It can be used as a framework for several metrics defined earlier. Further models and empirical results are summarized in various text books on software measurement (see [474, 124, 204, 234]).

4.4 Related Work on Metrics for Process Models

In this section, we discuss related work on metrics for process models. Since the authors hardly refer to each other, it is difficult to group the contributions according to subject area. We will, therefore, present their work mainly chronologically.

In 1990, *Lee and Yoon* conducted pioneering work on the definition of metrics for Petri net process models and their empirical validation [243, 244]. The authors group their metrics into two categories: *structural metrics* include simple counts of places, transitions, arcs and the cyclomatic number of the control graph. *Dynamic metrics* cover the number of markings and the maximum and average number of tokens for the original and a reduced state space. In an empirical study of a set of 75 Petri nets, the authors find that a simple adaptation of the cyclomatic number is not a suitable complexity metric; that the number of places can serve as a predictor for the size of the reachability graph in an exponential equation; and that reduction techniques reduce the analysis problem by factor four for the sample nets.

Nissen was among the first to introduce measurement concepts for business process modeling and business process design in particular (see [318, 319, 320]). His work is motivated by the observation that business process design is an ill-structured process and that it is, therefore, a case for business process reengineering on itself. Based on a set of measurements for process models, he utilizes design heuristics and a knowledge-based system for reasoning on the quality of the design. The proposed metrics cover counts for *distinct paths*, *hierarchy levels*, *nodes* in the process model, *cycles*, *diameter* and *parallelism* as number of nodes divided by the diameter. These metrics are provided by the KOPeR tool which guides the process reengineering process [320].

Tjaden, Narasmihan and Gupta operationalize four characteristics of a business process that need to be balanced: simplicity, flexibility, integration and efficiency [430, 429]. *Simplicity* is calculated based on so-called basic complexity of the process, i.e. in essence the sum of nodes, arcs and roles. The overall simplicity is then formalized as the average activity complexity divided by the maximum activity complexity. *Flexibility* and *Integration* are determined based on a list of scores similar to function point analysis. Though it is mentioned, the technical report [429] does not operationalize efficiency. *Balasubramanian and Gupta* criticize the high level of abstraction of the metrics by Tjaden (see [37]). A function point approach, such as it is proposed for flexibility and integration, is difficult to automate.

Building on measurement efforts for concurrent programs (see [396]), *Morasca* proposes a set of metrics for Petri nets and a theoretical foundation [308]. He identifies size, length, structural complexity and coupling as interesting attributes of a Petri net and for each attribute he defines a set of axiomatic properties which a respective metric would have to fulfill. For size he proposes *number of places and transitions*, for length the maximum minimal distance (i.e. the *diameter*), for structural complexity the *number of base paths*, the *concurrent contribution* as the number of arcs minus two times the number of transitions, the *sequential contribution* as the number of transitions with one input places and for coupling the *number of inbound or outbound arcs of a subnet*. Since *Morasca's* contribution is theoretical, an empirical validation is not included in his paper.

Latva-Koivisto [239] proposes several complexity metrics for business process models including the *Coefficient of Network Connectivity, Cyclomatic Number, Reduction Complexity Index, Restrictiveness Estimator* and *Number of Trees in a Graph* as metrics. This work has two basic weaknesses. First, there is no distinction made between different kinds of routing elements and second a motivation to consider the restrictiveness estimator and the number of trees in a graph as a complexity metric is missing. The work by *Latva-Koivisto* did not receive much attention in the community since it was published only as a technical report.

A different stream of research adapts coupling and cohesion concepts from software engineering (see [397, 68, 393, 57]). In the tradition of this work, *Daneva et al.* [94] introduce a set of complexity metrics for EPCs based on the notational elements of the model: *function cohesion, event cohesion* and *cohesion of a logical connector*. From a limited validation with 11 EPCs they conclude that these metrics help to identify error-prone model fragments. In [347, 348], *Reijers and Vanderfeesten* develop a set of coupling and cohesion metrics to guide the design of workflow processes. The coupling of an activity is calculated based on its relation cohesion and its information cohesion. The *activity relation cohesion* λ describes in how far an activity shares control flow input and output with other activities. It is defined as the sum of overlaps between each activity pair divided by the maximum number of pairs with choices not being considered as overlap. The *activity information cohesion* μ determines how many information objects are used by an activity more than once in relation to all information objects in use. The cohesion of an activity is calculated as $\lambda \cdot \mu$. The overall *process cohesion* c is then defined as the average activity cohesion. The *process coupling* k metric is calculated as the number of connected activities divided by the maximum number of connections. That is, process coupling is equated with the density Δ of the process graph. Inspired by [394], the authors define a process coupling/cohesion ratio as $\rho = k/c$ with a low value indicating good design.

The work of *Cardoso* is centered around an adaptation of the cyclomatic number for business processes he calls *control-flow complexity (CFC)* [69, 72]. CFC is calculated from a model by summing up the split connectors weighted by the combinations of output markings they can produce: 1 for an AND-split S_{and}, $|S_{xor} \bullet|$ for an XOR-split S_{xor}, and $2^{|S_{or}\bullet|} - 1$ for an OR-split. The CFC metric was validated against a set of complexity axioms proposed by *Weyuker* [454] in [70, 71] and tested with respect to their correlation with perceived complexity [73]. In an analysis of the SAP Reference Model, however, the CFC metric was found unsuitable for the prediction of errors in business process models [276].

The research conducted by a group including *Canfora, Rolón, García, Piattini, Ruiz and Visaggio* extends work related to measurement of the software process. In [67], *Canfora et al.* present a set of metrics and evaluate their suitability to serve as predictors for maintainability of the process model. The operational definition of maintainability covers *analyzability* as the likeliness of discovering errors or deficiencies in the model, *understandability* as the likeliness of comprehending a model and *modifiability* as the likeliness of correctly changing the structure of the model. The metrics address structural properties of the process model related to size, complexity and coupling. For *size* they include count metrics based on the number of activities, work products, process roles, input and output dependencies of work products with activities, ratio of work products to activities and ratio of process roles to activities. For *complexity* they consider number of dependencies between work products and activities and ratio between input or output dependencies of work products with activities and total number of dependencies. *Coupling* is measured as number of precedence dependencies between activities and activity coupling. In a set of related experiments, the authors find that most of the metrics are correlated to maintainability: the numbers of activities, work products, work product dependencies and precedence dependencies show good results while activities coupling and the ratio of roles to activities are only correlated to a limited extent. The number of roles and the ratios related to work product dependencies are not correlated. *Rolón et al.* extend this set of metrics and tailor it to the specifics of BPMN reflecting additional numbers for events, gateways, message flows and pools [354, 355, 356, 353].

Inspired by *Nissen's* and *Tjaden's* work, *Balasubramanian and Gupta* propose a set of metrics to support business process design (see [37]). This set includes, among others, metrics to quantify the degree of automatic decision making (*branching automation*), *activity automation*, *role integration*, *role dependency*, *activity parallelism* and *transition delay risk*. These metrics are applied in a case study for identifying the best of two alternative process designs.

Cognitive considerations play an important role for understanding good design in software engineering, for example [58]. This is explicitly reflected in some approaches to metrics. The work by *Gruhn and Laue* adapts cognitive weights from software engineering to business process models [152, 153]. The approach by *Vanderfeesten et al.* defines the cross-connectivity metric. Its aim is to capture how difficult it is to understand how two nodes in a process model relate to each other [437]. This metric is validated for predicting errors and understanding of process models.

Only partially related is the work by *Etien and Rolland* on measuring the fitness of a business process model with a real-world process [121]. The authors define several metrics related to concepts of the Bunge-Wand-Weber ontology which express in how far certain concepts are represented in a model that is present in the real world. In practice, such a measurement maps to a comparison of a business process model with a potentially more complete model that captures entities of the BWW-ontology related to the real-world process. Such a measurement is accordingly more of theoretical interest than of benefit in the design process.

Modularity is another concept that builds on insights on software design. In essence, modularity relates to the number, the size and the depth of nesting of modules. The approach by *Lassen and Van der Aalst* identifies structured components in arbitrary process models for the translation to structured BPEL [14, 17]. These components can also be used to describe the process model in a quantitative way. The work by *Vanhatalo et al.* builds on the program structure tree concept for formal computer program analysis [438]. Using a linear time algorithm, a program structure tree can be derived that includes a nesting of all single-entry-single-exit components of the process model. The authors use maximum, average and minimum component size to describe their model sample. The structuredness of the process model can be defined depending on the structure of the components [242].

The two survey papers by *Cardoso, Mendling, Neumann and Reijers* [74] and *Gruhn and Laue* [241] summarize a great share of the earlier mentioned work. They reveal that several metrics for business process models are adaptations of software complexity metrics. This also holds true for an adaptation of complexity metrics for EPCs as reported in [155]. Only some authors provide operationalizations for central concepts of business process models such as parallelism, cycles and sequentiality (see [320]). Several process-related aspects like structuredness and mismatch of connectors are covered only to a limited extent or not at all. In the following section, we will identify several metrics that are specifically tailored for predicting errors in business process models.

4.5 Definition of Metrics for Process Models

In the previous sections we have discussed several metrics for business process models. Many of them aim to operationalize the structural complexity of the process graph. The term complexity is discussed in software measurement and authors try to identify axioms that a complexity metric would have to fulfill (see the work by *Weyuker* [454]). Such an axiomatic approach is criticized from different perspectives. In [79], the authors show that the *Weyuker* axioms do not guarantee that the metric is meaningful by defining an obviously useless metric that meets the axioms. More serious is the criticism by *Zuse* who shows that the aspects subsumed under the term complexity cannot be captured by a single metric alone [474]. *Fenton and Pfleeger* reinforce this finding by pointing to measurement theory [124, pp.322], saying that every valid measurement should obey the rules of representational theory of measurement. This implies that first an empirical concept or relationship in the real world should be identified, followed by suitable measurements. In other words, the concept guides the measurement and the metric does not define the concept. This principle is incorporated in several software measurement approaches such as the Goal Question Metric (GQM) approach by *Basili et al.* [45, 44] or the Concept, Definition, Operational Definition, Measurement approach by *Kan* [204].

Following this line of argument, we consider the comprehensibility of the business process model as the main determinant for error probability. This is based on the assumption that process models are constructed by human modelers and that their design is subject to bounded rationality [404]. The comprehensibility of any model by a person is influenced by a variety of factors including *model-related* factors like size, *personal factors* like modeling competence, *purpose* of modeling like documentation or execution, *domain knowledge*, *modeling language* or *graphical layout* of the model. In this chapter, we only investigate the model-related aspect. More precisely, we analyze several metrics that capture various aspects related to either the *process model structure*, the *process model state space*, or both (see [244]) and discuss their impact on error probability. Each metric is presented by giving its (1) symbol, (2) definition, (3) rationale why it should be considered, (4) limitations, (5) the hypothesis related to it and (6) related work that mentions similar metrics in previous research. We consider a business process model to be a special kind of graph $G = (N, A)$ with at least three node types $N = T \cup S \cup J$, that is *tasks T*, *splits S*, *joins J* and *control flow arcs* $A \subseteq N \times N$ to connect them. We use the generic term connectors $C = S \cup J$ for splits and joins collectively. Each connector has a *label* AND, OR or XOR that gives its routing of merging semantics. For presentation purposes we subdivide the set of metrics into the categories *size, density, partitionability, connector interplay, cyclicity* and *concurrency*.

4.5.1 Size

Several papers point to *size* as an important factor for the comprehensibility of software and process models (see [324, 67, 74, 241, 474, 124, 204]). While the size of software is frequently equated with lines of code, the size of a process model is often related to the number of nodes N of the process model. Furthermore, we consider the *diameter* of the process graph.

Symbol	S_N
Definition	Number of nodes of the process model graph G
Metric	$S_N(G) = |N|$
Rationale	A larger business process model in terms of $S_N(G)$ should be more likely to contain errors than a small one since the modeler would only be able to perceive a certain amount of nodes in a certain period of time.
Limitations	There are obviously large models in terms of $S_N(G)$ that are unlikely to have errors, e.g. if the model is sequential without any connectors.
Hypothesis	An increase in $S_N(G)$ should imply an increase in error probability of the overall model.
Related Work	*LoC* [474, 124, 204]; Number of nodes [244, 320, 308, 37, 67, 74, 241, 356].

The size metric S_N does not differentiate between the several node types and its subsets of an EPC. We define size metrics for each EPC element type and its subsets by mentioning it as the index of S, i.e. S_{E_E} refers to the number of end events of an EPC, and S_F to the number of functions of an EPC. The size of the model might be closer related to the longest path of it and we, therefore, define the diameter *diam* of a process model.

Symbol	$diam$
Definition	The diameter gives the length of the longest path from a start node to an end node in the process model.
Metric	$diam(G)$ is calculated either based on the distance matrix of a process model or based on shortest path algorithms (see [65])
Rationale	A larger business process model in terms of $diam(G)$ should be more likely to contain errors than a small one since the modeler would only be able to perceive a certain amount of consecutive nodes in a certain period of time.
Limitations	There are obviously large models in terms of $diam(G)$ that are unlikely to have errors, for example if the model is sequential.
Hypothesis	An increase in $diam(G)$ should imply an increase in error probability of the overall model.
Related Work	The diameter was also proposed in [320, 308].

Figure 4.2 illustrates one particular shortcoming of size as a simple count metric. The left and the right model have exactly the same number of nodes but the diameter of the right EPC is longer. This difference between the models does not become apparent if only the size metric S_N is considered.

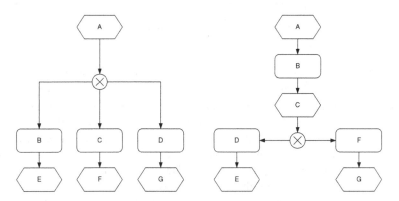

Figure 4.2. Two EPCs of the same size with different diameter

4.5.2 Density

In the context of this book we use density as a generic term to refer to any metric that relates numbers of nodes to numbers of arcs. There are several metrics that provide information about the relation of arcs and nodes. Here we consider the *density* metric, the *coefficient of network connectivity*, *average connector degree* and *maximum degree*.

Symbol	Δ
Definition	The density of the process graph refers to the number of arcs divided by the number of the maximum number of arcs for the same number of nodes.
Metric	$\Delta(G) = \dfrac{|A|}{|N| \cdot (|N| - 1)}$
Rationale	A business process model with a high density $\Delta(G)$ should be more likely to contain errors than a less dense model with the same number of nodes.
Limitations	The density in terms of Δ is difficult to compare for models with a different number of nodes: larger models with the same average degree have a smaller density since the maximum possible number of arcs grows by the square of $|N|$. Many natural graphs seem to obey a power law (see [64]) which implies that larger models would be less dense in terms of Δ.
Hypothesis	An increase in $\Delta(G)$ should imply an increase in error probability of the overall model.
Related Work	Δ is mentioned as process coupling metric in [348].

Symbol	CNC
Definition	The coefficient of connectivity gives the ratio of arcs to nodes.
Metric	$CNC(G) = \dfrac{|A|}{|N|}$
Rationale	A denser business process model in terms of $CNC(G)$ should be more likely to contain errors since the modeler has to perceive more connections between nodes than in a model that is less dense.
Limitations	There are process models with the same CNC value that might differ in error probability. Consider, for example, a sequential model without any connector and a model with the same number of nodes having one split-connector. The two models also have the same number of arcs, therefore CNC is equivalent.
Hypothesis	An increase in $CNC(G)$ should imply an increase in error probability of the overall model.
Related Work	CNC is listed in [239, 74]. The inverse of CNC called activity coupling $NCA = |N|/|A| = 1/CNC$ is proposed in [67, 356].

Symbol	$\overline{d_C}$
Definition	The average degree of connectors gives the number of nodes a connector is in average connected to.
Metric	$\overline{d_C}(G) = \dfrac{1}{|C|} \sum_{c \in C} d(c)$

Rationale	A denser business process model in terms of $\overline{d_C}(G)$ should be more likely to contain errors since the modeler has to perceive more connections between nodes than in a model that is less dense.
Limitations	There are process models with the same $\overline{d_C}$ value which differ in size. They should, therefore, also differ in error probability.
Hypothesis	An increase in $\overline{d_C}(G)$ should imply an increase in error probability of the overall model.
Related Work	$\overline{d_C}$ is related to the information flow metric by *Henry and Kafura* [177] and its adaptation to process models in [74, 241].

Symbol	$\widehat{d_C}$
Definition	The maximum degree of a connector.
Metric	$\widehat{d_C}(G) = max\{d(c) \mid c \in C\}$
Rationale	A business process model with a high maximum degree $\widehat{d_C}(G)$ should be more likely to contain errors since the modeler has to perceive more connections between the connector of maximum degree than in a model that has a lower maximum degree.
Limitations	There are obviously process models with a high maximum degree and the same $\widehat{d_C}$, but with a low average degree.
Hypothesis	An increase in $\widehat{d_C}(G)$ should imply an increase in error probability of the overall model.
Related Work	$\widehat{d_C}$ is closely related to the information flow metric by *Henry and Kafura* [177]. The idea of information flow is to identify modules whose interactions are difficult to comprehend and the connector of maximum degree is the most difficult following this line of argumentation.

Figure 4.3 illustrates the sensitivity of the different density metrics to size. The EPC on the left-hand side has 18 nodes and 17 arcs while the one on the right-hand side only has 8 nodes and 7 arcs. The density metric Δ of the smaller model is more than twice as high (0.055 to 0.125) than that of the larger one although the structure is quite similar. This fact reinforces the statements of Section 4.2 on the difficulty to compare graphs of different size by the density value. The CNC metric reflects the similar structure much better with similar values (0.945 to 0.875). The average and the maximum degree of connectors $\overline{d_C}$ and $\widehat{d_C}$ yield 3 for both models. In this case, they underline the similarity of the models well.

4.5.3 Partitionability

We use the term partitionability for referring to those aspects of a process model that relate to the relationship of subcomponents to the overall model. We discuss *separability* and *sequentiality* in particular, both of which capture how far certain parts of the model can be considered in isolation. Furthermore, *structuredness* quantifies

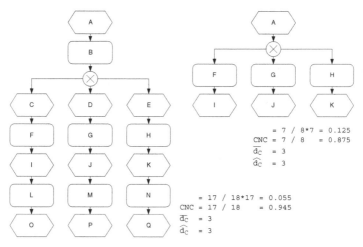

Figure 4.3. Two EPCs of the same average and maximum connector degree and varying density and CNC values

to which degree components are composed in a structured way while *depth* defines how far a certain node is from a start or end event.

Separability is closely related to the notion of a cut-vertex (or articulation point), i.e. a node whose deletion separates the process model into multiple components. We define the separability ratio as the number of cut-vertices to number of nodes. Cut-vertices can be found using depth-first search.

Symbol	Π
Definition	The separability ratio relates the number of cut-vertices to the number of nodes.
Metric	$\Pi(G) = \dfrac{\|\{n \in N \mid n \text{ is cut-vertex}\}\|}{\|N\| - 2}$
Rationale	A model with a high ratio of cut-vertices should be less likely to contain errors than a model with a low ratio. If every node except the start and the end node is a cut-vertex, the model is sequential and should, thus, be easy to understand.
Limitations	The separability ratio Π can be low if there are two long sequential paths in parallel since none of the parallel nodes is a cut-vertex.
Hypothesis	An increase in $\Pi(G)$ should imply a decrease in error probability of the overall model.
Related Work	Π has not yet been considered as a business process model metric.

Sequentiality relates to the fact that sequences of consecutive tasks are the most simple components of a process model. The sequentiality ratio relates arcs of a sequence to the total number of arcs.

Symbol	Ξ
Definition	The sequentiality ratio is the number of arcs between none-connector nodes divided by the number of arcs.
Metric	$\Xi(G) = \dfrac{\lvert A \cap (T \times T)\}\rvert}{\lvert A \rvert}$
Rationale	A process model with a high sequentiality ratio should be less likely to contain errors than one with a low sequentiality ratio. In contrast to the separability ratio Π, the sequentiality ratio Ξ also considers sequences that are in parallel or exclusive. If every arc connects only non-connector nodes, the model is sequential and the sequentiality ratio is 1.
Limitations	There are models with the same sequentiality ratio but whose non-sequential arcs might differ in their degree of comprehensibility.
Hypothesis	An increase in $\Xi(G)$ should imply a decrease in error probability of the overall model.
Related Work	Ξ has not yet been considered as a business process model metric. It is related to sequential contribution of *Morasca* [308].

Figure 4.4 illustrates the difference between the separability and the sequentiality ratio. The model on the left-hand side includes two cut vertices (the XOR-split and the XOR-join) while the model on the right-hand side additionally has the cut vertices B, C, F and G. Even though the number of nodes is the same in both models, the separability ratio is 0.25 for the left model and 0.75 for the right model. The sequentiality ratio counts sequence arcs no matter in which part of the EPC they appear. The sequential components B to F and C to G, therefore, contribute as much to the sequentiality ratio of the left model as the sequences A to C and F to H in the right model (40%).

Structuredness relates to how far a process model can be built by nesting blocks of matching join and split connectors (see [215]). The degree of structuredness can be determined by applying reduction rules and comparing the size of the reduced model to the original size. We consider the reduction of trivial constructs, structured blocks and loops and of structured start and end components as defined in Section 3.3.2.

Symbol	Φ
Definition	The structuredness ratio of the process graph is one minus the number of nodes in the reduced process graph G' divided by the number of nodes in the original process graph G.
Metric	$\Phi_N = 1 - \dfrac{S_N(G')}{S_N(G)}$
Rationale	A process model with a high structuredness ratio should be more likely to contain errors than one with a low ratio. If every node is part of a structured block, the model is structured and the structuredness ratio is 1.
Limitations	There are models with the same structuredness ratio but which differ in their degree of comprehensibility, e.g. if one is larger.

Hypothesis   An increase in $\Phi(G)$ should imply a decrease in error probability of
the overall model.

Related Work Φ has not yet been formalized in literature but mentioned in [241, 154]. It is related to essential cyclomatic complexity [260].

Figure 4.5 illustrates the structuredness ratio by the help of two EPCs. The EPC on the left-hand side is totally structured and yields a structuredness value[2] of 1. The EPC on the right-hand side contains one additional arc and two XOR-connectors that affect the structuredness. While the nodes B to G are deleted by the reduction rule for trivial constructs, the connectors cannot be eliminated. Only 6 out of 12 nodes are deleted yielding a structuredness ratio of 0.5. In the EPC on the right-hand side, the arc between the left and the right column blocks the application of further reduction rules.

Depth relates to the maximum nesting of structured blocks in a process. To calculate depth also for unstructured models we define an algorithm that calculates the in-depth $\lambda_{in}(n)$ of a node n relative to its predecessor nodes $\bullet n$. All nodes are initialized with an in-depth value of 0. The process model is then traversed along all paths starting from a start node and ending with either an end node or a node that was visited before in this path.[3] At each visited node n, the new in-depth value $\lambda'_{in}(n)$ is updated based on the value of the previously visited predecessor node $\lambda_{in}(pre)$ and the current value $\lambda_{in}(n)$ according to the following rule:

$$\lambda'_{in}(n) = \begin{cases} max(\lambda_{in}(n), \lambda_{in}(pre) + 1) & \text{if } pre \in S \wedge n \notin J \\ max(\lambda_{in}(n), \lambda_{in}(pre)) & \text{if } pre \in S \wedge n \in J \\ max(\lambda_{in}(n), \lambda_{in}(pre)) & \text{if } pre \notin S \wedge n \notin J \\ max(\lambda_{in}(n), \lambda_{in}(pre) - 1) & \text{if } pre_i \notin S \wedge n \in J \end{cases}$$

This definition of in-depth captures the maximum number of split connectors that have to be visited to arrive at a node minus the number of joins on this path. The out-depth $\lambda_{out}(n)$ is defined analogously with respect to the successor nodes and decreased for splits and increased for joins. In a structured model, $\lambda_{in}(n)$ equates with $\lambda_{out}(n)$. We define depth $\lambda(n)$ as the minimum of in-depth $\lambda_{in}(n)$ and out-depth $\lambda_{out}(n)$. The depth of the process model Λ is then the maximum depth $\lambda(n)$ over n.

Symbol	Λ
Definition	The depth is the maximum depth of all nodes.
Metric	$\Lambda(G) = max\{\lambda(n) \mid n \in N\}$
Rationale	A process model with a high depth should be more likely to contain errors since connectors are deeply nested.
Limitations	There are models with the same depth that differ in size.

[2] Please note that if the reduced EPC has the minimum size of 2, i.e. if only one start and one end event are connected by an arc, then the value of Φ is set to 1.

[3] This definition addresses potential problems with the existence of a fixed point by visiting each node only once for each path even if it is on a loop.

Hypothesis   An increase in $\Lambda(G)$ should imply an increase in error probability of the overall model.

Related Work Λ has not yet been formalized but mentioned in [320, 241].

Figure 4.6 shows a structured EPC with its in-depth and out-depth values next to the nodes. It can be seen that both in-depth and out-depth increase with each visit to an XOR-split while visiting an XOR-join decreases both parameters. It must be mentioned that joins are used as entries to loops and splits as exits. The depth calculation algorithm is not able to identify such loops as deeper nested structures. Still, it offers a way to quantify the depth of any process model, no matter if it is structured or not.

4.5.4 Connector Interplay

In this section, we present metrics related to connectors and their interplay. In particular, we discuss connector mismatch, connector heterogeneity and the control flow complexity metric.

Structuredness implies that each split-connector matches a corresponding join of the same type. A mismatch might be the source of an error. Depending on the connector label and the degree, we define the connector mismatch as $MM_l = |\sum_{c \in S_l} d(c) - \sum_{c \in J_l} d(c)|$ where l is the connector type. The mismatch ratio MM gives the sum of mismatch for each connector type.

Symbol	MM
Definition	The connector mismatch gives the sum of mismatches for each connector type.
Metric	$MM(G) = MM_{or} + MM_{xor} + MM_{and}$
Rationale	A process model with a high mismatch is likely to include errors since parallel tokens might not be synchronized or alternative branches might run into AND-joins and deadlock. If the model is structured with matching split- and join connectors MM is zero.
Limitations	Languages like EPCs offer multiple start and end events. They, therefore, might show a mismatch without having errors.
Hypothesis	An increase in $MM(G)$ should imply an increase in error probability of the overall model.
Related Work	MM has not yet been formalized in literature.

Connector heterogeneity refers to which extent different connectors are used in a business process model. For defining a suitable metric that ranges from 0 in the case that there are only connectors of one type, to 1 in the case that there are the same amount of connectors of all three types, we refer to the information entropy measure which has exactly these characteristics. In contrast to the original work of *Shannon and Weaver* [395], we do not consider a binary encoding but a ternary because of the three connector types. The base of the logarithm is therefore three, not two. We also utilize the relative frequency $p(l) = |C_l|/|C|$. The connector heterogeneity is

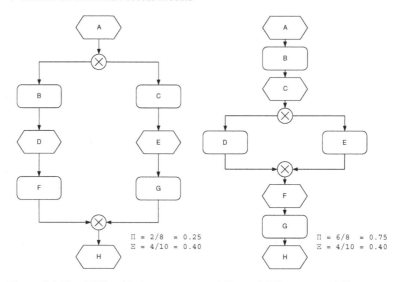

Figure 4.4. Two EPCs with the same sequentiality and different separability

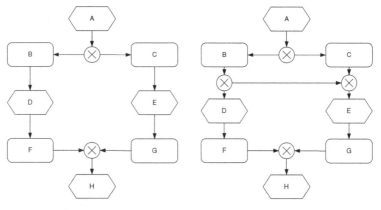

Figure 4.5. Two EPCs with the same functions and events but different degree of structured-ness

then calculated analogously to information entropy as the negative sum over the three connector types of $p(l) \cdot log_3(p(l))$.

Symbol	CH
Definition	The connector heterogeneity gives the entropy over the different connector types.
Metric	$CH(G) = -\sum_{l \in \{and, xor, or\}} p(l) \cdot log_3(p(l))$
Rationale	A process model with a high heterogeneity is likely to include errors since connectors can be mismatched more easily. If the model includes only one connector type then CH is 0.

Limitations	Process models might have a high connector heterogeneity but if the model is structured an error is less likely.
Hypothesis	An increase in $CH(G)$ should imply an increase in error probability of the overall model.
Related Work	CH has not yet been formalized in literature.

The Control Flow Complexity metric was introduced in [72] for measuring how difficult it is to consider all potential states after a split depending on its type.

Symbol	CFC
Definition	CFC is the sum over all connectors weighted by their potential combinations of states after the split.
Metric	$CFC(G) = \sum_{c \in S_{and}} 1 + \sum_{c \in S_{xor}} |c_{xor} \bullet| + \sum_{c \in S_{or}} 2^{|c_{or} \bullet|} - 1$
Rationale	A process model with a high CFC should be more likely to contain errors according to the above argument.
Limitations	Models with the same structure but with different connector labels may have a huge difference in CFC while they are equally easy to understand.
Hypothesis	An increase in $CFC(G)$ should imply an increase in error probability of the overall model.
Related Work	CFC is inspired by [260] and introduced in [72].

Figure 4.7 illustrates the three connector metrics by the help of two example EPCs. The EPC on the left-hand side has six XOR-connectors, each with a matching counterpart. The mismatch value is 0. Since there are only XOR-connectors, the heterogeneity value is also 0. The CFC value is 6 since each of the three split connectors represents a binary choice. The EPC on the right-hand side has the same structure but partially different connector types. There is one AND-split and an OR-join that do not have a matching counterpart. This results in a mismatch value of 4. Three OR, two XOR and one AND-connector yield a high heterogeneity value of 0.92. Finally, the CFC value is calculated by summing up 2 for the XOR-split and 3 for the OR-split which gives a result of 5.

4.5.5 Cyclicity

Cyclic parts of a model are presumably more difficult to understand than sequential parts. $|N_C|$ gives the number of nodes n_i for which a cycle exists such that $n_i \hookrightarrow n_i$, and cyclicity relates it to the total number of nodes.

Symbol	CYC
Definition	Cyclicity relates nodes on a cycle to the number of nodes.
Metric	$CYC_N = |N_C|/|N|$
Rationale	A process model with a high cyclicity should be more likely to contain errors. For a sequential model cyclicity is 0.

Limitations	There are models with the same cyclicity but which differ in comprehensibility, e.g. if one is larger.
Hypothesis	An increase in $CYC(G)$ should imply an increase in error probability of the overall model.
Related Work	CYC has not yet been mentioned in literature. *Nissen* proposes to count the number of cycles instead [320].

Figure 4.8 depicts two similar EPCs. They have the same cyclicity since they have the same number of nodes that are on a loop. The difference is that the model on the right-hand side has two cycles that are nested in another cycle while the EPC on the left side has two structured XOR-blocks on one loop. Since the cyclicity metric only captures how many nodes are on a cycle it cannot distinguish between models with a different number of cycles.

4.5.6 Concurrency

Modelers have to keep track of concurrent paths that need to be synchronized. AND-splits and OR-splits introduce new threads of control, so that the number of control tokens potentially increases by the number of the output degree minus one. The Token Split metric counts these newly introduced tokens. Concurrent tokens from the initial marking are not considered.

Symbol	TS
Definition	The token split sums up the output-degree of AND-joins and OR-joins minus one.
Metric	$$TS(G) = \sum_{c \in C_{or} \cup C_{and}} d_{out}(n) - 1$$
Rationale	A process model with a high token split value should be more likely to contain errors since it introduces a high degree of parallelism. A model with $TS = 0$ does not introduce new threads of execution after instantiation.[4]
Limitations	There are models with the same token split value but which differ in comprehensibility, e.g. if one is structured.
Hypothesis	An increase in $TS(G)$ should imply an increase in error probability of the overall model.
Related Work	The maximum number of tokens was proposed by *Lee and Yoon* in [244]. While that approach is appealing, it is more computation intense than the token split metric. In *Nissen* [320], the concept of parallelism is captured by an approximation as number of nodes divided by diameter assuming that all splits introduce parallelism. *Morasca* proposes concurrent contribution which is related to token splits [308]. *Balasubramanian and Gupta* relate parallel nodes to nodes in total [37].

---

[4] There may still be concurrency due to multiple start events.

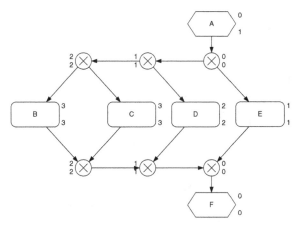

Figure 4.6. EPC with depth values next to nodes (top: in-depth, bottom: out-depth)

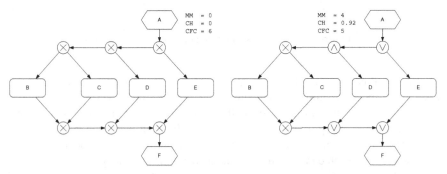

Figure 4.7. Two EPCs with different connector types

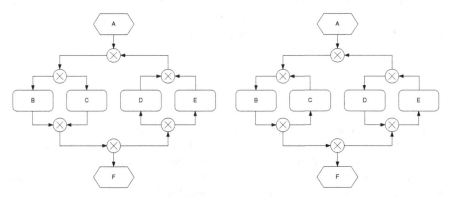

Figure 4.8. Two EPCs, one with nested cycles

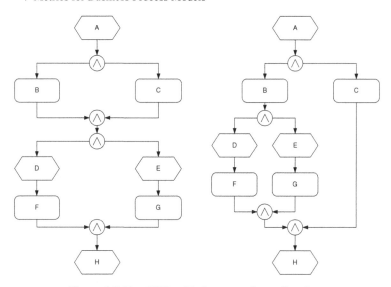

Figure 4.9. Two EPCs with the same token split values

Figure 4.9 illustrates that the token split gives an upper bound for the number of tokens in a model assuming boundedness. The EPC on the left-hand side contains two blocks of concurrency is sequence. Its maximum number of tokens is, therefore, lower than the token split value. In the model on the right-hand side the two blocks are nested. In this case, the maximum number of tokens matches the token split value.

The set of presented metrics reveals that there are several independent factors that presumably affect error probability. Approaches trying to squeeze the complexity of a process model[5] into a single metric consequently seem doomed to fail. A similar observation is made by *Zuse* [474] who describes software complexity as a multi-dimensional phenomenon. In the subsequent section, we revisit the example EPC from Figure 2.1 to illustrate the metrics.

4.6 Calculating Metrics

In Section 2.1, we introduced the example of a loan request EPC taken from [325]. Table 4.1 summarizes the different metrics and Figure 4.10 illustrates which nodes and arcs contribute to the more elaborate metrics. Since the different count metrics, for size in particular, can be easily read from the model, we focus on those that need to be calculated from the process graph (separability, sequentiality, structuredness, depth, cyclicity and diameter).

The *separability ratio* Π depends on the identification of cut vertices (articulation points); those nodes whose deletion breaks up the graph in two or more disconnected

---

[5] The complexity of a process model can be defined as the degree to which a process model is difficult to analyze, understand or explain (see [194]).

Table 4.1. Metrics derived from the EPC example

Size S_N	27	density Δ	0.040
Size S_E	11	density CNC	1.074
Size S_{E_S}	1	av. connector degree $\overline{d_C}$	3
Size $S_{E_{Int}}$	8	max. connector degree $\widehat{d_C}$	3
Size S_{E_E}	2	separability Π	0.440
Size S_F	8	sequentiality Ξ	0.345
Size S_C	8	structuredness Φ	0.556
Size $S_{S_{XOR}}$	3	depth Λ	1
Size $S_{J_{XOR}}$	2	mismatch MM	8
Size $S_{S_{AND}}$	0	heterogeneity CH	0.819
Size $S_{J_{AND}}$	2	control flow complexity CFC	8
Size $S_{S_{OR}}$	0	cyclicity CYC	0.259
Size $S_{J_{OR}}$	1	token splits TS	2
Size S_A	29		
Size $diam$	14		

components. Figure 4.10 displays articulation points with a letter A written next to the top left-hand side of the node. For example, if the function *record loan request* is deleted the start event is no longer connected with the rest of the process model. There are eleven articulation points in total yielding a separability ratio of $11/(27 - 2) = 0.440$. Note that start and end events do not belong to the set of articulation points since their removal does not increase the number of separate components.

The *sequentiality ratio* Ξ is calculated by relating the number of sequence arcs (arcs that connect functions and events) to the total number of arcs. Figure 4.10 highlights sequence arcs with an s label. There are ten sequence arcs and 29 arcs altogether which results in a sequentiality ratio of $10/29 = 0.345$. The degree of *structuredness* Φ relates the size of a reduced process model to the size of the original one. Figure 4.10 shows those elements with a cross on the left-hand side that are eliminated by reduction of trivial constructs. Other structured reduction rules are not applicable. Since 15 elements are deleted by reduction, the structuredness ratio is $1 - 15/27 = 0.556$. The *in-depth and out-depth* is also indicated for each node in Figure 4.10. The depth of a node is then the minimum of in-depth and out-depth. Several nodes have a depth of 1, which is a maximum, and therefore also the depth of the overall process. The *cyclicity* is based on the relation between number of nodes on a cycle and nodes in total. Figure 4.10 shows nodes on a cycle with a letter C written to the left-hand side bottom. There are seven such nodes yielding a cyclicity ratio of $7/27 = 0.259$. Figure 4.10 connects those 14 nodes that are on the *diameter* with a bold line.

We implemented the calculation of the various metrics as an extension to *xoEPC* (see Section 3.3.2). For each EPC that is analyzed by the program, the whole set of metrics is calculated and written to the entry for the model in the errorreport.xml file. We will use this feature in the following chapter for the analysis of an extensive collection of real-world EPC business process models.

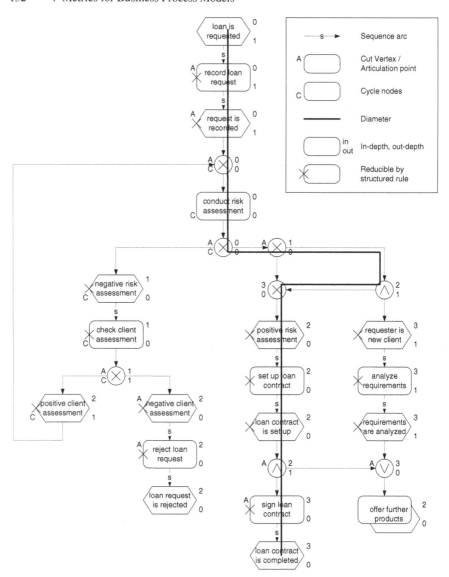

Figure 4.10. EPC example with sequence arcs, articulation points, cycle nodes, diameter, depth, and reducible nodes

4.7 Summary

In this chapter, we discussed the suitability of metrics for error prediction from a theoretical point of view. Revisiting related research in the area of network analysis, software measurement and metrics for business process models, we found that several aspects of process models were not yet combined in an overall measurement framework. Based on theoretical considerations, *we presented a set of 15 metrics related to size and 13 metrics that capture various aspects of the structure and the state space of the process model.* For each of the metrics we discussed a plausible connection with error probability and formulated respective hypotheses. In the following chapter, we will test these hypotheses for a large set of EPC business process models from practice using statistical methods.

5

Validation of Metrics as Error Predictors

In this chapter, we test the validity of metrics that were defined in the previous chapter for predicting errors in EPC business process models. In Section 5.1, we provide an overview of how the analysis data is generated. Section 5.2 describes the sample of EPCs from practice that we use for the analysis. Here we discuss a disaggregation by the EPC model group and by error as well as a correlation analysis between metrics and error. Based on this sample, we calculate a logistic regression model for predicting error probability with the metrics as input variables in Section 5.3. In Section 5.4, we then test the regression function for an independent sample of EPC models from textbooks as a cross-validation. Section 5.5 summarizes the findings.

5.1 Analysis Data Generation

Figure 5.1 gives an overview of the analysis data generation process. As input, we use four sets of EPC business process models that are available in the XML interchange format of ARIS Toolset of IDS Scheer AG. In Section 5.2, we describe these sets of EPC models in detail. As a first step, the set of ARIS XML files is read and processed by *xoEPC*, the batch program we introduced in Chapter 3. *xoEPC* applies the set of reduction rules that we described in Section 3.3.3, and generates an XML error report file that includes, among others, the following information for each EPC:

- processing time for the EPC,
- references to syntactical problems,
- references to errors,
- statistics about how often a certain reduction rule was applied,
- information about whether the model is reduced completely and finally
- values for each of the metrics that we described in Section 4.5.

The error report XML file is then transformed to an HTML table by an XSLT program. Each incompletely reduced EPC is then written to an EPML file. The reduced EPCs are analyzed with the help of the reachability graph analysis plug-in for ProM

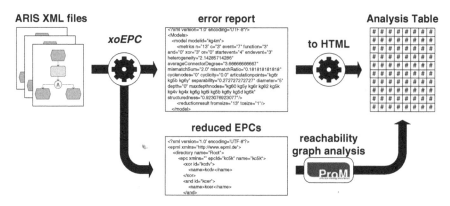

Figure 5.1. Overview of the analysis

introduced in Section 3.2. The results of this analysis are added to the analysis table. The table is stored as an MS Excel file, as this format can be loaded by SPSS; the software package that we use for the statistical analysis. The complete list of variables of the analysis table is described in Appendix C.1 of [266].

5.2 The Sample of EPC Models

This section describes the sample of EPC models that we use for the validation of the set of metrics that we defined in the previous chapter. We present descriptive statistics disaggregated by group and error as well as a correlation analysis between the variable *hasErrors* and each of the metrics.

The sample includes four collections of EPCs with a total of 2003 process models. All EPCs of the four groups were developed by practitioners.

1. *SAP Reference Model:* The first collection of EPCs is the SAP Reference Model. We already used this set of process models to illustrate the performance of the reduction rule verification approach as implemented in *xoEPC* (see Chapter 3). The development of the SAP reference model started in 1992 and the first models were presented at CEBIT'93 [211, p.VII]. It was subsequently developed further, up until version 4.6 of SAP R/3 which was released in 2000 [269]. The SAP reference model includes 604 non-trivial EPCs.
2. *Service Model:* The second collection of EPCs stems from a German process reengineering project in the service sector. The project was conducted in the late 1990s. The modeling task was carried out by a project team with academic supervision. As an organization principle, the business processes were modelled in two separate groups depending on whether they were supported by the ERP-system or not. The models that were defined in this project include 381 non-trivial EPCs. There are models describing the organization, data and information systems.

3. *Finance Model:* The third model collection contains the EPCs of a process documentation project in the Austrian financial industry. The project not only recorded the various business processes of the different functional units of the company but also information systems, organization and business forms. It includes 935 EPC process models altogether.

4. *Consulting Model:* The fourth collection covers a total of 83 EPCs from three different consulting companies. These companies reside in three different countries. The models of these collections also include organizational and functional models. The models are mainly used as reference models to support and streamline consulting activities of the companies.

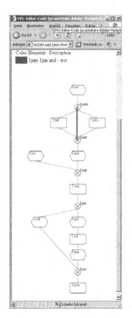 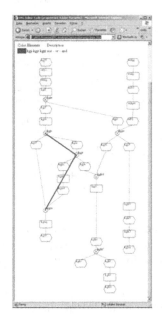 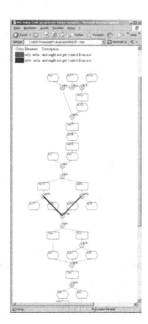

Figure 5.2. EPC with error from group 2   **Figure 5.3.** EPC with error from group 3   **Figure 5.4.** EPC with error from group 4

We will use the terms *group 1* synonymously for the SAP Reference Model, *group 2* for the Service Model, *group 3* for the Finance Model, and *group 4* for the Consulting Model. Figures 5.2 to 5.4 show example EPCs with errors from the service model, the finance model and the consulting model.

5.2.1 How Do the Four Groups Differ?

In this section, we use descriptive statistics to characterize the overall EPC sample and its four sub-groups. We give mean values μ and standard deviation σ for each metric including size S_N and its variants, diameter $diam$, density Δ, coefficient of

Table 5.1. Mean and Standard Deviation of model sets disaggregated by group

Parameter	Complete Sample		SAP Ref. Model		Services Model		Finance Model		Consulting Model	
	μ	σ	μ_1	σ_1	μ_2	σ_2	μ_3	σ_3	μ_4	σ_4
S_N	20.71	16.84	20.74	18.74	22.14	15.71	19.50	15.30	27.64	21.35
S_E	10.47	8.66	11.50	10.44	9.54	7.80	9.93	7.41	13.20	9.99
S_{E_S}	2.43	2.70	3.87	3.84	1.99	2.02	1.59	1.12	3.43	3.38
S_{E_E}	2.77	3.20	4.49	4.78	2.35	2.08	1.77	1.24	3.39	3.12
S_F	5.98	4.94	4.03	3.81	8.23	5.45	6.22	4.79	7.22	5.95
S_C	4.27	5.01	5.21	6.22	4.37	4.20	3.35	3.90	7.22	6.96
$S_{C_{AND}}$	2.25	3.00	2.18	2.75	1.26	1.88	0.48	1.27	3.37	3.71
$S_{C_{XOR}}$	1.26	2.24	1.95	2.78	2.34	3.01	2.29	2.99	3.49	4.05
$S_{C_{OR}}$	0.76	1.54	1.08	1.81	0.77	1.27	0.57	1.45	0.35	0.89
$S_{J_{AND}}$	0.63	1.23	1.09	1.60	0.56	0.93	0.27	0.71	1.64	2.01
$S_{J_{XOR}}$	1.01	1.46	1.02	1.51	0.94	1.38	1.00	1.41	1.49	1.93
$S_{J_{OR}}$	0.37	0.82	0.46	1.03	0.37	0.69	0.32	0.73	0.22	0.54
$S_{S_{AND}}$	0.62	1.17	1.08	1.48	0.68	1.06	0.22	0.64	1.51	1.79
$S_{S_{XOR}}$	1.24	1.75	0.93	1.50	1.27	1.76	1.36	1.81	1.88	2.19
$S_{S_{OR}}$	0.37	0.86	0.62	1.14	0.33	0.57	0.25	0.74	0.13	0.46
S_A	21.11	18.87	20.80	20.84	22.50	17.43	20.12	17.54	28.14	22.80
$diam$	11.45	8.21	9.20	6.46	12.25	7.90	12.27	8.78	14.83	10.50
Δ	0.09	0.07	0.09	0.08	0.07	0.05	0.09	0.07	0.06	0.05
CNC	0.96	0.13	0.94	0.13	0.97	0.13	0.96	0.13	1.00	0.12
$\overline{d_C}$	3.56	2.40	3.30	1.46	3.12	1.66	2.50	1.62	3.08	0.81
$\widehat{d_C}$	2.88	1.60	4.36	2.72	3.85	2.30	2.91	2.11	3.81	1.22
Π	0.56	0.27	0.52	0.22	0.56	0.25	0.60	0.30	0.50	0.21
Ξ	0.46	0.31	0.29	0.28	0.45	0.26	0.59	0.29	0.32	0.22
Φ	0.88	0.11	0.83	0.14	0.90	0.09	0.90	0.08	0.81	0.17
Λ	0.70	0.74	0.55	0.71	0.79	0.66	0.72	0.76	1.00	0.86
MM	3.31	4.55	6.02	6.19	2.84	3.42	1.68	2.49	3.95	3.47
CH	0.28	0.35	0.43	0.38	0.31	0.34	0.15	0.28	0.38	0.34
CFC	382.62	8849.48	1187.98	16040.30	101.80	1678.82	10.17	52.79	6.71	7.35
CYC	0.01	0.08	0.02	0.09	0.04	0.13	0.00	0.01	0.02	0.09
TS	1.82	3.53	3.16	4.89	1.84	2.66	0.91	2.39	2.13	2.63

connectivity CNC, average and maximum connector degree $\overline{d_C}$ and $\widehat{d_C}$, Separability Π, Sequentiality Ξ, Structuredness Φ, Depth Λ, connector mismatch MM and heterogeneity CH, control flow complexity CFC, cyclicity CYC and token splits TS.

Table 5.1 gives an overview of the mean μ and the standard deviation σ for all metrics disaggregated by the four model groups. Several of the disaggregated mean values are quite close to each other but the Finance Model in particular shows some striking differences. Notably, it uses start and end events very scarcely (1.59 and 1.77 compared to 3.87 and 4.49 in average in the SAP Reference Model) and has the highest mean in structuredness Φ and sequentiality Ξ. Figures 5.5 and 5.6 illustrate the distribution of both the latter metrics as box plots[1] disaggregated by group. In this type of diagram the median is depicted as a horizontal line in a box that represents the interval between lower and upper quartile; that is, the box refers to middle range EPCs ranked by the metric from 25% to 75%. Please note that the table indicates the *mean* while the box plot shows the *median*. The upper and lower lines outside the box define a one and a half multiple of the respective 25%–50% and 50%–75%

---

[1] The box plot is particularly useful for exploratory data analysis. It was invented by *Tukey* in 1977 (see [434]). Box plots of all variables disaggregated by group are included in Appendix C.2 of [266].

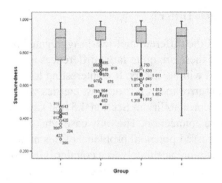

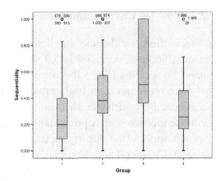

Figure 5.5. Box plot for structuredness Φ disaggregated by group

Figure 5.6. Box plot for sequentiality Ξ disaggregated by group

quartiles. Values outside these two intervals are drawn as individual points and are considered to be outliers. From the two observations on start and end events, as well as on structuredness Φ and sequentiality Ξ, we might be tempted to conclude that the Finance Model contains the more structured EPCs and thus might have less error models.

There is some evidence for such a hypothesis when we look at the number of errors in each of the four groups. Table 5.2 gives a respective overview. It can be seen that there are 2003 EPCs in the overall sample with 215 of them containing at least one error. This is an overall error ratio of 10.7%. 154 of the 215 errors were found by *xoEPC*. 156 EPCs could not be completely reduced and were analyzed with ProM. This analysis revealed that 115 of the unreduced EPCs still had errors. Please note that there are EPCs for which both *xoEPC* and ProM found errors. The number of EPCs with errors is, therefore, less than the sum of EPCs with *xoEPC* and ProM errors. The comparison of the groups shows that the error ratio is quite different. In the previous paragraph, we hypothesized that the finance model group might have less errors since it seems to follow certain guidelines that lead to more structured models. This might be an explanation for a low error ratio of only 3.3%. We might find some further evidence regarding the connection between metrics and errors in the subsequent section with a disaggregation by the boolean variable *hasErrors*.

Table 5.2. Errors in the sample models

Parameter	Complete Sample	SAP Ref. Model	Services Model	Finance Model	Consulting Models
xoEPC errors	154	90	28	26	10
Unreduced EPCs	156	103	18	17	18
ProM error EPCs	115	75	16	7	17
EPCs with errors	215	126	37	31	21
EPCs in total	2003	604	381	935	83
Error ratio	10.7%	20.9%	9.7%	3.3%	25.3%

5.2.2 How Do Correct and Incorrect Models Differ?

In this section, we discuss the distribution of the different metrics disaggregated by the variable *hasErrors*. Table 5.3 shows that there are quite large differences in the mean values of the EPC sub-sample with and without errors. It is interesting to note that the error mean μ_e is higher than the non-error mean μ_n for most metrics where we assumed a positive connection with error probability in Section 4.5 and smaller for those metrics with a presumably negative connection. The only case where this does not apply is the density metric. We discussed potential problems of this metric earlier in Chapter 4 and it seems that it works more accurately as a counter-indicator for size than as an indicator for the density of connections in the model. Indeed, there is a correlation of -0.659 between density and size. The two columns on the right-hand side of Table 5.3 might provide the basis for proposing potential error thresholds. The first of these columns gives a double σ_n deviation upwards from the non-error mean μ_n. Assuming a normal distribution, only 2.5% of the population can be expected to have a metric value greater than this. The comparison of this value with the mean μ_e of the error EPCs provides an idea of how well the two sub-samples can be separated by the metric. In several cases, the mean μ_e is outside the double σ_n interval around μ_n. The box plots in Figures 5.7 and 5.8 illustrate the different distributions. It can be seen that correct EPCs tend to have much higher structuredness values and lower connector heterogeneity values.[2] We verified the significance of the difference between the mean values by applying an analysis of variance (ANOVA). The result of the Kolmogorov-Smirnov test shows that the prerequisite of an approximate normal distribution is fulfilled by all variables. The F-statistic values of the analysis of variance indicate that the mean differences are significant with 99.9% confidence for all metrics. In the subsequent section, we gather further evidence regarding the direction of the connection between metrics and errors based on a correlation analysis. Details on the analysis are reported in [266].

5.2.3 Correlation Analysis

This section approaches the connection between error probability and metrics with a correlation analysis. The Appendix C.4 of [266] lists the complete correlation table calculated according to *Pearson* for interval scale data and to *Spearman* for ordinal scale data. The tendency is the same for both methods. As a confirmation of the previous observation, all variables have the expected direction of influence except for the density metric. Table 5.4 presents the Spearman correlation between *hasErrors* and the metrics ordered by strength of correlation. It can be seen that several correlations are quite considerable with absolute values between 0.30 and 0.50. The significance of all correlations is good with more than 99% confidence.

The ability of a metric to separate error from non-error models by ranking is illustrated in Figures 5.9 and 5.10. For Figure 5.9, all models are ranked according to their size. A point (x, y) in the graph relates a size x to the relative

---

[2] The two outliners in Figure 5.8 are cyclic models with only OR-connectors in the first case and only AND-connectors in the second case.

Table 5.3. Mean and Standard Deviation of the sample models disaggregated by error

Parameter	Complete Sample		Non-Error EPCs		Error EPCs		2σ dev. up	2σ dev. down
	μ	σ	μ_n	σ_n	μ_e	σ_e	$\mu_n + 2\sigma_n$	$\mu_n - 2\sigma_n$
S_N	20.71	16.84	18.04	13.48	42.97	24.08	$44.99 \approx \mu_e$	
S_E	10.47	8.66	9.06	6.69	22.17	13.19	$22.45 \approx \mu_e$	
S_{E_S}	2.43	2.70	2.04	2.04	5.69	4.65	$6.12 \approx \mu_e$	
S_{E_E}	2.77	3.20	2.25	2.11	7.02	6.19	$6.47 < \mu_e$	
S_F	5.98	4.94	5.67	4.65	8.53	6.33	14.97	
S_C	4.27	5.01	3.30	3.47	12.26	7.89	$10.24 < \mu_e$	
$S_{C_{AND}}$	2.25	3.00	0.85	1.47	4.74	3.89	$3.78 < \mu_e$	
$S_{C_{XOR}}$	1.26	2.24	1.85	2.60	5.50	3.97	7.05	
$S_{C_{OR}}$	0.76	1.54	0.60	1.33	2.02	2.35	3.27	
$S_{J_{AND}}$	0.63	1.23	0.40	0.81	2.54	2.12	$2.02 < \mu_e$	
$S_{J_{XOR}}$	1.01	1.46	0.82	1.24	2.63	2.06	3.29	
$S_{J_{OR}}$	0.37	0.82	0.32	0.74	0.79	1.26	1.79	
$S_{S_{AND}}$	0.62	1.17	0.44	0.84	2.13	2.09	$2.12 \approx \mu_e$	
$S_{S_{XOR}}$	1.24	1.75	1.04	1.56	2.86	2.31	4.16	
$S_{S_{OR}}$	0.37	0.86	0.27	0.68	1.22	1.51	1.63	
S_A	21.11	18.87	18.14	15.20	45.79	26.78	$48.54 \approx \mu_e$	
$diam$	11.45	8.21	10.63	7.71	18.25	9.01	26.06	
Δ	0.09	0.07	0.09	0.07	0.03	0.02	0.23	
CNC	0.96	0.13	0.95	0.13	1.05	0.08	1.21	
$\overline{d_C}$	3.56	2.40	2.80	1.66	3.57	0.68	6.11	
$\widehat{d_C}$	2.88	1.60	3.31	2.28	5.64	2.41	7.87	
Π	0.56	0.27	0.59	0.27	0.35	0.13		0.06
Ξ	0.46	0.31	0.49	0.30	0.18	0.14		-0.12
Φ	0.88	0.11	0.90	0.09	0.70	0.16		$0.72 > \mu_e$
Λ	0.70	0.74	0.61	0.69	1.45	0.73	1.98	
MM	3.31	4.55	2.54	3.45	9.71	6.92	$9.44 < \mu_e$	
CH	0.28	0.35	0.22	0.32	0.75	0.19	0.85	
CFC	382.62	8849.48	202.19	6306.23	1883.17	19950.26	12814.64	
CYC	0.01	0.08	0.01	0.06	0.07	0.17	0.12	
TS	1.82	3.53	1.28	2.46	6.26	6.62	$6.20 < \mu_e$	

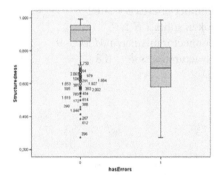

Figure 5.7. Box plot for structuredness Φ disaggregated by error

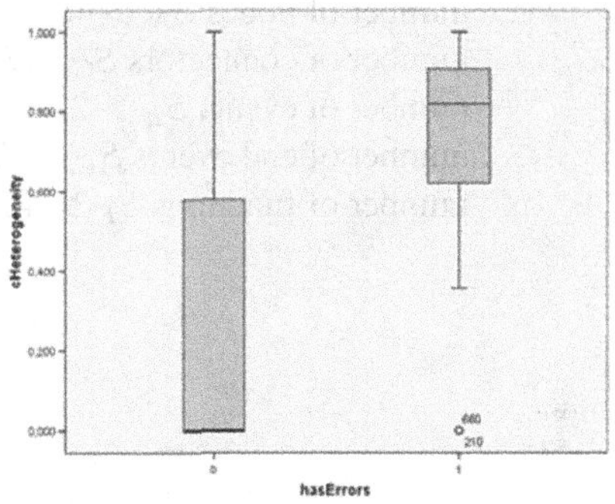

Figure 5.8. Box plot for connector heterogeneity CH disaggregated by error

Table 5.4. Spearman correlation between hasError and metrics ordered by absolute correlation

	hasError		hasError		hasError
$S_{J_{AND}}$	0,48	S_{E_E}	0,38	$S_{S_{OR}}$	0,31
CH	0,46	Δ	-0,37	$S_{S_{XOR}}$	0,31
$S_{C_{AND}}$	0,45	$S_{S_{AND}}$	0,37	CYC	0,30
S_C	0,43	Φ	-0,36	$S_{C_{OR}}$	0,30
MM	0,42	Ξ	-0,35	$diam$	0,30
CFC	0,39	$S_{C_{XOR}}$	0,35	Π	-0,29
S_A	0,38	S_{E_S}	0,35	CNC	0,28
TS	0,38	Λ	0,34	$\overline{d_C}$	0,23
S_N	0,38	$S_{J_{XOR}}$	0,33	S_F	0,19
S_E	0,38	$\widehat{d_C}$	0,33	$S_{J_{OR}}$	0,15

frequency of error models in a subset of models that have at least size x, i.e. $y = |\{\frac{errorEPC}{EPC} \mid S_N(EPC) > x\}|$. It can be seen that the relative frequency of error EPCs increases by increasing the minimum number of nodes. The relative frequency of error EPCs in particular is higher than 50% for all EPCs of at least 48 nodes. In Figure 5.10, all models are ranked according to their structuredness and (x, y) relates the structuredness x to the subset y of models that have at most structuredness x. Here the graph decreases and drops below 50% at a structuredness value of 0.80. Similar observations can also be made for some other metrics. The relative frequency of error models above 50% is reached if

number of nodes $S_N > 48$ number of arcs $S_A > 62$
number of connectors $S_C > 8$ token splits $TS > 7$
number of events $S_E > 22$ connector mismatch $MM > 9$
number of end events $S_{E_e} > 7$ structuredness $\Phi < 0.8$
number of functions $S_F > 40$

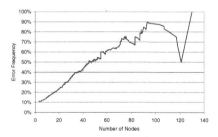

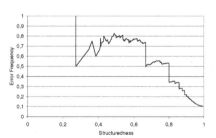

Figure 5.9. Error frequency to ordered number of nodes

Figure 5.10. Error frequency to ordered structuredness

In this section, we have gathered some evidence that the hypothetical connections between metrics and error probability as postulated in Section 4.5 might actually hold. We have found considerable and statistically significant differences in the metrics' mean values for the sub-samples of EPCs with and without errors. The mean values of error EPCs in particular tend to be larger or smaller as expected by the hypotheses. Correlation analysis has also confirmed the hypothetical direction of the connection between metrics and errors. The only exception is the density metric. It seems that this metric might be more suitable as a counter-indicator for size than as an indicator of the relative number of arcs in the EPCs. It must be kept in mind, however, that correlation alone does not provide a means to predict error probability. In contrast, logistic regression allows a precise prediction by estimating the parameters of the logistic function. We will, therefore, investigate logistic regression in the following section.

5.3 Logistic Regression

This section provides an introduction to logistic regression analysis and presents the result of its application for estimating the prediction model for error probability based on metrics.

5.3.1 Introduction to Logistic Regression

Logistic regression is a statistical model designed to estimate binary choices. It is perfectly suited to deal with dependent variables such as *hasErrors* with its range *error* and *no error*. The idea of binary choice models is to describe the probability of a binary event by its odds; that is, the ratio of event probability divided by non-event probability. In the *logistic regression* (or *logit*) model the odds are defined as $logit(p_i) = ln(\frac{p_i}{1-p_i}) = \beta_0 + \beta_1 x_{1,i} + \cdots + \beta_k x_{k,i}$ for k input variables and i observations (EPC i here). From this follows that

$$p_i = \frac{e^{\beta_0 + \beta_1 x_{1,i} + \cdots + \beta_k x_{k,i}}}{1 + e^{\beta_0 + \beta_1 x_{1,i} + \cdots + \beta_k x_{k,i}}}$$

The relationship between input and dependent variables is represented by an S-shaped curve of the logistic function that converges to 0 for $-\infty$ and to 1 for ∞ (see Figure 5.11). The cut value of 0.5 defines whether event or non-event is predicted. $Exp(\beta_k)$ gives the multiplicative change of the odds if the input variable β_k is increased by one unit ($Exp(\beta_k) > 1$ increases and $Exp(\beta_k) < 1$ decreases error probability). The actual value $Exp(\beta_k)$ cannot be interpreted in isolation since its impact depends upon the position on the non-linear curve [202, p.791].

The significance of the overall model is assessed by the help of two statistics. First, the *Hosmer & Lemeshow* Test should be greater than 5% to indicate a good fit based on the difference between observed and predicted frequencies (see [188]). Second, *Nagelkerke's* R^2 ranging from 0 to 1 serves as a coefficient of determination indicating which fraction of the variability is explained [314]. Each estimated

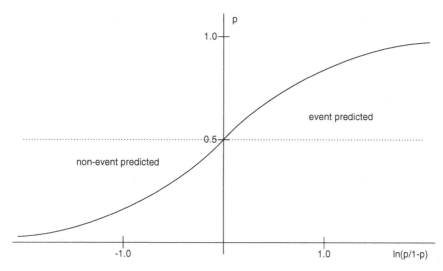

Figure 5.11. S-shaped curve of the logistic regression model

coefficient of the logit model is tested using the *Wald* statistic for values significantly different from zero. The significance should be less than 5%. We calculate the logistic regression model based on a stepwise introduction of those variables that provide the greatest increase in likelihood. For more details on logistic regression see [188, 161, 35].

5.3.2 Preparatory Analyses

Before calculating a multivariate logistic regression model for error probability, we carry out two preparatory analyses. We check collinearity, then determine which variables are included in the regression model. We also exclude 29 EPCs from the analysis that are not relaxed syntactically correct. While it is possible to find errors in these models (as we did in Section 3.3.4), it is not appropriate to use them in a regression analysis for predicting errors in EPCs that fulfill relaxed syntactical correctness.[3]

Collinearity describes the phenomenon of at least one of the independent variables being representable as a linear combination of other variables. The absence of collinearity is not a hard criterion for the applicability of logistic regression, but it is desirable. In a variable set without collinearity, every variable has a so-called tolerance value[4] higher than 0.1, otherwise there is a collinearity problem. There are

---

[3] Still, the effect of this choice is minimal. Including the 29 EPCs with syntax problems yields a logistic regression model with the same metrics and similar coefficients, and the same *Nagelkerke* R^2.

[4] The tolerance value is calculated based on the variance inflation factor. For an overview of multicollinearity detection methods refer to [202, Ch.21].

several collinearity problems in the original variable set. We dropped all count metrics apart from S_N as they were highly correlated. This resulted in a reduced variable set with almost no collinearity problems. The S_N metric is close to the 0.1 threshold and, therefore, kept in the metrics set.

As a second step, we calculated univariate models with and without a constant in order to check whether all inputs (the constant and each metric) were significantly different from zero. As a conclusion from these models we drop the constant and the control flow complexity CFC for the multivariate analysis. The constant is not significantly different from zero (Wald statistic of 0.872 and 0.117) in the separability and the sequentiality model which suggests that it is not necessary. The CFC metric is also not significantly different from zero (Wald statistic of 0.531 and 0.382) in both models with and without constant. All other metrics stay in the set of input variables from the multivariate logistic regression model.

5.3.3 Multivariate Logistic Regression Model

This section presents the results of the multivariate logistic regression model. We use a stepwise introduction of the variables to the logit model selected for its potential to improve the likelihood. Variables are only introduced if their *Wald* statistic is better than 0.05. They are excluded if this statistic becomes worse than 0.1. Such a stepwise approach for determining the best set of variables is particularly appropriate for a setting where little is known about the relative importance of the variables (see [188, p.116]). The final model was calculated in nine steps and includes seven variables. It is interesting to note that the hypothetical impact direction of the included metrics is reconfirmed. All variables have an excellent *Wald* statistic value (better than 0.001) indicating that they are significantly different from zero. The *Hosmer & Lemeshow* test is also greater than 0.05; another good value. The *Nagelkerke* R^2 has an excellent value of 0.901, indicating a high degree of explanation.

Based on the regression results, we can derive a classification function $p(EPC)$ for EPCs. It predicts that the EPC has errors if the result is greater than 0.5. Otherwise it predicts that there are no errors in the EPC. It is calculated by the help of the metrics coefficient of connectivity CNC, connector mismatch MM, cyclicity CYC, separability Π, structuredness Φ, connector heterogeneity CH and the diameter $diam$.

$$p(EPC) = \frac{e^{logit(EPC)}}{1 + e^{logit(EPC)}}$$

with

$$\begin{aligned}
logit(EPC) = &+4.008\,CNC \\
&+0.094\,MM \\
&+3.409\,CYC \\
&-2.338\,\Pi \\
&-9.957\,\Phi \\
&+3.003\,CH \\
&+0.064\,diam
\end{aligned}$$

It is easy to calculate an error prediction for an EPC based on this function. The results are as follows:

- 1724 EPCs are correctly predicted to have no errors,
- 155 EPCs are correctly predicted to have errors,
- 58 EPCs are predicted to have no errors, but actually have errors, and
- 37 EPCs are predicted to have errors, but actually have none.

Altogether 1879 EPCs have the correct prediction. The overall percentage is 95.2% which is 6% better than the naive model that always predicts no error (89.2%). There are also 213 EPCs with errors in the reduced sample and 155 of them are correctly predicted (72.7%). The prediction function gives a clue about the relative importance of the different metrics. Structuredness Φ appears to be the most important parameter since its absolute value is three times as high as the second. The coefficient of connectivity CNC, cyclicity CYC, separability Π, and connector heterogeneity CH likewise seem to be of comparable importance. Finally, connector mismatch MM and the diameter $diam$ might be of minor importance.

We then excluded the metrics of the regression model and calculated a second best model without the coefficient of network connectivity CNC, connector mismatch MM, cyclicity CYC, separability Π, structuredness Φ, connector heterogeneity CH, and without the diameter $diam$; the idea being to gain insight into the direction of the influence of further metrics on error probability. This second best model includes sequentiality Ξ, density Δ and size S_N. The *Hosmer & Lemeshow* Test fails to indicate a good fit since the value is less than 5% after the second step. The value of *Nagelkerke's* R^2 still indicates a high fraction of explanation of the variability with a value of 0.824 and 91.4% if all cases are classified correctly. These figures indicate that the second best regression model is less powerful than the first model. The estimated equation is

$$logit_2(EPC) = -6.540\ \Xi - 23.873\ \Delta + 0.034\ S_N$$

We also excluded the metrics of the second best regression model (only token split TS, average and maximum connector degree $\overline{d_C}$ and $\widehat{d_C}$, and Depth Λ were considered). The *Hosmer & Lemeshow* Test fails to indicate a good fit since the value is less than 5% and the *Nagelkerke's* R^2 reaches only (compared to the previous models) a value of 0.627. 72.9% of all cases are classified correctly indicating a weaker capability to predict errors correctly compared to the other models. The estimated equation is

$$logit_3(EPC) = 0.194\ TS - 1.371\ \overline{d_C} + 0.405\ \widehat{d_C} + 0.440\ \Lambda$$

It is interesting to note that most coefficients of the different regression models confirm the expected direction of influence on error probability. Beyond that, two variables have an impact opposite to the expectation: the density Δ and the average connector degree $\overline{d_C}$. We have already identified potential problems with density in Sections 4.2 and 4.5.2. It appears that this metric is more strongly negatively connected with size than with the degree of connections in the process model. In contrast, the unexpected sign of the coefficient for average connector degree $\overline{d_C}$ seems to be due to a positive correlation with structuredness of 0.251 which is significant at a 99% confidence level. Since structuredness is not included in the variable set of the third best regression model, the average connector degree $\overline{d_C}$ apparently captures some of its negative impact on error probability. Additional details on the logistic regression analysis are reported in [266].

In the following section, we analyze how well the different regression function is able to forecast errors in a sample of EPCs that was not included in the estimation.

5.4 External Validation

In this section, we utilize the estimated function to predict errors in EPCs from a *holdout sample*. This external validation step is of paramount importance for establishing the criterion validity of the measurements (to demonstrate that the model is not overfitting the data, see Section 4.1) and that it can also be used to predict errors in other model samples (see [188, pp.186]). A holdout sample is only one option for external validation. There are several techniques for *cross-validation* in which the original sample is partitioned into a training set and a test set. In k-fold cross-validation, the data set is split into k mutually exclusive subsets that each serve as a test set for an estimation that is calculated using the respective rest set. In the leave-one-out case (also called jackknife) only one case is left out and it is used to validate the estimation done with the rest. For a sample size N this procedure is repeated N/k times; that is, N times for the jackknife method. Another technique is *bootstrapping*. In the validation phase the bootstrap sample is built by sampling n instances from the data with replacement. Several papers compare the three validation methods theoretically and by running simulations (see e.g. [418, 143, 223]). Cross-validation and bootstrapping are particularly important when the sample size is small relative to the number of parameters; in case of there being 19 independent variables with 155 observations as discussed in [143], for example. Since our sample size is more than 100 times as large as the number of input variables (15 metrics without collinearity to 2003 EPC models), we deem it justified to consider an independent holdout sample and disregard cross-validation and bootstrapping.

For testing the performance of the prediction function, we gathered a holdout sample from popular German EPC business process modeling textbooks. The sample includes 113 models from the following books in alphabetical order:

- Becker and Schütte: *Handelsinformationssysteme*, 2004 [52]. This book discusses information systems in the retail sector with a special focus on conceptual modeling. It covers 65 EPC models that we include in the holdout sample.
- Scheer: *Wirtschaftsinformatik: Referenzmodelle für industrielle Geschäftsprozesse*, 1998 [379]. This textbook is an introduction to the ARIS framework and uses reference models for production companies to illustrate it. We included 27 EPC reference models in the holdout sample from this book.

Classification Table

Observed		Predicted		
		hasErrors		Percentage
		0	1	Correct
hasErrors	0	86	2	97,73%
	1	9	16	64,00%
Overall Percentage				90,27%

The cut value is ,500
113 cases included

Figure 5.12. Classification table for EPCs from the holdout sample

- Seidlmeier: *Prozessmodellierung mit ARIS*, 2002 [392]. This is another introduction to the ARIS framework. It features 10 EPCs that we included in the holdout sample.
- Staud: *Geschäftsprozessanalyse: Ereignisgesteuerte Prozessketten und Objektorientierte Geschäftsprozessmodellierung für Betriebswirtschaftliche Standardsoftware*, 2006 [415]. This book focuses on business process modeling and EPCs in particular. We included 13 EPCs from this book in the holdout sample.[5]

All EPCs in the holdout sample were checked for errors: first with *xoEPC* and then with the ProM plug-in if the rest size was greater than two. Altogether, there are 25 of the 113 models that have errors (21.43%). Based on the metrics generated by *xoEPC*, we can easily apply the prediction function. The result of this calculation is summarized in the classification table in Figure 5.12. It can be seen that 102 of the 113 EPCs are classified correctly (86 models without errors are predicted to have none and 16 with errors are predicted to have at least one). Altogether, 90.27% of the 113 EPCs were predicted correctly (81.25% with the second best model and 78.57% with the third best model). Please note that there is a difference between the interpretation of this classification result and the one in Section 5.3.3. During the estimation of the logistic regression, the sample is known. The lowest possible classification result is, therefore, defined by predicting no error for every EPC which would yield a correct prediction (89.2% of the cases for the sample in Section 5.3.3). The classification result of applying the estimated function on the estimation sample must accordingly be compared to this trivial classification. In Section 5.3.3, the regression function improves the result from 89.2% to 95.2%. Here we used a given function to classify an independent sample. The lowest possible classification result in this setting is 0%, while 50% might be expected for a random function. Using the regression function for the independent sample increases the classification result from 50% to 90.27%.

Based on the De Moivre-Laplace theorem we are also able to calculate a confidence interval for the accuracy of the prediction function. Using Equation 3 of [223] with a confidence value of 95% yields an accuracy interval from 81.15% to 96.77% (the prediction can be expected to be correct in at least 81.15% of the cases with a 95% confidence). This result strongly supports the validity of the regression function (and also the second and the third best model) for predicting error probability.

---

[5] The largest EPC of this book has 288 nodes and required 113 minutes processing time.

Table 5.5. Hypothetical and empirical connection between metrics and errors

	Hypothetical connection	$\mu_e - \mu_n$	Correlation	Regression coefficient	Direction
S_N	+	24.93	0.38	$0.034^{b)}$	confirmed
S_E	+	13.11	0.38		confirmed
S_{E_S}	+	3.65	0.35		confirmed
S_{E_E}	+	4.76	0.38		confirmed
S_F	+	2.86	0.19		confirmed
S_C	+	8.96	0.43		confirmed
$S_{C_{AND}}$	+	3.89	0.45		confirmed
$S_{C_{XOR}}$	+	3.65	0.35		confirmed
$S_{C_{OR}}$	+	1.41	0.30		confirmed
$S_{J_{AND}}$	+	2.14	0.48		confirmed
$S_{J_{XOR}}$	+	1.81	0.33		confirmed
$S_{J_{OR}}$	+	0.47	0.15		confirmed
$S_{S_{AND}}$	+	1.70	0.37		confirmed
$S_{S_{XOR}}$	+	1.82	0.31		confirmed
$S_{S_{OR}}$	+	0.95	0.31		confirmed
S_A	+	27.64	0.38		confirmed
$diam$	+	7.62	0.30	$0.064^{a)}$	confirmed
Δ	+	-0.06	-0.37	$-23.873^{b)}$	not confirmed
CNC	+	0.11	0.28	$4.008^{a)}$	confirmed
$\overline{d_C}$	+	0.76	0.23	$-1.371^{c)}$	partially confirmed
$\widehat{d_C}$	+	2.33	0.33	$0.405^{c)}$	confirmed
Π	-	-0.24	-0.29	$-2.338^{a)}$	confirmed
Ξ	-	-0.31	-0.35	$-6.540^{b)}$	confirmed
Φ	-	-0.20	-0.36	$-9.957^{a)}$	confirmed
Λ	+	0.85	0.34	$0.440^{c)}$	confirmed
MM	+	7.18	0.42	$0.094^{a)}$	confirmed
CH	+	0.54	0.46	$3.003^{a)}$	confirmed
CFC	+	1680.99	0.39		confirmed
CYC	+	0.06	0.30	$3.409^{a)}$	confirmed
TS	+	4.97	0.38	$0.194^{c)}$	confirmed

[a)] first regression model, [b)] second best, [c)] third best

5.5 Summary

In this section, we conducted several statistical analyses related to the hypotheses on a connection between metrics and error probability. The results strongly support the hypotheses since the mean difference between error and non-error models, the correlation coefficients and the regression coefficients confirm the hypothetical impact direction of all metrics except the density metric Δ (see Table 5.5) and partially the average connector degree $\overline{d_C}$. The density metric appears to be more closely related to the inverse of size than the relative number of arcs of an EPC. The wrong sign of the average connector degree in the regression model seems to be caused by a positive correlation with structuredness Φ, which tends to reduce error probability.

Implications for Business Process Modeling

In the previous chapters, we presented a novel holistic approach for the verification and metrics-based prediction of errors in EPC business process models. Against the state of the art, the technical results of this research can be summarized as follows.

Formalization of the OR-join: Existing formalizations of the OR-join suffer from a restriction of the EPC syntax or from non-intuitive behavior. In Chapter 2, we presented a novel formalization of EPC semantics including OR-joins that is applicable for any EPC that is relaxed syntactically correct and provides intuitive semantics for blocks of matching OR-splits and OR-joins. The calculation of the reachability graph is implemented as a plug-in for ProM as a proof of concept.

Verification of process models with OR-joins and multiple start and end events: Verification techniques for EPC process models with OR-joins and multiple start and end events suffer from a problem of using an approximation of the actual behavior, building on non-intuitive semantics or not being tailored to cope with multiple start and end events. In Chapter 3, we specified a dedicated soundness criterion for EPC business process models with OR-joins and multiple start and end events. We also defined two verification approaches for EPC soundness: one as an explicit analysis of the reachability graph and a second based on reduction rules to provide a better verification performance. Both approaches were implemented as a proof of concept.

Metrics for business process models: Metrics play an important role in operationalizing various quality-related aspects of business process models. While the current research on business process model measurement is mainly inspired by software metrics and not consolidated, Chapter 4 provides an extensive overview of existing work. We also introduced new metrics that capture important process model concepts such as partionability, connector interplay, cyclicity and concurrency and discussed their theoretical connection with error probability.

Validation of metrics as error predictors: Up until now there has been little empirical evidence for the validity of business process model metrics as predictors for error probability. In Chapter 5, we used statistical methods to confirm the hypothetical connection between metrics and errors. We then used logistic regression to estimate a error prediction function. This function not only fits an extensive EPC sample nicely, but shows a good performance in terms of external validity to predict errors in an independent EPC sample.

In the following sections, we discuss the implications of this research. Section 6.1 presents a set of seven process modeling guidelines that help the modeler to come up with less error-prone and more understandable process models. Section 6.2 discusses more general implications for business process modeling. Section 6.3 identifies some areas where future research is required.

6.1 Seven Process Modeling Guidelines (7PMG)

The results of Chapter 5 confirm that process models in practice suffer from quality problems and suggests that industry process model collections are likely to have error rates of 10% to 20%. There are clearly differences in error rates and different structural metrics that are closely connected with error probability exist. Based on these connections and on work on activity labeling [295], *Mendling, Reijers and Van der Aalst* propose a set of seven process modeling guidelines (7PMG) that are supposed to direct the modeler to creating understandable models that are less prone to errors [297].

Table 6.1. Seven Process Modeling Guidelines [297]

G1	Use as few elements in the model as possible
G2	Minimize the routing paths per element
G3	Use one start and one end event
G4	Model as structured as possible
G5	Avoid OR routing elements
G6	Use verb-object activity labels
G7	Decompose a model with more than 50 elements

Table 6.1 summarizes the 7PMG guidelines. Each of them is supported by empirical insight into the connection of structural metrics and errors or understanding. Parts of these foundations have been established by the research reported in Chapter 5. The size of the model has undesirable effects on understandability and likelihood of errors [296, 301, 278]. **G1**, therefore, recommends the use of as few elements as possible. **G2** suggests minimizing the routing paths per element. The higher the degree of elements in the process model the harder it becomes to understand the model [296, 278]. **G3** demands using one start and one end event since the number of start and end events is positively connected with an increase in error probability [278]. Following **G4**, models should be structured as much as possible. Unstructured models tend to have more errors and are understood less well [278, 154, 242, 296]. **G5** suggests avoiding OR routing elements since models that have only AND and

XOR connectors are less error-prone [278]. **G6** recommends using the verb-object labeling style because it is less ambiguous compared to other styles [295] According to **G7**, models should be decomposed if they have more than 50 elements.

6.2 Discussion

The results of this research have some more general implications for business process modeling. In the following pages, we discuss the implications for 1) the importance of verification in real-world projects, 2) for improvements of the business process modeling process, 3) for future business process modeling tools and 4) for teaching of business process modeling languages.

1. *Importance of Verification:* The amount of errors in the different EPC model collections from real-world projects that we used in this book emphasizes the importance of verification. We showed that an error ratio of about 10% is the average over the samples, with 3.3% the minimum. Other recent studies find similar error ratios [113, 438, 154]. While verification has been discussed for some time, this book demonstrates that the different techniques have matured to handle large sets of several thousand business process models on a common desktop computer. This observation relates to the gap between business analysis and information systems engineering in business process modeling (see [384, p.141] or [178, pp.424]), demonstrated by the refusal of engineers to reuse process documentations for systems implementation. While this gap is frequently accepted as a natural breach, this research tells a different story. The considerable amount of formal errors in documentation models hardly makes it possible to directly reuse them in the implementation. The utilization of verification techniques in practice might, therefore, be the key to eventually closing this gap in the future.

2. *Business Process Modeling Process:* In this research, we gathered substantial theoretical and statistical evidence that formal errors are connected with several characteristics of the process model. This finding provides the opportunity to use process model metrics for the management of the design process and of process model quality. This is the case especially if different design options have to be evaluated and one of multiple models might be considered to be superior regarding error-probability based on some metric. The strong connection between size and errors offers objective input for decisions regarding the question when a model should be split up or when model parts should be put in a sub-process. The seven process modeling guidelines (7PMG) summarize some of these findings [297]. There is clearly a need for further research in this area. Our findings nevertheless represent a major step towards establishing business process modeling as an engineering discipline beyond the intuition of the modeler.

3. *Business Process Modeling Tools:* Both items 1) and 2) call for respective tool support. While the verification techniques are apparently capable of dealing with large real-world models, there seems to be too little attention paid to this issue

by tool vendors. Indeed, tool vendors should have an interest in these topics as the lack of respective features has a negative impact on the productivity of the business process modeling exercise: models cannot be reused for system development, business users cannot interpret the models properly and conclusions can not be drawn from the models regarding process performance. Beyond verification support, modeling tools could easily calculate process metrics to assist the modeler in the design task. Building on such features, the tool vendors could easily provide a greater benefit to their customers and help to improve the process of designing business process models.

4. *Teaching Process Modeling:* There is apparently a weakness in business process modeling teaching methods if practitioners introduce a formal error in every tenth model (at least in our sample). The four textbooks on business process modeling that we used to build the holdout sample had an even higher error ratio. While these rates might be partially attributed to missing verification support in the tools, there seems to be a problem for many modelers to understand the behavioral implications of their design. This observation is confirmed by recent experiments [296, 300]. This has two consequences. Teaching of business process modeling should focus less on specific business process modeling language and instead concentrate on conveying the general principles behind it (concurrency, synchronization, repetition, and other aspects as captured by the workflow patterns). Formal errors also seem to get too little attention. Concepts like deadlocks should not only be taught as a technical property of a business process model, but also an erroneous business rule that leads to problems in real-world business processes that are not supported by information systems. The metrics are a good starting point for teaching patterns that are unlikely to result in errors. A high degree of structuredness, for example, appears to be less prone to cause errors. Such an approach might eventually deliver a better awareness and attention of formal errors in business process modeling practice.

6.3 Future Research

There are several open questions that could not be addressed in detail in this book. We focused in particular on business process model metrics and their capability to predict errors in business process models. We found strong evidence that our set of metrics can indeed explain a great share of the variation in error probability. There are other factors we did not investigate in detail including personal factors, modeling purpose, domain knowledge, modeling language or graphical layout, all of which might be connected with error probability [296, 300]. They might also be related to other important quality aspects, like maintainability or understandability, that we did not analyze. We strongly agree with *Moody* [306], who calls for more empirical research in business process modeling. This book and its findings give an idea of the benefits we might gain from this research and therefore may be regarded as an encouragement to follow *Moody's* call.

A

Transition Relation of EPCs Based on State and Context

In this appendix, we formalize the semantics of EPCs based on state and context. In particular, we define the transition relations R^d, R^w, R^{-1} and R^{+1} for each phase based on markings, i.e. state and context mappings σ and κ collectively.

A.1 Phase 1: Transition Relation for Dead Context Propagation

Given the definition of an EPC marking , we define the transition relations for each phase. We can summarize the different dead context rules of Figure 2.12 in a single one: if one input arc of the respective node has a dead context, then this is propagated to the output arcs.

Definition A.1 (Transition Relations for Dead Context Propagation). *Let $EPC = (E, F, C, l, A)$ be a relaxed syntactically correct EPC, $N = E \cup F \cup C$ its set of nodes, and M_{EPC} its marking space. Then $R^d \subseteq M_{EPC} \times N \times M_{EPC}$ is the transition relation for dead context propagation and $(m, n, m') \in R^d$ if and only if:*

$$(\exists_{a \in n_{in}} : \kappa_m(a) = dead) \wedge$$
$$(\forall_{a \in A} : \sigma_m(a) = \sigma_{m'}(a)) \wedge$$
$$(\exists_{X \neq \emptyset} : X = \{a \in n_{out} \mid \sigma_m(a) = 0 \wedge \kappa_m(a) = wait\} \wedge$$
$$(\forall_{a \in X} : \kappa_{m'}(a) = dead) \wedge$$
$$(\forall_{a \in A \backslash X} : \kappa_{m'}(a) = \kappa_m(a))$$

Furthermore, we define the following notations:

- $m_1 \xrightarrow[d]{n} m_2$ *if and only if $(m_1, n, m_2) \in R^d$. We say that in the dead context propagation phase marking m_1 enables node n and its firing results in m_2.*
- $m \xrightarrow[d]{} m'$ *if and only if $\exists n : m_1 \xrightarrow[d]{n} m_2$.*
- $m \xrightarrow[d]{\tau} m'$ *if and only if $\exists_{n_1,...,n_q,m_1,...,m_{q+1}} : \tau = n_1 n_2 ... n_q \in N * \wedge$*
  $m_1 = m \wedge m_{q+1} = m' \wedge m_1 \xrightarrow[d]{n_1} m_2, m_2 \xrightarrow[d]{n_2} ... \xrightarrow[d]{n_q} m_{q+1}.$

- $m \xrightarrow[d]{*} m'$ *if and only if* $\exists_\tau : m \xrightarrow[d]{\tau} m'$.
- $m \xrightarrow[d]{max} m'$ *if and only if* $\exists_\tau : m \xrightarrow[d]{\tau} m' \wedge \not\exists_{m'' \neq m'} : m' \xrightarrow[d]{} m''$.
- $max_d : M_{EPC} \to M_{EPC}$ *such that* $max_d(m) = m'$ *if and only if* $m \xrightarrow[d]{max} m'$. *The existence of a unique* $max_d(m)$ *is the subject of Theorem A.2 below.*

Theorem A.2 (Dead Context Propagation terminates). *For an EPC and a given marking* m, *there exists a unique* $max_d(m)$ *which is determined in a finite number of propagation steps.*

Proof. Regarding *uniqueness*, by contradiction: Consider an original marking $m_0 \in M_{EPC}$ and two markings $m_{max1}, m_{max2} \in M_{EPC}$ such that $m_0 \xrightarrow[d]{max} m_{max1}$, $m_0 \xrightarrow[d]{max} m_{max2}$, and $m_{max1} \neq m_{max2}$. Since both m_{max1} and m_{max2} can be produced from m_0 they share at least those arcs with dead context that were already dead in m_0. Furthermore, following from the inequality, there must be an arc a that has a wait context in one marking, but not in the other. Let us assume that this marking is m_{max1}. But if $\exists_\tau : m_0 \xrightarrow[d]{\tau} m_{max2}$ such that $\kappa_{m_{max2}}(a) = dead$, then there must also $\exists_{\tau'} : m_{max1} \xrightarrow[d]{\tau'} m'$ such that $\kappa_{m'}(a) = dead$ because m_{max2} is produced applying the propagation rules without ever changing a dead context to a wait context. Accordingly, there are further propagation rules that can be applied on m_{max1} and the assumption $m_0 \xrightarrow[d]{max} m_{max1}$ is wrong. Therefore, if there are two m_{max1} and m_{max2}, they must have the same set of arcs with dead context, and therefore also the same set of arcs with wait context. Since both their states are equal to the state of m_0 they are equivalent, i.e., $max_d(m)$ is unique.

Regarding *finiteness*: Following Definition 2.1 on page 22, the number of nodes of an EPC is finite, and therefore the set of arcs is also finite. Since the number of dead context arcs is increased in each propagation step, no new propagation rule can be applied, at the latest after each arc has a dead context. Accordingly, dead context propagation terminates at the latest after $|A|$ steps.

A.2 Phase 2: Transition Relation for Wait Context Propagation

For the wait context propagation, we also distinguish two cases based on the wait context transition relations of Figure 2.12. The first case covers (a) function, (b) intermediate event, (c) split, (d) and-join nodes. If the node belongs to this group and all input arcs are in a wait context, then the wait context is propagated to those output arcs that have a dead context and no state token on them. The second case, if the node is an XOR-join or an OR-join and one of the input arcs is in a wait context, then this is propagated to the dead output arc.

Definition A.3 (Transition Relations for Wait Context Propagation). *Let* $EPC = (E, F, C, l, A)$ *be a relaxed syntactically correct EPC,* $N = E \cup F \cup C$ *its set of* *nodes, and M_{EPC} its marking space. Then $R^w \subseteq M_{EPC} \times N \times M_{EPC}$ is the transition relation for wait context propagation and $(m, n, m') \in R^w$ if and only if:*

$$((n \in F \cup E_{int} \cup S \cup J_{and}) \wedge$$
$$(\forall_{a \in n_{in}} : \kappa_m(a) = wait) \wedge$$
$$(\forall_{a \in A} : \sigma_m(a) = \sigma_{m'}(a)) \wedge$$
$$(\exists_{X \neq \emptyset} : X = \{a \in n_{out} \mid \sigma_m(a) = 0 \ \wedge \kappa_m(a) = dead\} \wedge$$
$$(\forall_{a \in X} : \kappa_{m'}(a) = wait) \wedge$$
$$(\forall_{a \in A \backslash X} : \kappa_{m'}(a) = \kappa_m(a)))$$

$$\vee$$

$$((n \in J_{xor} \cup J_{or}) \wedge$$
$$(\exists_{a \in n_{in}} : \kappa_m(a) = wait) \wedge$$
$$(\forall_{a \in A} : \sigma_m(a) = \sigma_{m'}(a)) \wedge$$
$$(\exists_{X \neq \emptyset} : X = \{a \in n_{out} \mid \sigma_m(a) = 0 \ \wedge \kappa_m(a) = dead\} \wedge$$
$$(\forall_{a \in X} : \kappa_{m'}(a) = wait) \wedge$$
$$(\forall_{a \in A \backslash X} : \kappa_{m'}(a) = \kappa_m(a)))$$

Furthermore, we define the following notations:

- $m_1 \xrightarrow[w]{n} m_2$ *if and only if* $(m_1, n, m_2) \in R^w$. *We say that in the wait context propagation phase marking m_1 enables node n and its firing results in m_2.*
- $m \xrightarrow[w]{} m'$ *if and only if* $\exists n : m_1 \xrightarrow[w]{n} m_2$.
- $m \xrightarrow[w]{\tau} m'$ *if and only if* $\exists_{n_1,...,n_q, m_1,...,m_{q+1}} : \tau = n_1 n_2 ... n_q \in N* \wedge$
  $m_1 = m \wedge m_{q+1} = m' \wedge m_1 \xrightarrow[w]{n_1} m_2, m_2 \xrightarrow[w]{n_2} ... \xrightarrow[w]{n_q} m_{q+1}$.
- $m \xrightarrow[w]{*} m'$ *if and only if* $\exists_\tau : m \xrightarrow[w]{\tau} m'$.
- $m \xrightarrow[w]{max} m'$ *if and only if* $\exists_\tau : m \xrightarrow[w]{\tau} m' \wedge \nexists_{m'' \neq m'} : m' \xrightarrow[w]{} m''$.
- $max_w : M_{EPC} \to M_{EPC}$ *such that* $max_w(m) = m'$ *if and only if* $m \xrightarrow[w]{max} m'$.
  The existence of a unique $max_w(m)$ is the subject of Theorem A.4 below.

Theorem A.4 (Wait Context Propagation terminates). *For an EPC and a given marking m, there exists a unique $max_w(m)$ which is determined in a finite number of propagation steps.*

Proof. Analogous proof as for Theorem A.2.

The transition relations of context propagation permit the following observations:

- *Context changes terminate:* The Theorems A.2 and A.4 show that dead and wait context propagation cannot run in an infinite loop. As a consequence, the context change phase will always terminate and enable the consideration of new state changes in the subsequent phase.
- *State tokens block context propagation:* The transition relations for context propagation require that the output arcs to be changed do not hold any state token, i.e., arcs with a positive token always have a wait context and arcs with a negative token always have a dead context.

- *Context propagating elements:* Functions, events and split nodes reproduce the context that they receive at their input arcs.
- *OR- and XOR-joins:* Both these connectors reproduce a dead and also a wait context if at least one of the input arcs has the respective context.
- *AND-joins:* AND-joins produce wait context status only if all inputs are wait. Otherwise, the output context remains in a dead context.

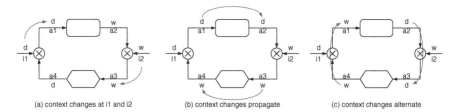

(a) context changes at i1 and i2   (b) context changes propagate   (c) context changes alternate

Figure A.1. Situation of unstable context changes without two phases

Figure A.1 illustrates the need to perform context propagation in two separate phases as opposed to together in one phase. If there are context changes (a) at $i1$ and $i2$, the current context enables the firing of the transition rules for both connectors producing a *dead* context status in $a1$ and a *wait* context status in $a3$. This leads to a new context in (b) with an additional *dead* context status in $a2$ and a new *wait* context status in $a4$. Since both arcs from outside the loop to the connectors are marked in such a way that incoming context changes on the other arc is simply propagated, there is a new context in (c) with a *wait* status in $a1$ and a *dead* context status in $a3$. Note that this new context can be propagated and this way the initial situation is reproduced. This can be repeated again and again. Without a sequence of two phases, the transitions could continue infinitely and the result would be undefined.

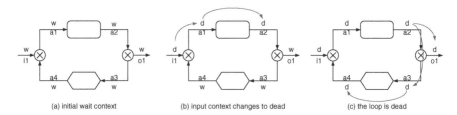

(a) initial wait context   (b) input context changes to dead   (c) the loop is dead

Figure A.2. Propagating dead context in a loop

The precedence of the two phases can also be motivated using an example EPC containing a loop. The propagation of dead context with only one dead input is needed to accurately mark loops as dead. Figure A.2 shows the picture of a simple loop with one XOR-join as entrance and one XOR-split as exit. Initially, the loop might be in a wait context (a). If the path to the loop becomes dead, this context is propagated into the loop (b) and to its output (c). If not all join-connectors would propagate dead context with one dead input, the loop could never become dead. But since this often results in too many dead arcs, the wait context propagation must be performed afterwards. It guarantees that arcs that can still be receive a positive token get a wait context.

A.3 Phase 3: Transition Relation for Negative State Propagation

The transition rules for the various node types in this phase can be easily summarized in one transition relation: if all input arcs carry a negative token and all output arcs hold no negative or positive token, then consume all negative tokens on the input arcs and produce negative tokens on each output arc.

Definition A.5 (Transition Relations for Negative State Propagation). *Let* EPC *=* (E, F, C, l, A) *be a relaxed syntactically correct EPC,* $N = E \cup F \cup C$ *its set of nodes, and* M_{EPC} *its marking space. Then* $R^{-1} \subseteq M_{EPC} \times N \times M_{EPC}$ *is the transition relation for negative state propagation and* $(m, n, m') \in R^{-1}$ *if and only if:*

$$(\forall_{a \in n_{in}} : \sigma_m(a) = -1) \land$$
$$(\forall_{a \in n_{out}} : \sigma_m(a) = 0) \land$$
$$(\forall_{a \in n_{in}} : \sigma_{m'}(a) = 0) \land$$
$$(\forall_{a \in n_{out}} : \sigma_{m'}(a) = -1) \land$$
$$(\forall_{a \in A \setminus n_{out}} : \kappa_{m'}(a) = \kappa_m(a)) \land$$
$$(\forall_{a \in n_{out}} : \kappa_{m'}(a) = dead) \land$$
$$(\forall_{a \in A \setminus (n_{in} \cup n_{out})} : \sigma_{m'}(a) = \sigma_m(a))$$

Furthermore, we define the following notations:

- $m_1 \xrightarrow[-1]{n} m_2$ *if and only if* $(m_1, n, m_2) \in R^{-1}$. *We say that in the negative state propagation phase marking* m_1 *enables node* n *and its firing results in* m_2.
- $m \xrightarrow[-1]{} m'$ *if and only if* $\exists n : m_1 \xrightarrow[-1]{n} m_2$.
- $m \xrightarrow[-1]{\tau} m'$ *if and only if* $\exists_{n_1,...,n_q,m_1,...,m_{q+1}} : \tau = n_1 n_2 ... n_q \in N * \land$
  $m_1 = m \land m_{q+1} = m' \land m_1 \xrightarrow[-1]{n_1} m_2, m_2 \xrightarrow[-1]{n_2} ... \xrightarrow[-1]{n_q} m_{q+1}$.
- $m \xrightarrow[-1]{*} m'$ *if and only if* $\exists_\tau : m \xrightarrow[-1]{\tau} m'$.
- $m \xrightarrow[-1]{max} m'$ *if and only if* $\exists_\tau : m \xrightarrow[-1]{\tau} m' \land \nexists_{m'' \neq m'} : m' \xrightarrow[-1]{} m''$.
- $max_{-1} : M_{EPC} \to M_{EPC}$ *such that* $max_{-1}(m) = m'$ *if and only if* $m \xrightarrow[-1]{max} m'$.
  The existence of a unique $max_{-1}(m)$ *is discussed below in Theorem A.6.*

Theorem A.6 (Negative State Propagation terminates). *For an EPC and a given marking* m, *there exists a unique* $max_{-1}(m)$ *which is determined in a finite number of propagation steps.*

Proof. Regarding finiteness, by contradiction. Since an EPC is safe, i.e. there is at maximum one token per arc, it is a prerequisite for an infinite propagation that there is a cyclic structure in the process in which the negative token runs into an infinite loop. Due to the coherence property of an EPC, and the minimum number of one start and one end node (Definition 2.1), two cases of a cyclic path can be distinguished:

(i) cyclic path $a \hookrightarrow a$ with $\nexists e \in E_s : e \hookrightarrow a$: in this case the loop could potentially propagate a negative token infinitely, but it will never receive a token since there is no path from a start node into the cyclic path. Furthermore, relaxed syntactically correct EPCs do not contain such paths according to Definition 2.8.

(ii) cyclic path $a \hookrightarrow a$ with $\exists e \in E_s : e \hookrightarrow a$: In this case, there must be a join j on a cyclic path $a \hookrightarrow a$ such that there exists an arc (x, j) and there is no path $a \hookrightarrow x$. Therefore, a negative token could only be propagated infinitely on the path $a \hookrightarrow a$ if the join j would receive repeatedly ad infinitum negative tokens on the arc (x, j) in order to allow j to fire according to Definition A.5. Since the number of tokens on arcs is limited to one, this is only possible if there is another cyclic path $b \hookrightarrow b$ that produces negative tokens ad infinitum on a split node s. Again, for this cyclic path $b \hookrightarrow b$, the two cases (i) and (ii) can be distinguished. Accordingly, there must be another cyclic path $c \hookrightarrow c$ that feeds the path with b, and so forth.

Since the existence of a cyclic path that propagates negative tokens infinitely depends on the existence of another such path, there is a contradiction.

Regarding uniqueness we do not provide a formal proof here. Consider that there exist an original marking $m_0 \in M_{EPC}$ and two markings $m_{max1}, m_{max2} \in M_{EPC}$ such that $m_0 \overset{max}{\underset{-1}{\rightarrow}} m_{max1}$, $m_0 \overset{max}{\underset{-1}{\rightarrow}} m_{max2}$, and $m_{max1} \neq m_{max2}$. According to the transition relation, there are no transitions that could compete for tokens such as in non free-choice Petri nets, i.e. the firing of a transition cannot disable another one, and there are no alternative transitions for an enabled node. Furthermore, a context change of an arc has no impact on the applicability of a rule and no positive tokens are involved in firings. Therefore, m_{max1} and m_{max2} must either be equivalent or there must be a transition enabled in one of them such that the max property of it does not hold.

A.4 Phase 4: Transition Relation for Positive State Propagation

The positive state firing rules of the OR-join in Figure 2.12 deserve some further comments. Beyond the removal of all positive and negative tokens on the input arcs, also those negative tokens on the *negative upper corona* of the OR-join are removed. The motivation for this concept is that loops can propagate dead context, but negative tokens get stuck at the entry join of a loop. After the loop, a dead context can make the firing condition of an OR-join become true, while negative tokens that were generated for synchronization purposes still reside before the loop. Not removing such negative tokens with the firing of an OR-join might cause non-intuitive behavior.

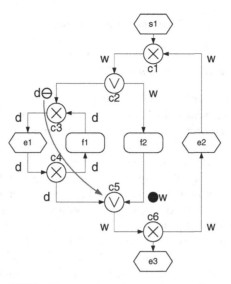

Figure A.3. A structured EPC with a negative token on the negative upper corona of OR-join $c5$

Therefore, in addition to the positive and negative tokens on the input arcs of the OR-join, also those negative tokens with a path leading to the OR-join via arcs that all have a dead context, i.e. on the negative corona, are also removed.

Figure A.3 gives the example of a structured EPC with an outer XOR-loop between $c1$ and $c6$ and an inner XOR-loop between $c3$ and $c4$. The inner loop is also nested in an OR-block between $c2$ and $c5$. The current marking is produced by firing the OR-split with a negative token to the left and a positive token to the right, and then propagating the positive token via $f2$. Now, the OR-join $c5$ is enabled with a dead context on one of the input arcs. Moreover, there is a negative token before the inner XOR-loop which cannot be propagated. If the OR-join would now simply fire and navigate via $e2$ back to $c2$ the EPC would be in a deadlock since the firing rules for tokens require the output arcs to be empty. Therefore, the negative token before $c3$ has to be removed when firing the OR-join $c5$. Accordingly, if an OR-join fires, it has to remove all negative tokens on its so-called negative upper corona, i.e. the arcs carrying a negative token that have a path to the OR-join on which each arc has a dead context and no token on it. The following Definition A.7 formalizes the notion of a negative upper corona.

Definition A.7 (Dead Empty Path, Negative Upper Corona). *Let* $EPC = (E, F,$ $C, l, A)$ *be a relaxed syntactically correct EPC,* $N = E \cup F \cup C$ *its set of nodes, and a marking* $m \in M_{EPC}$. *Then, we define the negative upper corona of a node* $n \in N$ *based on a dead empty path. A dead empty path* $a \overset{d}{\underset{m}{\hookrightarrow}} b$ *refers to a sequence of nodes* $n_1, \ldots, n_k \in N$ *with* $a = n_1$ *and* $b = n_k$ *such that for* $(n_1, n_2) \in A :$ $\sigma_m(n_1, n_2) = -1$ *and* $\forall i \in 2, \ldots, k - 1$ *holds:* $(n_i, n_{i+1}) \in A \wedge \sigma_m(n_i, n_{i+1}) =$

$0 \wedge \kappa_m(n_i, n_{i+1}) = dead$. *Then, the* negative upper corona $\overset{-1}{\underset{m}{\rightarrow}} n = \{a \in A | a =$
$(s,t) \wedge \sigma(a) = -1 \wedge t \overset{d}{\underset{m}{\rightarrow}} n\}$ *refers to those arcs with a negative token whose target node t is a transitive predecessor of n and has a dead empty path to n in marking m.*

The transition rules for the various node types can be easily summarized as follows: (1) for function, event and AND-connector nodes, positive tokens on all input arcs are consumed and propagated to all output arcs if all of them are empty. The input context is set to dead and the output context to wait. (2) For XOR-connectors, one input token is consumed from one input arc and propagated to one of the output arcs if all of them are empty. The respective input arc is set to a dead context, as well as those output arcs that do not receive the token. The output arc with the positive token gets a wait context. (3) For OR-splits, the positive token is consumed from the input, and a combination of positive and negative tokens is produced at the output arcs such that at least one positive token is available. Furthermore, each output arc with a positive token gets a wait context while the others get a dead context. (4) OR-joins fire either if all input arcs are not empty and one of them has a positive token or if there is no empty arc with a wait context and at least one positive token on the inputs. Then, all input tokens are consumed plus potentially negative tokens on the negative upper corona, the input arcs are set to a dead context, and a positive token is produced on the output with a wait context.

Definition A.8 (Transition Relation for Positive State Propagation). *Let $EPC = (E, F, C, l, A)$ be a relaxed syntactically correct EPC, $N = E \cup F \cup C$ its set of nodes, and M_{EPC} its marking space. Then $R^{+1} \subseteq M_{EPC} \times N \times M_{EPC}$ is the transition relation for positive state propagation and $(m, n, m') \in R^{+1}$ if and only if:*

$$((n \in F \cup E_{int} \cup C_{and}) \wedge$$
$$(\forall_{a \in n_{in}} : \sigma_m(a) = +1) \wedge$$
$$(\forall_{a \in n_{out}} : \sigma_m(a) = 0) \wedge$$
$$(\forall_{a \in n_{in}} : \sigma_{m'}(a) = 0 \wedge \kappa_{m'}(a) = dead) \wedge$$
$$(\forall_{a \in n_{out}} : \sigma_{m'}(a) = +1 \wedge \kappa_{m'}(a) = wait) \wedge$$
$$(\forall_{a \in A \setminus (n_{in} \cup n_{out})} : \kappa_{m'}(a) = \kappa_m(a)) \wedge$$
$$(\forall_{a \in A \setminus (n_{in} \cup n_{out})} : \sigma_{m'}(a) = \sigma_m(a)))$$
$$\vee$$
$$((n \in C_{xor}) \wedge$$
$$(\exists_{a_1 \in n_{in}} : (\sigma_m(a_1) = +1 \wedge \sigma_{m'}(a_1) = 0 \wedge$$
$$\kappa_m(a_1) = wait \wedge \kappa_{m'}(a_1) = dead) \wedge$$
$$(\forall_{a \in n_{out}} : \sigma_m(a) = 0) \wedge$$
$$(\exists_{X \wedge a_2 \in n_{out}} : X = \{a \in n_{in} \mid \sigma_m(a) = -1 \wedge \kappa_m(a) = dead\} \wedge$$
$$(\sigma_{m'}(a_2) = +1 \wedge \kappa_{m'}(a_2) = wait) \wedge$$
$$(\forall_{a \in A \setminus \{a_1, a_2\}} : \kappa_{m'}(a) = \kappa_m(a)) \wedge$$
$$(\forall_{a \in X} : \sigma_{m'}(a) = 0 \wedge \kappa_{m'}(a) = \kappa_m(a)) \wedge$$
$$(\forall_{a \in A \setminus (X \cup \{a_1, a_2\})} : \sigma_{m'}(a) = \sigma_m(a)))))$$
$$\vee$$

$$((n \in S_{or}) \wedge$$
$$(\forall_{a \in n_{in}} : \sigma_m(a) = +1) \wedge$$
$$(\forall_{a \in n_{out}} : \sigma_m(a) = 0) \wedge$$
$$(\forall_{a \in n_{in}} : \sigma_{m'}(a) = 0 \wedge \kappa_{m'}(a) = dead) \wedge$$
$$(\exists_{X \neq \emptyset} : X = \{a \in n_{out} \mid \sigma_{m'}(a) = +1 \wedge \kappa_{m'}(a) = wait\} \wedge$$
$$\quad (\forall_{a \in n_{out} \backslash X} : \sigma_{m'}(a) = -1 \wedge \kappa_{m'}(a) = dead) \wedge$$
$$\quad (\forall_{a \in A \backslash (n_{in} \cup n_{out})} : \kappa_{m'}(a) = \kappa_m(a) \wedge \sigma_{m'}(a) = \sigma_m(a)))$$
$$\vee$$
$$((n \in J_{or}) \wedge$$
$$(\exists_{X \neq \emptyset} : X = \{a \in n_{in} \mid \sigma_m(a) = +1 \wedge \kappa_m(a) = wait\}) \wedge$$
$$(\exists_Y : Y = \{a \in n_{in} \mid \sigma_m(a) = -1 \wedge \kappa_m(a) = dead\}) \wedge$$
$$(\exists_Z : Z = \{a \in n_{in} \mid \sigma_m(a) = 0 \wedge \kappa_m(a) = dead\}) \wedge$$
$$(X \cup Y \cup Z = n_{in}) \wedge$$
$$(\forall_{a \in n_{out}} : \sigma_m(a) = 0) \wedge$$
$$(\forall_{a \in n_{in}} : \sigma_{m'}(a) = 0 \wedge \kappa_{m'}(a) = dead)) \wedge$$
$$(\forall_{a \in n_{out}} : \sigma_{m'}(a) = +1 \wedge \kappa_{m'}(a) = wait) \wedge$$
$$(\exists_{U \subset A} : U = \overset{-1}{\underset{m}{\rightsquigarrow}} n \wedge$$
$$\quad (\forall_{a \in U} : \sigma_{m'}(a) = 0 \wedge \kappa_{m'}(a) = \kappa_m(a)) \wedge$$
$$\quad (\forall_{a \in A \backslash (U \cup n_{in} \cup n_{out})} : \sigma_{m'}(a) = \sigma_m(a) \wedge \kappa_{m'}(a) = \kappa_m(a)))).$$

Furthermore, we define the following notations:

- $m_1 \xrightarrow[+1]{n} m_2$ *if and only if* $(m_1, n, m_2) \in R^{+1}$. *We say that in the positive state propagation phase marking* m_1 *enables node* n *and its firing results in* m_2.
- $m \xrightarrow[+1]{} m'$ *if and only if* $\exists n : m_1 \xrightarrow[+1]{n} m_2$.
- $m \xrightarrow[+1]{\tau} m'$ *if and only if* $\exists_{n_1, \dots, n_q, m_1, \dots, m_{q+1}} : \tau = n_1 n_2 \dots n_q \in N * \wedge$
  $m_1 = m \wedge m_{q+1} = m' \wedge m_1 \xrightarrow[+1]{n_1} m_2, m_2 \xrightarrow[+1]{n_2} \dots \xrightarrow[+1]{n_q} m_{q+1}$.
- $m \xrightarrow[+1]{*} m'$ *if and only if* $\exists_\tau : m \xrightarrow[+1]{\tau} m'$.

The transition relations cover several marking changes that are not interesting for an observer of the process. The reachability graph RG of an EPC as defined in Definition 2.17 abstracts from dead context, wait context and negative context propagation and includes only transitions of the positive state propagation phase.

References

1. van der Aalst, W.M.P.: Patterns and XPDL: A Critical Evaluation of the XML Process Definition Language. QUT Technical report FIT-TR–06. Queensland University of Technology, Brisbane (2003)
2. van der Aalst, W.M.P.: Verification of Workflow Nets. In: Azéma, P., Balbo, G. (eds.) ICATPN 1997. LNCS, vol. 1248, pp. 407–426. Springer, Heidelberg (1997)
3. van der Aalst, W.M.P.: The Application of Petri Nets to Workflow Management. The Journal of Circuits, Systems and Computers 8(1), 21–66 (1998)
4. van der Aalst, W.M.P.: Formalization and Verification of Event-driven Process Chains. Information and Software Technology 41(10), 639–650 (1999)
5. van der Aalst, W.M.P., Benatallah, B., Casati, F., Curbera, F. (eds.): BPM 2005. LNCS, vol. 3649. Springer, Heidelberg (2005)
6. van der Aalst, W.M.P., Desel, J., Kindler, E.: On the semantics of EPCs: A vicious circle. In: Proc. of the 1st GI-Workshop on Business Process Management with Event-Driven Process Chains (EPK 2002), Trier, Germany, pp. 71–79 (2002)
7. van der Aalst, W.M.P., Desel, J., Oberweis, A. (eds.): Business Process Management. LNCS, vol. 1806. Springer, Heidelberg (2000)
8. van der Aalst, W.M.P., van Dongen, B.F., Herbst, J., Maruster, L., Schimm, G., Weijters, A.J.M.M.: Workflow Mining: A Survey of Issues and Approaches. Data and Knowledge Engineering 47(2), 237–267 (2003)
9. van der Aalst, W.M.P., van Hee, K.: Workflow Management: Models, Methods, and Systems. MIT Press, Cambridge (2002)
10. van der Aalst, W.M.P., Hirnschall, A., Verbeek, H.M.W.: An Alternative Way to Analyze Workflow Graphs. In: Pidduck, A.B., Mylopoulos, J., Woo, C.C., Ozsu, M.T. (eds.) CAiSE 2002. LNCS, vol. 2348, pp. 535–552. Springer, Heidelberg (2002)
11. van der Aalst, W.M.P., ter Hofstede, A.H.M.: YAWL: Yet Another Workflow Language. Information Systems 30(4), 245–275 (2005)
12. van der Aalst, W.M.P., ter Hofstede, A.H.M., Kiepuszewski, B., Barros, A.P.: Workflow Patterns. Distributed and Parallel Databases 14(1), 5–51 (2003)
13. van der Aalst, W.M.P., ter Hofstede, A.H.M., Weske, M. (eds.): BPM 2003. LNCS, vol. 2678. Springer, Heidelberg (2003)
14. van der Aalst, W.M.P., Jørgensen, J.B., Lassen, K.B.: Let's Go All the Way: From Requirements via Colored Workflow Nets to a BPEL Implementation of a New Bank System. In: Meersman, R., Tari, Z. (eds.) OTM 2005. LNCS, vol. 3760, pp. 22–39. Springer, Heidelberg (2005)

15. van der Aalst, W.M.P., Jørgensen, J.B., Lassen, K.B.: Let's Go All the Way: From Requirements via Colored Workflow Nets to a BPEL Implementation of a New Bank System Paper. In: Meersman, R., Tari, Z. (eds.) OTM 2005. LNCS, vol. 3760, pp. 22–39. Springer, Heidelberg (2005)

16. van der Aalst, W.M.P., Lassen, K.B.: Translating Workflow Nets to BPEL4WS. BETA Working Paper Series, WP 145. Eindhoven University of Technology, Eindhoven (2005)

17. van der Aalst, W.M.P., Lassen, K.B.: Translating unstructured workflow processes to readable BPEL: Theory and implementation. Information and Software Technology 50(3), 131–159 (2008)

18. van der Aalst, W.M.P., Rubin, V., van Dongen, B.F., Kindler, E., Günther, C.W.: Process mining: A two-step approach using transition systems and regions. BPMCenter Report BPM-06-30, BPMcenter.org (2006)

19. van der Aalst, W.M.P., Weijters, A.J.M.M., Maruster, L.: Workflow Mining: Discovering Process Models from Event Logs. IEEE Transactions on Knowledge and Data Engineering 16(9), 1128–1142 (2004)

20. Aczel, A.D., Sounderpandian, J.: Complete Business Statistics, 5th edn. McGraw-Hill, New York (2002)

21. Adam, O., Thomas, O., Martin, G.: Fuzzy enhanced process management for the industrial order handling. In: Scheer, A.-W. (ed.) Proceedings of the 5th International Conference; The Modern Information Technology in the Innovation Processes of the Industrial Enterprises, MITIP 2003. Veröffentlichungen des Instituts für Wirtschaftsinformatik, vol. 176, pp. 15–20. German Research Center for Artificial Intelligence (2003)

22. Albrecht, A.J.: Measuring application development productivity. In: Proceeding IBM Applications Development Symposium, GUIDE Int and Share Inc., IBM Corp., Monterey, CA, Oct. 14–17, 1979, p. 83ff. (1979)

23. Alonso, G., Dadam, P., Rosemann, M. (eds.): BPM 2007. LNCS, vol. 4714. Springer, Heidelberg (2007)

24. Alves, A., Arkin, A., Askary, S., Barreto, C., Bloch, B., Curbera, F., Ford, M., Goland, Y., Guizar, A., Kartha, N., Liu, C.K., Khalaf, R., Koenig, D., Marin, M., Mehta, V., Thatte, S., van der Rijn, D., Yendluri, P., Yiu, A.: Web services business process execution language version version 2.0. Committee specification 31 january 2007, OASIS (2007)

25. Ami, T., Sommer, R.: Comparison and evaluation of business process modelling and management tools. International Journal of Services and Standards 3(2), 249–261 (2007)

26. Andrews, T., Curbera, F., Dholakia, H., Goland, Y., Klein, J., Leymann, F., Liu, K., Roller, D., Smith, D., Thatte, S., Trickovic, I., Weerawarana, S.: Business Process Execution Language for Web Services, Version 1.1. Specification, BEA Systems, IBM Corp., Microsoft Corp., SAP AG, Siebel Systems (2003)

27. Anupindi, R., Chopra, S., Deshmukh, S.D., van Mieghem, J.A., Zemel, E.: Managing Business Process Flows. Prentice-Hall, Englewood Cliffs (1999)

28. Armistead, C.G., Machin, S.: Implications of business process management for operations management. International Journal of Operations & Production Management 17(9), 886–898 (1997)

29. Astrahan, M.M., Blasgen, M.W., Chamberlin, D.D., Eswaran, K.P., Gray, J., Griffiths, P.P., King III, W.F., Lorie, R.A., McJones, P.R., Mehl, J.W., Putzolu, G.R., Traiger, I.L., Wade, B.W., Watson, V.: System R: Relational Approach to Database Management. ACM Transactions on Database Systems 1(2), 97–137 (1976)

30. Astrahan, M.M., Chamberlin, D.D.: Implementation of a Structured English Query Language. Commun. ACM 18(10), 580–588 (1975)

31. Atkinson, C., Kühne, T.: The essence of multilevel metamodeling. In: Gogolla, M., Kobryn, C. (eds.) UML 2001. LNCS, vol. 2185, pp. 19–33. Springer, Heidelberg (2001)
32. Atkinson, C., Kühne, T.: Processes and products in a multi-level metamodeling architecture. International Journal of Software Engineering and Knowledge Engineering 11(6), 761–783 (2001)
33. Atkinson, C., Kühne, T.: Model-driven development: A metamodeling foundation. IEEE Software 20(5), 36–41 (2003)
34. Austin, J.L.: How to Do Things with Words. Harvard University Press, Cambridge, Mass (1962)
35. Backhaus, K., Erichson, B., Plinke, W., Weiber, R.: Multivariate Analysemethoden. Eine anwendungsorientierte Einführung, 10th edn. Springer, Heidelberg (2003)
36. Badouel, E., Darondeau, P.: Theory of regions. In: Reisig, W., Rozenberg, G. (eds.) APN 1998. LNCS, vol. 1491, pp. 529–586. Springer, Heidelberg (1998)
37. Balasubramanian, S., Gupta, M.: Structural metrics for goal based business process design and evaluation. Business Process Management Journal 11(6), 680–694 (2005)
38. Balzert, H.: Lehrbuch der Software-Technik: Software-Management, Software-Qualitätssicherung, Unternehmensmodellierung. Spektrum Akademischer Verlag (1998)
39. Bandara, W., Gable, G.G., Rosemann, M.: Factors and measures of business process modelling: model building through a multiple case study. European Journal of Information Systems 14, 347–360 (2005)
40. Barabási, A.-L., Albert, R.: Emergence of scaling in random networks. Science 286, 509–512 (1999)
41. Barborka, P., Helm, L., Köldorfer, G., Mendling, J., Neumann, G., van Dongen, B.F., Verbeek, H.M.W., van der Aalst, W.M.P.: Integration of EPC-related Tools with ProM. In: Proceedings of the 5th GI Workshop on Business Process Management with Event-Driven Process Chains (EPK 2006), Vienna, Austria, December 2006, pp. 105–120. German Informatics Society (2006)
42. Barkaoui, K., Petrucci, L.: Structural Analysis of Workflow Nets with Shared Resources. In: Aalst, W.M.P.v.d., Michelis, G.D., Ellis, C.A. (eds.) Proceedings of Workflow Management: Net-based Concepts, Models, Techniques and Tools (WFM'98), Lisbon, Portugal. Computing Science Reports, vol. 98/7, pp. 82–95. Eindhoven University of Technology, Eindhoven (1998)
43. Basili, V.R., Perricone, B.T.: Software errors and complexity: An empirical investigation. Communications of the ACM 27(1), 42–52 (1984)
44. Basili, V.R., Rombach, H.D.: The TAME project: Towards improvement-oriented software environments. IEEE Transactions on Software Engineering 14(6), 758–773 (1988)
45. Basili, V.R., Weiss, D.M.: A methodology for collecting valid software engineering data. IEEE Transactions on Software Engineering 10(6), 728–738 (1984)
46. Batini, C., Lenzerini, M., Navathe, S.B.: A Comparative Analysis of Methodologies for Database Schema Integration. ACM Computing Surveys 18(4), 323–364 (1986)
47. Becker, J., Algermissen, L., Niehaves, B.: Prozessmodellierung in eGovernment-Projekten mit der eEPK. In: Proc. of the 2nd GI-Workshop on Business Process Management with Event-Driven Process Chains (EPK 2003), Bamberg, Germany, pp. 31–44.
48. Becker, J., Kugeler, M.: The Process in Focus. In: Becker, J., Kugeler, M., Rosemann, M. (eds.) Process Management: A Guide for the Design of Business Processes, pp. 1–12. Springer, Heidelberg (2003)
49. Becker, J., Kugeler, M., Rosemann, M.: Process Management: A Guide for the Design of Business Processes. Springer, Heidelberg (2003)
50. Becker, J., Rosemann, M., Schütte, R.: Grundsätze ordnungsmässiger Modellierung. Wirtschaftsinformatik 37(5), 435–445 (1995)

51. Becker, J., Rosemann, M., von Uthmann, C.: Guidelines of Business Process Modeling. In: van der Aalst, W.M.P., Desel, J., Oberweis, A. (eds.) Business Process Management, Models, Techniques, and Empirical Studies. lncs, vol. 1806, pp. 30–49. Springer, Berlin (2000)

52. Becker, J., Schütte, R.: Handelsinformationssysteme, 2nd edn. Moderne Industrie, Landsberg/Lech (2004)

53. Bernauer, M., Kappel, G., Kramler, G., Retschitzegger, W.: Specification of Interorganizational Workflows - A Comparison of Approaches. In: Proceedings of the 7th World Multiconference on Systemics, Cybernetics and Informatics, pp. 30–36 (2003)

54. Berners-Lee, T., Hendler, J., Lassila, O.: The semantic web. Scientific American (Mai 2001)

55. Berthelot, G.: Checking Properties of Nets Using Transformations. In: Rozenberg, G. (ed.) APN 1985. LNCS, vol. 222, pp. 19–40. Springer, Heidelberg (1986)

56. Berthelot, G.: Transformations and Decompositions of Nets. In: Brauer, W., Reisig, W., Rozenberg, G. (eds.) APN 1986. LNCS, vol. 254, pp. 360–376. Springer, Heidelberg (1987)

57. Bieman, J.M., Kang, B.-K.: Measuring design-level cohesion. IEEE Transactions on Software Engineering 24(2), 111–124 (1998)

58. Blackwell, A.F., Britton, C., Cox, A.L., Green, T.R.G., Gurr, C.A., Kadoda, G.F., Kutar, M., Loomes, M., Nehaniv, C.L., Petre, M., Roast, C., Roe, C., Wong, A., Young, R.M.: Cognitive dimensions of notations: Design tools for cognitive technology. In: Beynon, M., Nehaniv, C.L., Dautenhahn, K. (eds.) CT 2001. LNCS (LNAI), vol. 2117, pp. 325–341. Springer, Heidelberg (2001)

59. Boehm, B.W.: Software engineering; R & D trends and defense needs. In: Wegner, P. (ed.) Research Directions in Software Technology, MIT Press, Cambridge (1979)

60. Boehm, B.W.: Software Engineering Economics. Prentice-Hall, Englewood Cliffs (1981)

61. Brabänder, E., Ochs, J.: Analyse und Gestaltung prozessorientierter Risikomanagementsysteme mit Ereignisgesteuerten Prozessketten. In: Proc. of the 1st GI-Workshop on Business Process Management with Event-Driven Process Chains (EPK 2002), Trier, Germany, pp. 17–35 (2002)

62. Brandes, U., Erlebach, T.: Fundamentals. In: Brandes, U., Erlebach, T. (eds.) Network Analysis. LNCS, vol. 3418, pp. 7–15. Springer, Heidelberg (2005)

63. Brandes, U., Erlebach, T.: Introduction. In: Brandes, U., Erlebach, T. (eds.) Network Analysis. LNCS, vol. 3418, pp. 1–6. Springer, Heidelberg (2005)

64. Brandes, U., Erlebach, T. (eds.): Network Analysis. LNCS, vol. 3418. Springer, Heidelberg (2005)

65. Brinkmeier, M., Schank, T.: Network statistics. In: Brandes, U., Erlebach, T. (eds.) Network Analysis. LNCS, vol. 3418, pp. 293–317. Springer, Heidelberg (2005)

66. Bunge, M.: Treatise on Basic Philosophy. Vol.3. Ontology I. The Furniture of the World. D. Reidel Publishing, New York (1977)

67. Canfora, G., García, F., Piattini, M., Ruiz, F., Visaggio, C.A.: A family of experiments to validate metrics for software process models. Journal of Systems and Software 77(2), 113–129 (2005)

68. Card, D.N., Church, V.E., Agresti, W.W.: An empirical study of software design practices. IEEE Transactions on Software Engineering 12(2), 264–271 (1986)

69. Cardoso, J.: About the complexity of teamwork and collaboration processes. In: 2005 IEEE/IPSJ International Symposium on Applications and the Internet Workshops (SAINT 2005 Workshops), 31 January - 4 February 2005, Trento, Italy, pp. 218–221. IEEE Computer Society Press, Los Alamitos (2005)

70. Cardoso, J.: Control-flow Complexity Measurement of Processes and Weyuker's Properties. In: 6th International Enformatika Conference. Transactions on Enformatika, Systems Sciences and Engineering, vol. 8, pp. 213–218 (2005)
71. Cardoso, J.: Evaluating the process control-flow complexity measure. In: 2005 IEEE International Conference on Web Services (ICWS 2005), 11-15 July 2005, Orlando, FL, USA, pp. 803–804. IEEE Computer Society Press, Los Alamitos (2005)
72. Cardoso, J.: Evaluating Workflows and Web Process Complexity. In: Fischer, L. (ed.) Workflow Handbook 2005, pp. 284–290. Future Strategies, Inc., Lighthouse Point (2005)
73. Cardoso, J.: Process control-flow complexity metric: An empirical validation. In: Proceedings of IEEE International Conference on Services Computing (IEEE SCC 06), Chicago, USA, September 18-22, pp. 167–173. IEEE Computer Society Press, Los Alamitos (2006)
74. Cardoso, J., Mendling, J., Neumann, G., Reijers, H.A.: A Discourse on Complexity of Process Models. In: Eder, J., Dustdar, S. (eds.) BPM Workshops 2006. LNCS, vol. 4103, pp. 117–128. Springer, Heidelberg (2006)
75. Casati, F., Ceri, S., Pernici, B., Pozzi, G.: Conceptual modeling of workflows. In: Proceedings of the OOER International Conference, Gold Cost, Australia (1995)
76. Chamberlin, D.D., Astrahan, M.M., Eswaran, K.P., Griffiths, P.P., Lorie, R.A., Mehl, J.W., Reisner, P., Wade, B.W.: SEQUEL 2: A Unified Approach to Data Definition, Manipulation, and Control. IBM Journal of Research and Development 20(6), 560–575 (1976)
77. Chen, P.: The Entity-Relationship Model - Towards a Unified View of Data. ACM Transactions on Database Systems (TODS) 1, 9–36 (1976)
78. Chen, R., Scheer, A.W.: Modellierung von Prozessketten mittels Petri-Netz-Theorie. Heft 107, Institut für Wirtschaftsinformatik, Saarbrücken, Germany (1994)
79. Cherniavsky, J.C., Smith, C.H.: On weyuker's axioms for software complexity measures. IEEE Transactions on Software Engineering 17(6), 636–638 (1991), doi:10.1109/32.87287
80. Chernowitz, G.: Review: Office work and automation and electronic data processing for business and industry. Management Science 4(4), 475–477 (1958)
81. Chidamber, S.R., Kemerer, C.F.: A metrics suite for object oriented design. IEEE Transaction on Software Engineering 20(6), 476–493 (1994)
82. Codd, E.F.: A relational model for large shared data banks. Communications of the ACM 13(6), 377–387 (1970)
83. Cook, J.E., Wolf, A.L.: Discovering Models of Software Processes from Event-Based Data. ACM Transactions on Software Engineering and Methodology 7(3), 215–249 (1998)
84. Cormen, T.H., Leiserson, C.E., Rivest, R.L., Stein, C.: Introduction to Algorithms, 2nd edn. MIT Press, Cambridge (2001)
85. Cortadella, J.: Petrify: a tutorial for the designer of asychronous circuits. Universitat Politécnica de Catalunya (December 1998), http://www.lsi.upc.es/petrify
86. Cortadella, J., Kishinevsky, M., Lavagno, L., Yakovlev, A.: Deriving petri nets from finite transition systems. IEEE Transactions on Computers 47(8), 859–882 (1998)
87. Cuntz, N.: Über die effiziente Simulation von Ereignisgesteuerten Prozessketten (in German). Master's thesis, University of Paderborn (June 2004)
88. Cuntz, N., Freiheit, J., Kindler, E.: On the semantics of EPCs: Faster calculation for EPCs with small state spaces. In: Proceedings of the 4th GI Workshop on Business Process Management with Event-Driven Process Chains (EPK 2005), Hamburg, Germany, December 2005, pp. 7–23. German Informatics Society (2005)

89. Cuntz, N., Kindler, E.: On the semantics of EPCs: Efficient calculation and simulation. In: Proceedings of the 3rd GI Workshop on Business Process Management with Event-Driven Process Chains (EPK 2004), pp. 7–26 (2004)

90. Cuntz, N., Kindler, E.: On the semantics of ePCs: Efficient calculation and simulation. In: van der Aalst, W.M.P., Benatallah, B., Casati, F., Curbera, F. (eds.) BPM 2005. LNCS, vol. 3649, pp. 398–403. Springer, Heidelberg (2005)

91. Curbera, F., Goland, Y., Klein, J., Leymann, F., Roller, D., Thatte, S., Weerawarana, S.: Business Process Execution Language for Web Services, Version 1.0. Specification, BEA Systems, IBM Corp., Microsoft Corp. (2002)

92. Curran, T., Keller, G., Ladd, A.: SAP R/3 Business Blueprint: Understanding the Business Process Reference Model. Enterprise Resource Planning Series. Prentice Hall PTR, Upper Saddle River (1997)

93. Curtis, B., Kellner, M.I., Over, J.: Process modeling. Commun. ACM 35(9), 75–90 (1992)

94. Daneva, M., Heib, R., Scheer, A.-W.: Benchmarking Business Process Models. IWi Research Report 136, Institute for Information Systems. University of the Saarland, Germany (1996)

95. Davenport, T.H.: Process Innovation: Reengineering Work Through Information Technology. Harvard Business School Press, Boston (1993)

96. Davies, I., Green, P., Rosemann, M., Indulska, M., Gallo, S.: How do practitioners use conceptual modeling in practice? Data & Knowledge Engineering 58(3), 358–380 (2006)

97. Dayal, U., Hsu, M., Ladin, R.: Business Process Coordination: State of the Art, Trends, and Open Issues. In: Proc. of 27th International Conference on Very Large Data Bases (VLDB), Roma, Italy, Sept. 2001 (2001)

98. Decker, G., Mendling, J.: Instantiation semantics for process models. In: Dumas, M., Reichert, M., Shan, M.-C. (eds.) BPM 2008. LNCS, vol. 5240, Springer, Heidelberg (2008)

99. Dehnert, J.: Making EPC's fit for Workflow Management. In: Proc. of the 1st GI-Workshop on Business Process Management with Event-Driven Process Chains (EPK 2002), Trier, Germany, pp. 51–69 (2002)

100. Dehnert, J., van der Aalst, W.M.P.: Bridging The Gap Between Business Models And Workflow Specifications. International J. Cooperative Inf. Syst. 13(3), 289–332 (2004)

101. Dehnert, J., Rittgen, P.: Relaxed Soundness of Business Processes. In: Dittrich, K.R., Geppert, A., Norrie, M.C. (eds.) CAiSE 2001. LNCS, vol. 2068, pp. 157–170. Springer, Heidelberg (2001)

102. Dehnert, J., Zimmermann, A.: On the suitability of correctness criteria for business process models. In: van der Aalst, W.M.P., Benatallah, B., Casati, F., Curbera, F. (eds.) BPM 2005. LNCS, vol. 3649, pp. 386–391. Springer, Heidelberg (2005)

103. DeMarco, T.: Controlling Software Projects. Yourdon Press, New York (1982)

104. Desel, J.: Process Modeling Using Petri Nets. In: Dumas, M., ter Hofstede, A., van der Aalst, W.M.P. (eds.) Process Aware Information Systems: Bridging People and Software Through Process Technology, pp. 147–178. Wiley, Chichester (2005)

105. Desel, J., Esparza, J.: Free Choice Petri Nets. Cambridge Tracts in Theoretical Computer Science, vol. 40. Cambridge University Press, Cambridge (1995)

106. Desel, J., Pernici, B., Weske, M. (eds.): BPM 2004. LNCS, vol. 3080. Springer, Heidelberg (2004)

107. Dietz, J.L.G.: The deep structure of business processes. Communications of the ACM 49(5), 58–64 (2006)

108. van Dongen, B.F.: Process Mining and Verification. PhD thesis. Eindhoven University of Technology, Eindhoven, The Netherlands (2007)
109. van Dongen, B.F., van der Aalst, W.M.P., Verbeek, H.M.W.: Verification of ePCs: Using reduction rules and petri nets. In: Pastor, Ó., Falcão e Cunha, J. (eds.) CAiSE 2005. LNCS, vol. 3520, pp. 372–386. Springer, Heidelberg (2005)
110. van Dongen, B.F., Jansen-Vullers, M.H.: Verification of SAP reference models. In: van der Aalst, W.M.P., Benatallah, B., Casati, F., Curbera, F. (eds.) BPM 2005. LNCS, vol. 3649, pp. 464–469. Springer, Heidelberg (2005)
111. van Dongen, B.F., de Medeiros, A.K.A., Verbeek, H.M.W., Weijters, A.J.M.M.T., van der Aalst, W.M.P.: The ProM Framework: A New Era in Process Mining Tool Support. In: Ciardo, G., Darondeau, P. (eds.) ICATPN 2005. LNCS, vol. 3536, pp. 444–454. Springer, Heidelberg (2005)
112. van Dongen, B.F., Mendling, J., van der Aalst, W.M.P.: Structural Patterns for Soundness of Business Process Models. In: Proceedings of the 10th IEEE International Enterprise Distributed Object Computing Conference (EDOC'06), Hong Kong, China, pp. 116–128. IEEE Computer Society Press, Los Alamitos (2006)
113. Dongen, B.F.v., Vullers-Jansen, M.H., Verbeek, H.M.W., Aalst, W.M.P.v.d.: Verification of the sap reference models using epc reduction, state-space analysis, and invariants. Computers in Industry 58(6), 578–601 (2007)
114. Dumas, M., ter Hofstede, A., van der Aalst, W.M.P.: Process Aware Information Systems: Bridging People and Software Through Process Technology, chapter Introduction, pp. 3–20. Wiley, Chichester (2005)
115. Dustdar, S., Fiadeiro, J.L., Sheth, A.P. (eds.): BPM 2006. LNCS, vol. 4102. Springer, Heidelberg (2006)
116. Ehrenfeucht, A., Rozenberg, G.: Partial (Set) 2-Structures - Part 1 and Part 2. Acta Informatica 27(4), 315–368 (1989)
117. Ellis, C.A.: Information Control Nets: A Mathematical Model of Office Information Flow. In: Proceedings of the Conference on Simulation, Measurement and Modeling of Computer Systems, Boulder, Colorado, pp. 225–240. ACM Press, New York (1979)
118. Ellis, C.A., Nutt, G.J.: Office information systems and computer science. ACM Computing Surveys 12(1), 27–60 (1980)
119. Ellis, C.A., Nutt, G.J.: Modelling and Enactment of Workflow Systems. In: Ajmone Marsan, M. (ed.) ICATPN 1993. LNCS, vol. 691, pp. 1–16. Springer, Heidelberg (1993)
120. Esparza, J.: Reduction and synthesis of live and bounded free choice petri nets. Information and Computation 114(1), 50–87 (1994)
121. Etien, A., Rolland, C.: Measuring the fitness relationship. Requir. Eng. 10(3), 184–197 (2005)
122. Fayol, H.: Administration industrielle et générale. Prévoyance, Organisation, Commandement, Coordination, Control, Extrait du Bulletin de la Société de l'Industrie Minéeale. 3e livraison de 1916 edition, Dunod, Paris (1966)
123. Fenton, N.E., Ohlsson, N.: Quantitative analysis of faults and failures in a complex software system. IEEE Transactions on Software Engineering 26(8), 797–814 (2000)
124. Fenton, N.E., Pfleeger, S.L.: Software Metrics. A Rigorous and Practical Approach, 2nd edn. PWS, Boston (1997)
125. Ferraiolo, J., Jun, F., Jackson, D.: Scalable Vector Graphics (SVG) 1.1. W3C Recommendation 14 January 2003, World Wide Web Consortium (2003)
126. Fettke, P.: Referenzmodellevaluation - Konzeption der strukturalistischen Referenzmodellierung und Entfaltung ontologischer Gütekriterien. PhD thesis, Universität des Saarlandes (2006)

127. Fettke, P., Loos, P.: Classification of reference models - a methodology and its application. Information Systems and e-Business Management 1(1), 35–53 (2003)
128. Finkel, A., Schnoebelen, P.: Well-structured Transition Systems everywhere!. Theoretical Computer Science 256(1–2), 63–92 (2001)
129. Flatscher, R.G.: Meta-Modellierung in EIA/CDIF. ADV-Verlag, Wien (1998)
130. Ford, H.: Today and Tomorrow. Doubleday, Page and Company (1926)
131. Frank, U.: Conceptual Modelling as the Core of Information Systems Discipline - Perspectives and Epistemological Challenges. In: Proceedings of the America Conference on Information Systems - AMCIS '99, Milwaukee, pp. 695–698 (1999)
132. Frederiks, P.J.M., van der Weide, T.P.: Information modeling: The process and the required competencies of its participants. Data & Knowledge Engineering 58(1), 4–20 (2006)
133. Freeman, L.C.: Centrality in social networks conceptual clarification. Social Networks 1(3), 215–239 (1979)
134. Galler, J., Scheer, A.-W.: Workflow-Projekte: Vom Geschäftsprozeßmodell zur unternehmensspezifischen Workflow-Anwendung. Information Management 10(1), 20–27 (1995)
135. Gemino, A., Wand, Y.: Evaluating modeling techniques based on models of learning. Commun. ACM 46(10), 79–84 (2003)
136. Gemino, A., Wand, Y.: A framework for empirical evaluation of conceptual modeling techniques. Requir. Eng. 9(4), 248–260 (2004)
137. Gemino, A., Wand, Y.: Complexity and clarity in conceptual modeling: Comparison of mandatory and optional properties. Data & Knowledge Engineering 55(3), 301–326 (2005)
138. Genero, M., Poels, G., Piattini, M.: Defining and validating metrics for assessing the understandability of entity-relationship diagrams. Data and Knowledge Engineering 64(3), 534–557 (2008)
139. Georgakopoulos, D., Hornick, M., Sheth, A.: An Overview of Workflow Management: From Process Modeling to Workflow Automation Infrastructure. Distributed and Parallel Databases 3, 119–153 (1995)
140. Ghezzi, C., Jazayeri, M., Mandrioli, D.: Fundamentals of Software Engineering, 2nd edn. Prentice-Hall, Englewood Cliffs (2003)
141. Gilb, T.: Principles of Software Engineering Management. Addison-Wesley, Reading (1988)
142. Gill, G.K., Kemerer, C.F.: Cyclomatic complexity density and software maintenance productivity. IEEE Transaction on Software Engineering 17(9), 1284–1288 (1991)
143. Gong, G.: Cross-validation, the jackknife, and the bootstrap: Excess error estimation in forward logistic regression. Journal of the American Statistical Association 81(393), 108–113 (1986)
144. Grigori, D., Casati, F., Castellanos, M., Dayal, U., Sayal, M., Shan, M.C.: Business Process Intelligence. Computers in Industry 53(3), 321–343 (2004)
145. Grochla, E.: Automation und Organisation. Betriebswirtschaftlicher Verlag Dr. Th. Gabler (1966)
146. Grochla, E.: Die Integration der Datenverarbeitung. Durchführung anhand eines integrierten Unternehmensmodells. Bürotechnik und Automation 9, 108–120 (1968)
147. Grochla, E.: Integrierte Gesamtmodelle der Datenverarbeitung. Entwicklung und Anwendung des Kölner Integrationsmodells (KIM). Hanser, München (1974)
148. Grochla, E., Szyperski, N.: Information Systems and Organizational Structure. Walter de Gruyter, Berlin (1975)

149. Groote, J.F., van Ham, F.: Large state space visualization. In: Garavel, H., Hatcliff, J. (eds.) TACAS 2003. LNCS, vol. 2619, pp. 585–590. Springer, Heidelberg (2003)

150. Groote, J.F., van Ham, F.: Interactive visualization of large state spaces. International Journal on Software Tools for Technology Transfer 8(1), 77–91 (2006)

151. Grossmann, G., Ren, Y., Schrefl, M., Stumptner, M.: Behavior based integration of composite business processes. In: van der Aalst, W.M.P., Benatallah, B., Casati, F., Curbera, F. (eds.) BPM 2005. LNCS, vol. 3649, pp. 186–204. Springer, Heidelberg (2005)

152. Gruhn, V., Laue, R.: Adopting the cognitive complexity measure for business process models. In: Yao, Y., Shi, Z., Wang, Y., Kinsner, W. (eds.) Proceedings of the Firth IEEE International Conference on Cognitive Informatics, ICCI 2006, July 17-19, Beijing, China, pp. 236–241. IEEE Computer Society Press, Los Alamitos (2006)

153. Gruhn, V., Laue, R.: On experiments for measuring cognitive weights for software control structures. In: Zhang, D., Wang, Y., Kinsner, W. (eds.) Proceedings of the Six IEEE International Conference on Cognitive Informatics, ICCI 2007, August 6-8, Lake Tahoe, CA, USA, pp. 116–119. IEEE Computer Society Press, Los Alamitos (2007)

154. Gruhn, V., Laue, R.: What business process modelers can learn from programmers. Science of Computer Programming 65(1), 4–13 (2007), doi:10.1016/j.scico.2006.08.003

155. Gruhn, V., Laue, R., Meyer, F.: Berechnung von Komplexitätsmetriken für ereignisgesteuerte Prozessketten. In: Proceedings of the 5th GI Workshop on Business Process Management with Event-Driven Process Chains (EPK 2006), Vienna, Austria, December 2006, pp. 189–202. German Informatics Society (2006)

156. Guceglioglu, A.S., Demirors, O.: A process based model for measuring process quality attributes. In: Richardson, I., Abrahamsson, P., Messnarz, R. (eds.) EuroSPI 2005. LNCS, vol. 3792, pp. 118–129. Springer, Heidelberg (2005)

157. Guceglioglu, A.S., Demirors, O.: Using software quality characteristics to measure business process quality. In: van der Aalst, W.M.P., Benatallah, B., Casati, F., Curbera, F. (eds.) BPM 2005. LNCS, vol. 3649, pp. 374–379. Springer, Heidelberg (2005)

158. Guizzardi, G., Herre, H., Wagner, G.: On the general ontological foundations of conceptual modeling. In: Spaccapietra, S., March, S.T., Kambayashi, Y. (eds.) ER 2002. LNCS, vol. 2503, pp. 65–78. Springer, Heidelberg (2002)

159. Gulla, J.A., Brasethvik, T.: On the Challenges of Business Modeling in Large-Scale Reengineering Projects. In: Chen, P.P., Embley, D.W., Kouloumdjian, J., Liddle, S.W., Roddick, J.F. (eds.) 4th International Conference on Requirements Engineering, Schaumburg, pp. 17–26. IEEE Computer Society Press, Los Alamitos (2000)

160. Guttman, L.: What is not what in statistics. The statistician 26, 81–107 (1977)

161. Hair jr., J.F., Anderson, R.E., Tatham, R.L., Black, W.C.: Multivariate Data Analysis, 5th edn. Prentice-Hall, Englewood Cliffs (1998)

162. Halstead, M.H.: Elements of Software Science. Operating, and Programming Systems Series, vol. 7. Elsevier, Amsterdam (1977)

163. van Ham, F., van de Wetering, H., van Wijk, J.J.: Interactive visualization of state transition systems. IEEE Transactions on Visualization and Computer Graphics 8(4), 319–329 (2002)

164. Hammer, M., Champy, J.: Reengineering the Corporation: A Manifesto for Business Revolution. Harpercollins, New York (1993)

165. Hammer, M.: Reengineering work: Don't automate, obliterate. Harvard Business Review 68(4), 104–112 (1990)

166. Hansen, H.R.: Bestimmungsfaktoren fü den Einsatz elektronischer Datenverarbeitungsanlagen in Unternehmungen. Betriebspolitische Schriften – Beiträge zur Unternehmenspolitik. Duncker & Humblot, Berlin (1970)

167. Hansen, H.R., Neumann, G.: Wirtschaftsinformatik 1: Grundlagen und Anwendungen, 9th edn. Lucius & Lucius (2005)
168. Hars, A.: Referenzdatenmodelle. Grundlagen effizienter Datenmodellierung. Gabler Verlag (1994)
169. Hauser, R., Fries, M., Küster, J.M., Vanhatalo, J.: Combining analysis of unstructured workflows with transformation to structured workflows. In: Proceedings of EDOC 2006, October 2006, IEEE Computer Society Press, Los Alamitos (2006)
170. Havey, M.: Essential Business Process Modeling. O'Reilly, Sebastopol (2005)
171. van Hee, K.M., Oanea, O., Serebrenik, A., Sidorova, N., Voorhoeve, M.: History-based joins: Semantics, soundness and implementation. In: Dustdar, S., Fiadeiro, J.L., Sheth, A.P. (eds.) BPM 2006. LNCS, vol. 4102, pp. 225–240. Springer, Heidelberg (2006)
172. van Hee, K., Oanea, O., Sidorova, N.: Colored Petri Nets to Verify Extended Event-Driven Process Chains. In: Meersman, R., Tari, Z. (eds.) OTM 2005. LNCS, vol. 3760, pp. 183–201. Springer, Heidelberg (2005)
173. van Hee, K.M., Oanea, O., Sidorova, N., Voorhoeve, M.: Verifying generalized soundness of workflow nets. In: Virbitskaite, I., Voronkov, A. (eds.) PSI 2006. LNCS, vol. 4378, pp. 235–247. Springer, Heidelberg (2007)
174. van Hee, K., Sidorova, N., Somers, L., Voorhoeve, M.: Consistency in model integration. Data & Knowledge Engineering 56, 4–22 (2006)
175. van Hee, K.M., Sidorova, N., Voorhoeve, M.: Generalised Soundness of Workflow Nets Is Decidable. In: Cortadella, J., Reisig, W. (eds.) ICATPN 2004. LNCS, vol. 3099, pp. 197–215. Springer, Heidelberg (2004)
176. Heilmann, H., Heinrich, L.J., Roithmayr, F.: Information Engineering, chapter Die Integration der Aufbauorganisation in Workflow-Management-Systemen, pp. 147–165 (1996)
177. Henry, S., Kafura, D.: Software structure metrics based on information-flow. IEEE Transactions On Software Engineering 7(5), 510–518 (1981)
178. Hepp, M., Roman, D.: An ontology framework for semantic business process management. In: Oberweis, A., Weinhardt, C., Gimpel, H., Koschmider, A., Pankratius, V., Schnizler, B. (eds.) eOrganisation: Service-, Prozess-, Market Engineering, Tagungsband der 8. Internationalen Tagung Wirtschaftsinformatik. Band 1, pp. 423–440. Universitätsverlag, Karlsruhe (2007)
179. Herbst, J.: A Machine Learning Approach to Workflow Management. In: López de Mántaras, R., Plaza, E. (eds.) ECML 2000. LNCS (LNAI), vol. 1810, pp. 183–194. Springer, Heidelberg (2000)
180. Hevner, A.R., March, S.T., Park, J., Ram, S.: Design science in information systems research. MIS Quarterly 28(1), 75–105 (2004)
181. Hirschheim, R., Klein, H.K.: Four paradigms of information systems development. Commun. ACM 32(10), 1199–1216 (1989)
182. Hoffmann, W., Wein, R., Scheer, A.-W.: Konzeption eines Steuerungsmodelles für Informationssysteme - Basis für Real-Time-Erweiterung der EPK (rEPK). Heft 106, Institut für Wirtschaftsinformatik, Saarbrücken, Germany (1993)
183. Hofreiter, B., Huemer, C., Kim, J.-H.: Choreography of ebxml business collaborations. Information Systems and E-Business Management (2006)
184. Hollingsworth, D.: The Workflow Reference Model. TC00-1003 Issue 1.1, Workflow Management Coalition, 24 November (1994)
185. Hollingsworth, D.: The Workflow Reference Model: 10 Years On. In: Fischer, L. (ed.) The Workflow Handbook 2004, pp. 295–312. Workflow Management Coalition (2004)
186. Hopcroft, J.E., Tarjan, R.E.: Efficient planarity testing. Journal of the ACM 21(4), 549–568 (1974)

187. Hoppenbrouwers, S.J.B.A., Proper, H.A., van der Weide, T.P.: A fundamental view on the process of conceptual modeling. In: Delcambre, L.M.L., Kop, C., Mayr, H.C., Mylopoulos, J., Pastor, Ó. (eds.) ER 2005. LNCS, vol. 3716, pp. 128–143. Springer, Heidelberg (2005)

188. Hosmer, D.W., Lemeshow, S.: Applied Logistic Regression, 2nd edn. John Wiley & Sons, Chichester (2000)

189. Hsu, M., Kleissner, C.: Objectflow: Towards a process management infrastructure. Distributed and Parallel Databases 4(2), 169–194 (1996)

190. IDS Scheer AG: XML-Export und -Import mit ARIS 5.0, January 2001 (2001)

191. IDS Scheer AG: ARIS 6 Collaborative Suite – Methods Manual (2003)

192. IDS Scheer AG: XML-Export und -Import (ARIS 6 – Collaborative Suite Version 6.2 Schnittstellenbeschreibung). (Juni 2003), ftp://ftp.ids-scheer.de/pub/ARIS/HELPDESK/EXPORT/

193. IEEE: IEEE Standard 729: Glossary of Software Engineering Terminology. IEEE Computer Society Press, Los Alamitos (1983)

194. IEEE: IEEE Std 610.12-1990 IEEE Standard Glossary of Software Engineering Terminology . IEEE Computer Society Press, Los Alamitos (1990)

195. International Standards Organisation ISO: Information technology - software product evaluation - quality characteristics and guide lines for their use. Iso/iec is 9126 (1991)

196. Jablonski, S., Bussler, C.: Workflow Management: Modeling Concepts, Architecture, and Implementation. International Thomson Computer Press, London (1996)

197. Jansen-Vullers, M.H., van der Aalst, W.M.P., Rosemann, M.: Mining configurable enterprise information systems. Data & Knowledge Engineering 56(3), 195–244 (2006)

198. Jensen, K., Kristensen, L.M., Wells, L.: Coloured Petri nets and CPN tools for modelling and validation of concurrent systems. International Journal on Software Tools for Technology Transfer (2007)

199. Jeston, J.: Business Process Management. Practical Guidelines to Successful Implementations. Butterworth Heinemann (2006)

200. Johannesson, P.: Representation and communication - a speech act based approach to information systems design. information systems 20(4), 291–303 (1995)

201. Jones, T.C.: Programming Productivity. McGraw-Hill, New York, New York (1986)

202. Judge, G.G., Hill, R.C., Griffiths, W.E., Lütkepohl, H., Lee, T.-C.: Introduction to the theory and practice of econometrics, 2nd edn. John Wiley & Sons, Chichester (1988)

203. Junginger, S., Kühn, H., Strobl, R., Karagiannis, D.: Ein geschäftsprozessmanagementwerkzeug der nächsten generation – adonis: Konzeption und anwendungen. Wirtschaftsinformatik 42(5), 392–401 (2000)

204. Kan, S.H.: Metrics and Models in Software Quality Engineering, 2nd edn. Addison-Wesley, Reading (2002)

205. Kaplan, R.S., Norton, D.P.: The balanced scorecard - measures that drive performance. Harvard Business Review 70 (1), 71–79 (1992)

206. Kaplan, R.S., Norton, D.P.: Having trouble with your strategy? then map it. Harvard Business Review 78(5), 167–176 (2000)

207. Karagiannis, D., Kühn, H.: Metamodelling platforms. In: Bauknecht, K., Tjoa, A.M., Quirchmayr, G. (eds.) EC-Web 2002. LNCS, vol. 2455, pp. 182–196. Springer, Heidelberg (2002)

208. Kavakli, E., Loucopoulos, P.: Experiences with goal-oriented modelling of organisational change. IEEE Transactions on Systems, Man and Cybernetics - Part C 36(2), 221–235 (2006)

209. Kavantzas, N., Burdett, D., Ritzinger, G., Fletcher, T., Lafon, Y., Barreto, C.: Web Services Choreography Description Language Version 1.0. W3C Candidate Recommendation 9 November 2005, World Wide Web Consortium (April 2005)

210. Keller, G., Nüttgens, M., Scheer, A.-W.: Semantische Prozessmodellierung auf der Grundlage "Ereignisgesteuerter Prozessketten (EPK)". Heft 89, Institut für Wirtschaftsinformatik, Saarbrücken, Germany (1992)

211. Keller, G., Teufel, T.: Sap R/3 Process Oriented Implementation: Iterative Process Prototyping. Addison-Wesley Longman Publishing Co., Inc., Boston (1998)

212. Kelly, S., Lyytinen, K., Rossi, M.: Metaedit+: A fully configurable multi-user and multi-tool case and came environment. In: Constantopoulos, P., Vassiliou, Y., Mylopoulos, J. (eds.) CAiSE 1996. LNCS, vol. 1080, pp. 1–21. Springer, Heidelberg (1996)

213. Khan, R.N.: Business Process Management: A Practical Guide. Meghan Kiffer (2004)

214. Kiepuszewski, B.: Expressiveness and Suitability of Languages for Control Flow Modelling in Workflows. PhD thesis, Queensland University of Technology, Brisbane, Australia (2003)

215. Kiepuszewski, B., ter Hofstede, A.H.M., Bussler, C.J.: On structured workflow modelling. In: Wangler, B., Bergman, L.D. (eds.) CAiSE 2000. LNCS, vol. 1789, pp. 431–445. Springer, Heidelberg (2000)

216. Kindler, E.: On the semantics of EPCs: A framework for resolving the vicious circle (Extended Abstract). In: Proc. of the 2nd GI-Workshop on Business Process Management with Event-Driven Process Chains (EPK 2003), Bamberg, Germany, pp. 7–18 (2003)

217. Kindler, E.: On the Semantics of EPCs: A Framework for Resolving the Vicious Circle. In: Desel, J., Pernici, B., Weske, M. (eds.) BPM 2004. LNCS, vol. 3080, pp. 82–97. Springer, Heidelberg (2004)

218. Kindler, E.: On the semantics of EPCs: Resolving the vicious circle. Data & Knowledge Engineering 56(1), 23–40 (2006)

219. Kindler, E., Rubin, V., Schäfer, W.: Incremental workflow mining based on document versioning information. In: Li, M., Boehm, B., Osterweil, L.J. (eds.) SPW 2005. LNCS, vol. 3840, pp. 287–301. Springer, Heidelberg (2006)

220. Kindler, E., Rubin, V., Schäfer, W.: Activity mining for discovering software process models. In: Biel, B., Book, M., Gruhn, V. (eds.) Proc. of the Software Engineering 2006 Conference, Leipzig, Germany, March 2006. LNI, vol. P-79, pp. 175–180. Gesellschaft für Informatik (2006)

221. Kindler, E., Rubin, V., Schäfer, W.: Process Mining and Petri Net Synthesis. In: Eder, J., Dustdar, S. (eds.) BPM Workshops 2006. LNCS, vol. 4103, pp. 105–116. Springer, Heidelberg (2006)

222. Kirn, S., Heine, C., Petsch, M., Puppe, F., Klügl, F., Herrler, R.: Agentenorientierte Modellierung vernetzter Logistikkreisläufe als Ausgangspunkt agentenbasierter Simulation. In: Kirn, S., Petsch, M. (eds.) Tagungsband zum 2. Kolloquium des DFG-Schwerpunktprogramms "Intelligente Softwareagenten und Betriebswirtschaftliche Anwendungen" (2000)

223. Kohavi, R.: A study of cross-validation and bootstrap for accuracy estimation and model selection. In: Proceedings of the Fourteenth International Joint Conference on Artificial Intelligence (IJCAI), pp. 1137–1145 (1995)

224. Kopp, O., Unger, T., Leymann, F.: Nautilus Event-driven Process Chains: Syntax, Semantics, and their mapping to BPEL. In: Proceedings of the 5th GI Workshop on Business Process Management with Event-Driven Process Chains (EPK 2006), Vienna, Austria, December 2006, pp. 85–104. German Informatics Society (2006)

225. Koschützki, D., Lehmann, K.A., Tenfelde-Podehl, D., Zlotowski, O.: Advanced central-ity concepts. In: Brandes, U., Erlebach, T. (eds.) Network Analysis. LNCS, vol. 3418, pp. 83–111. Springer, Heidelberg (2005)
226. Kosiol, E.: Modellanalyse als Grundlage unternehmerischer Entscheidungen. Zeitschrift für betriebswirtschaftlicher Forschung, 318–334 (1961)
227. Krajewski, L.J., Ritzman, L.P., Malhotra, M.K.: Operations Management. Processes and Value Chains: Process and Value Chains. Addison-Wesley, Reading (2006)
228. Krogstie, J., Sindre, G., Jørgensen, H.: Process models representing knowledge for ac-tion: a revised quality framework. European Journal of Information Systems 15(1), 91–102 (2006), doi:10.1057/palgrave.ejis.3000598
229. Kruse, C.: Referenzmodellgestütztes Geschäftsprozeßmanagement: Ein Ansatz zur prozeßorientierten Gestaltung betriebslogistischer Systeme. Gabler Verlag (1996)
230. Kruse, C., Hars, A., Heib, R., Scheer, A.-W.: Ways of utilizing reference models for data engineering in CIM. International Journal of Flexible Automation and Integrated Manufactoring (FAIM) 1(1), 47–58 (1993)
231. Kugeler, M.: SCM und CRM - Prozessmodellierung für Extende Enterprises. In: Becker, J., Kugeler, M., Rosemann, M. (eds.) Prozessmanagement, 3rd edn., pp. 457–485. Springer, Heidelberg (2002)
232. Kühne, T.: Matters of (meta-) modeling. Software and Systems Modeling 5(4), 369–385 (2006)
233. Laguna, M., Marklund, J.: Business Process Modeling, Simulation and Design. Prentice-Hall, Englewood Cliffs (2004)
234. Laird, L.M., Brennan, M.C.: Software Measurement and Estimation: A Practical Ap-proach. IEEE Computer Society Press, Los Alamitos (2006)
235. Lang, K.R., Schmidt, M.: Workflow-supported organizational memory systems: An in-dustrial application. In: 35th Hawaii International International Conference on Systems Science (HICSS-35 2002), CD-ROM / Abstracts Proceedings, p. 208. IEEE Computer Society Press, Los Alamitos (2002)
236. Langner, P., Schneider, C., Wehler, J.: Ereignisgesteuerte Prozeßketten und Petri-Netze (in German). Report Series of the Department of Computer Science 196, University of Hamburg - Computer Sience Department (March 1997)
237. Langner, P., Schneider, C., Wehler, J.: Prozeßmodellierung mit ereignisgesteuerten Prozeßketten (EPKs) und Petri-Netzen. Wirtschaftsinformatik 39(5), 479–489 (1997)
238. Langner, P., Schneider, C., Wehler, J.: Petri Net Based Certification of Event-Driven Process Chains. In: Desel, J., Silva, M. (eds.) ICATPN 1998. LNCS, vol. 1420, pp. 286–305. Springer, Heidelberg (1998)
239. Latva-Koivisto, A.M.: Finding a complexity for business process models. In: Research report, February 2001, Helsinki University of Technology (2001)
240. Laudon, K.C., Laudon, J.P., Schoder, D.: Wirtschaftsinformatik. Eine Einführung. Pear-son, London (2006)
241. Laue, R., Gruhn, V.: Complexity metrics for business process models. In: Abramowicz, W., Mayr, H.C. (eds.) 9th International Conference on Business Information Systems (BIS 2006). Lecture Notes in Informatics, vol. 85, pp. 1–12. Gesellschaft für Informatik (2006)
242. Laue, R., Mendling, J.: The impact of structuredness on error probability of process models. In: Kaschek, R., Kop, C., Steinberger, C., Fliedl, G. (eds.) Information Systems and e-Business Technologies: 2nd International United Information Systems Confer-ence, UNISCON 2008, Klagenfurt, Austria, April 22-25, 2008, Proceedings. Lectures Notes in Business Information Processing, vol. 5, Springer, Heidelberg (2008)

243. Lee, G.S., Yoon, J.-M.: An empirical study on the complexity metrics of petri nets. In: JTC-CSCC: Joint Technical Conference on Circuits Systems, Computers and Communications, 1990, pp. 327–332 (1990)

244. Lee, G.S., Yoon, J.-M.: An empirical study on the complexity metrics of petri nets. Microelectronics and Reliability 32(3), 323–329 (1992)

245. Leuschel, M.A., Lehmann, H.: Coverability of reset petri nets and other well-structured transition systems by partial deduction. In: Palamidessi, C., Moniz Pereira, L., Lloyd, J.W., Dahl, V., Furbach, U., Kerber, M., Lau, K.-K., Sagiv, Y., Stuckey, P.J. (eds.) CL 2000. LNCS (LNAI), vol. 1861, pp. 101–115. Springer, Heidelberg (2000)

246. Levin, H.S.: Office Work and Automation. John Wiley and Sons, Chichester (1956)

247. Leymann, F., Altenhuber, W.: Managing business processes as an information resource. IBM Systems Journal 33(2), 326–348 (1994)

248. Leymann, F., Roller, D.: Production Workflow - Concepts and Techniques. Prentice-Hall, Englewood Cliffs

249. Lin, H., Zhao, Z., Li, H., Chen, Z.: A novel graph reduction algorithm to identify structural conflicts. In: 35th Hawaii International Conference on System Sciences (HICSS-35 2002), CD-ROM / Abstracts Proceedings, 7-10 January 2002, Big Island, HI, USA. Track 9, p. 289. IEEE Computer Society Press, Los Alamitos (2002)

250. Lindland, O.I., Sindre, G., Sølvberg, A.: Understanding quality in conceptual modeling. IEEE Software 11(2), 42–49 (1994)

251. Lindsay, A., Downs, D., Lunn, K.: Business processes—attempts to find a definition. Information and Software Technology 45(15), 1015–1019 (2003)

252. List, B., Korherr, B.: An evaluation of conceptual business process modelling languages. In: Haddad, H. (ed.) Proceedings of the 2006 ACM Symposium on Applied Computing (SAC), Dijon, France, April 23-27, 2006, pp. 1532–1539. ACM Press, New York (2006)

253. Liu, R., Kumar, A.: An analysis and taxonomy of unstructured workflows. In: van der Aalst, W.M.P., Benatallah, B., Casati, F., Curbera, F. (eds.) BPM 2005. LNCS, vol. 3649, pp. 268–284. Springer, Heidelberg (2005)

254. Loos, P., Allweyer, T.: Process Orientation and Object-Orientation – An Approach for Integrating UML and Event-Driven Process Chains (EPC). In: Heft 144, Institut für Wirtschaftsinformatik, Saarbrücken, Germany, (1998)

255. Löwer, J.: tDOM – A fast XML/DOM/XPath package for Tcl written in C. In: Document to Talk at the First European Tcl/Tk User Meeting, June 2000, http://www.tdom.org/documents/tDOM3.pdf

256. Maes, A., Poels, G.: Evaluating quality of conceptual modelling scripts based on user perceptions. Data & Knowledge Engineering 63(3), 701–724 (2007)

257. Malone, T.W., Crowston, K., Herman, G.A.: Organizing Business Knowledge: The MIT Process Handbook. MIT Press, Cambridge (2003)

258. Marczyk, G., DeMatteo, D., Festinger, D.: Essentials of Research Design and Methodology. John Wiley & Sons, Chichester (2005)

259. Martens, A.: On Compatibility of Web Services. Petri Net Newsletter 65, 12–20 (2003)

260. McCabe, T.J.: A complexity measure. IEEE Transactions on Software Engineering 2(4), 308–320 (1976)

261. McCabe, T.J., Butler, C.W.: Design complexity measurement and testing. Communications of the ACM 32, 1415–1425 (1989)

262. McCabe, T.J., Watson, A.H.: Software complexity (Crosstalk). Journal of Defence Software Engineering 7(12), 5–9 (1994)

263. McGuinness, D.L., van Harmelen, F.: OWL Web Ontology Language Overview. W3c recommendation, World Wide Web Consortium (2004)

264. Melao, N., Pidd, M.: A conceptual framework for understanding business processes and business process modelling. Information Systems Journal 10(2), 105–129 (2000)

265. Melenovsky, M.J.: Business Process Management's Success Hinges on Business-Led Initiatives. Gartner Note G00129411 (2005)

266. Mendling, J.: Detection and Prediction of Errors in EPC Business Process Models. PhD thesis, Vienna University of Economics and Business Administration (2007), http://wi.wu-wien.ac.at/home/mendling/publications/Mendling %20Doctoral%20thesis.pdf

267. Mendling, J., Aalst, W.M.P.v.d.: Towards EPC Semantics based on State and Context. In: Proceedings of the 5th GI Workshop on Business Process Management with Event-Driven Process Chains (EPK 2006), Vienna, Austria, December 2006, pp. 25–48. German Informatics Society (2006)

268. Mendling, J., van der Aalst, W.M.P.: Formalization and Verification of EPCs with OR-Joins Based on State and Context. In: Krogstie, J., Opdahl, A., Sindre, G. (eds.) CAiSE 2007 and WES 2007. LNCS, vol. 4495, pp. 439–453. Springer, Heidelberg (2007)

269. Mendling, J., van der Aalst, W.M.P., van Dongen, B.F., Verbeek, H.M.W.: Referenzmodell: Sand im Getriebe - Webfehler. iX - Magazin für Professionelle Informationstechnik (in German), 131–133 (2006)

270. Mendling, J., Hafner, M.: From Inter-organizational Workflows to Process Execution: Generating BPEL from WS-CDL. In: Meersman, R., Tari, Z., Herrero, P. (eds.) OTM-WS 2005. LNCS, vol. 3762, pp. 506–515. Springer, Heidelberg (2005)

271. Mendling, J., Lassen, K.B., Zdun, U.: Transformation strategies between block-oriented and graph-oriented process modelling languages. Technical Report JM-2005-10-10, WU Vienna (October 2005)

272. Mendling, J., Lassen, K.B., Zdun, U.: Experiences in Enhancing Existing BPM Tools with BPEL Import and Export. In: Dustdar, S., Fiadeiro, J.L., Sheth, A.P. (eds.) BPM 2006. LNCS, vol. 4102, pp. 348–357. Springer, Heidelberg (2006)

273. Mendling, J., Lassen, K.B., Zdun, U.: Transformation strategies between block-oriented and graph-oriented process modelling languages. In: Lehner, F., Nösekabel, H., Kleinschmidt, P. (eds.) Multikonferenz Wirtschaftsinformatik 2006, XML4BPM Track, Band 2, Passau, Germany, February 2006, pp. 297–312. GITO-Verlag, Berlin (2006)

274. Mendling, J., Moser, M., Neumann, G.: Transformation of yEPC Business Process Models to YAWL. In: 21st Annual ACM Symposium on Applied Computing, Dijon, France, vol. 2, pp. 1262–1267. ACM, Dijon, France (2006)

275. Mendling, J., Moser, M., Neumann, G., Verbeek, H.M.W., van Dongen, B.F., van der Aalst, W.M.P.: A Quantitative Analysis of Faulty EPCs in the SAP Reference Model. BPM Center Report BPM-06-08, BPMCenter.org (2006)

276. Mendling, J., Moser, M., Neumann, G., Verbeek, H.M.W., van Dongen, B.F., van der Aalst, W.M.P.: Faulty EPCs in the SAP Reference Model. In: Dustdar, S., Fiadeiro, J.L., Sheth, A.P. (eds.) BPM 2006. LNCS, vol. 4102, pp. 451–457. Springer, Heidelberg (2006)

277. Mendling, J., zur Muehlen, M., Price, A.: Standards for Workflow Definition and Execution. In: Dumas, M., ter Hofstede, A., van der Aalst, W.M.P. (eds.) Process Aware Information Systems: Bridging People and Software Through Process Technology, pp. 281–316. Wiley, Chichester (2005)

278. Mendling, J., Neumann, G., van der Aalst, W.M.P.: Understanding the occurrence of errors in process models based on metrics. In: Meersman, R., Tari, Z. (eds.) OTM 2007, Part I. LNCS, vol. 4803, pp. 113–130. Springer, Heidelberg (2007)

279. Mendling, J., Neumann, G., Nüttgens, M.: Towards Workflow Pattern Support of Event-Driven Process Chains (EPC). In: Proc. of the 2nd Workshop XML4BPM 2005, Karlsruhe, Germany, Karlsruhe, Germany, March 2005. CEUR Workshop Proceedings, vol. 145, pp. 23–38. Sun SITE Central Europe (2005)

280. Mendling, J., Neumann, G., Nüttgens, M.: A Comparison of XML Interchange Formats for Business Process Modelling. In: Fischer, L. (ed.) Workflow Handbook 2005, pp. 185–198. Future Strategies Inc., Lighthouse Point (2005)

281. Mendling, J., Neumann, G., Nüttgens, M.: Yet Another Event-Driven Process Chain. In: van der Aalst, W.M.P., Benatallah, B., Casati, F., Curbera, F. (eds.) BPM 2005. LNCS, vol. 3649, pp. 428–433. Springer, Heidelberg (2005)

282. Mendling, J., Neumann, G., Nüttgens, M.: Yet Another Event-driven Process Chain - Modeling Workflow Patterns with yEPCs. Enterprise Modelling and Information Systems Architectures - an International Journal 11(1), 3–13 (2005)

283. Mendling, J., Nüttgens, M.: Event-Driven-Process-Chain-Markup-Language (EPML): Anforderungen zur Definition eines XML-Schemas für Ereignisgesteuerte Prozessketten (EPK). In: Proc. of the 1st GI-Workshop on Business Process Management with Event-Driven Process Chains (EPK 2002), Trier, Germany, pp. 87–93 (2002)

284. Mendling, J., Nüttgens, M.: EPC Modelling based on Implicit Arc Types. In: Proc. of the 2nd International Conference on Information Systems Technology and its Applications (ISTA), Kharkiv, Ukraine. Lecture Notes in Informatics, vol. 30, pp. 131–142 (2003)

285. Mendling, J., Nüttgens, M.: EPC Syntax Validation with XML Schema Languages. In: Proc. of the 2nd GI-Workshop on Business Process Management with Event-Driven Process Chains (EPK 2003), Bamberg, Germany, pp. 19–30 (2003)

286. Mendling, J., Nüttgens, M.: XML-basierte Geschäftsprozessmodellierung. In: Uhr, W., Esswein, W., Schoop, E. (eds.) Proc. of Wirtschaftsinformatik 2003 / Band II, Dresden, Germany, pp. 161–180 (2003)

287. Mendling, J., Nüttgens, M.: Exchanging EPC Business Process Models with EPML. In: Nüttgens, M., Mendling, J. (eds.) XML4BPM 2004, Proceedings of the 1st GI Workshop XML4BPM – XML Interchange Formats for Business Process Management at 7th GI Conference Modellierung 2004, Marburg, Germany, March 2004, pp. 61–80 (2004)

288. Mendling, J., Nüttgens, M.: Transformation of ARIS Markup Language to EPML. In: Nüttgens, M., Rump, F.J. (eds.) Proceedings of the 3rd GI Workshop on Business Process Management with Event-Driven Process Chains (EPK 2004), pp. 27–38 (2004)

289. Mendling, J., Nüttgens, M.: XML-based Reference Modelling: Foundations of an EPC Markup Language. In: Becker, J. (ed.) Referenzmodellierung - Proceedings of the 8th GI-Workshop on Reference Modelling, MKWI Essen, Germany, pp. 51–71 (2004)

290. Mendling, J., Nüttgens, M.: EPC Markup Language (EPML) - An XML-Based Interchange Format for Event-Driven Process Chains (EPC). Technical Report JM-2005-03-10, Vienna University of Economics and Business Administration, Austria (2005)

291. Mendling, J., Nüttgens, M.: EPC Markup Language (EPML) - An XML-Based Interchange Format for Event-Driven Process Chains (EPC). Information Systems and e-Business Management 4(3), 245–263 (2005)

292. Mendling, J., Nüttgens, M., Neumann, G.: A Comparison of XML Interchange Formats for Business Process Modelling. In: Feltz, F., Oberweis, A., Otjacques, B. (eds.) Proceedings of EMISA 2004 - Information Systems in E-Business and E-Government. Lecture Notes in Informatics, vol. 56, pp. 129–140 (2004)

293. Mendling, J., Recker, J.: Extending the discussion of model quality: Why clarity and completeness may not be enough. In: Krogstie, J., Opdahl, A., Sindre, G. (eds.) CAiSE 2007 and WES 2007. LNCS, vol. 4495, pp. 235–244. Springer, Heidelberg (2007)

294. Mendling, J., Recker, J., Rosemann, M., van der Aalst, W.M.P.: Generating Correct EPCs from Configured CEPCs. In: Proceedings of the 21st Annual ACM Symposium on Applied Computing, Dijon, France, April 23–27, 2006, vol. 2, pp. 1505–1511. ACM, New York (2006)

295. Mendling, J., Reijers, H.A.: How to define activity labels for business process models? In: Oberweis, A., Hesse, W. (eds.) Proc. of the Third AIS SIGSAND European Symposium on Analysis, Design, Use and Societal Impact of Information Systems (SIGSAND Europe 2008), Marburg, Germany. Lecture Notes in Informatics (2008)

296. Mendling, J., Reijers, H.A., Cardoso, J.: What makes process models understandable? In: Alonso, G., Dadam, P., Rosemann, M. (eds.) BPM 2007. LNCS, vol. 4714, pp. 48–63. Springer, Heidelberg (2007)

297. Mendling, J., Reijers, H.A., van der Aalst, W.M.P.: Seven Process Modeling Guidelines (7PMG). Qut eprint, Queensland University of Technology (2008)

298. Mendling, J., La Rosa, M., ter Hofstede, A.: Correctness of business process models with roles and objects. Qut eprint, Queensland University of Technology (2008)

299. Mendling, J., Simon, C.: Business Process Design by View Integration. In: Eder, J., Dustdar, S. (eds.) BPM Workshops 2006. LNCS, vol. 4103, pp. 55–64. Springer, Heidelberg (2006)

300. Mendling, J., Strembeck, M.: Influence factors of understanding business process models. In: Abramowicz, W., Fensel, D. (eds.) Proc. of the 11th International Conference on Business Information Systems (BIS 2008). Lecture Notes in Business Information Processing, vol. 7, p. 142. Springer, Heidelberg (2008)

301. Mendling, J., Verbeek, H.M.W., van Dongen, B.F., van der Aalst, W.M.P., Neumann, G.: Detection and Prediction of Errors in EPCs of the SAP Reference Model. Data and Knowledge Engineering 64(1), 312–329 (2008)

302. Mendling, J., Ziemann, J.: EPK-Visualisierung von BPEL4WS Prozessdefinitionen. In: Proc. of Workshop on Software Reengineering, Germany, Hamburg, Germany, December 2005, pp. 41–53. German Informatics Society (2005)

303. Mendling, J., Ziemann, J.: Transformation of BPEL Processes to EPCs. In: 4th GI Workshop on Event-Driven Process Chains, Hamburg, Germany, German Informatics Society (2005)

304. Moody, D.L.: Dealing With Complexity: A Practical Method For Representing Large Entity Relationship Models. PhD thesis, Department of Information Systems, University of Melbourne (June 2001)

305. Moody, D.L.: Measuring the quality of data models: an empirical evaluation of the use of quality metrics in practice. In: Proceedings of the 11th European Conference on Information Systems, ECIS 2003, Naples, Italy 16-21 June (2003)

306. Moody, D.L.: Theoretical and practical issues in evaluating the quality of conceptual models: current state and future directions. Data & Knowledge Engineering 55(3), 243–276 (2005)

307. Moody, D.L., Sindre, G., Brasethvik, T., Sølvberg, A.: Evaluating the quality of process models: Empirical testing of a quality framework. In: Spaccapietra, S., March, S.T., Kambayashi, Y. (eds.) ER 2002. LNCS, vol. 2503, pp. 380–396. Springer, Heidelberg (2002)

308. Morasca, S.: Measuring attributes of concurrent software specifications in petri nets. In: METRICS '99: Proceedings of the 6th International Symposium on Software Metrics, Washington, DC, USA, pp. 100–110. IEEE Computer Society Press, Los Alamitos (1999)

309. Mosteller, F., Tukey, J.W.: Data Analysis and Regression. Addison-Wesley, Reading (1977)

310. Muehlen, M.z.: Workflow-based Process Controlling. Foundation, Design, and Implementation of Workflow-driven Process Information Systems. Advances in Information Systems and Management Science, vol. 6. Logos, Berlin (2004)

311. Muehlen, M.z.: Research in business process management. BPTrends 4(5), 1–7 (2007)

312. Muehlen, M.z., Rosemann, M.: Multi-Paradigm Process Management. In: Proc. of the Fifth Workshop on Business Process Modeling, Development, and Support - CAiSE Workshops (2004)

313. Murata, T.: Petri Nets: Properties, Analysis and Applications. Proceedings of the IEEE 77(4), 541–580 (1989)

314. Nagelkerke, N.J.D.: A note on a general definition of the coefficient of determination. Biometrika 78(3), 691–692 (1991)

315. Neumann, G.: Metaprogrammierung und Prolog. Addison-Wesley, Reading (1988)

316. Neumann, G., Zdun, U.: XOTcl, an Object-Oriented Scripting Language. In: Proc. of the 7th USENIX Tcl/Tk Conference, Austin, Texas, USA,

317. Neumann, S., Probst, C., Wernsmann, C.: Continuous Process Management. In: Becker, J., Kugeler, M., Rosemann, M. (eds.) Process Management: A Guide for the Design of Business Processes, pp. 233–250. Springer, Berlin (2003)

318. Nissen, M.E.: Valuing it through virtual process measurement. In: Proc. 15th. International Conference on Information Systems, Vancouver, Canada, pp. 309–323 (1994)

319. Nissen, M.E.: Knowledge-based organizational process redesign: using process flow measures to transform procurement. PhD thesis, University of South California (1996)

320. Nissen, M.E.: Redesigning reengineering through measurement-driven inference. MIS Quarterly 22(4), 509–534 (1998)

321. Nordsieck, F.: Die Schaubildliche Erfassung und Untersuchung der Betriebsorganisation. Organisation - Eine Schriftenreihe. C. E. Poeschel Verlag, Stuttgart (1932)

322. Nordsieck, F.: Grundlagen der Organisationslehre. C.E. Poeschel Verlag, Stuttgart (1934)

323. Noy, N.F., Fergerson, R.W., Musen, M.A.: The knowledge model of protégé-2000: Combining interoperability and flexibility. In: Dieng, R., Corby, O. (eds.) EKAW 2000. LNCS (LNAI), vol. 1937, pp. 17–32. Springer, Heidelberg (2000)

324. Nüttgens, M.: Koordiniert-dezentrales Informationsmanagement: Rahmenkonzept, Koordinationsmodelle und Werkzeug-Shell. PhD thesis, Rechts- und Wirtschaftswissenschaftliche Fakultät der Universität des Saarlandes (1995)

325. Nüttgens, M., Rump, F.J.: Syntax und Semantik Ereignisgesteuerter Prozessketten (EPK). In: Proceedings of Promise 2002, Potsdam, Germany. Lecture Notes in Informatics, vol. 21, pp. 64–77 (2002)

326. Oberweis, A.: An integrated approach for the specification of processes and related complex structured objects in business applications. Decision Support Systems 17, 31–53 (1996)

327. Oberweis, A., Sander, P.: Information system behavior specification by high-level petri nets. ACM Transactions on Information Systems 14(4), 380–420 (1996)

328. Object Management Group: Business Process Modeling Notation (BPMN) Specification. Final Adopted Specification, dtc/06-02-01, Object Management Group (February 2006)

329. OMG (ed.): Meta Object Facility. Version 1.4, Object Management Group (2002)

330. OMG (ed.): Unified Modeling Language. Version 2.0, Object Management Group (2004)

331. Österle, H.: Business Engineering Prozeß- und Systementwicklung. Band 1: Entwurfstechniken. Springer, Heidelberg (1995)

332. Österle, H., Gutzwiller, T.: Konzepte angewandter Analyse- und Design-Methoden. Band 1: Ein Referenz-Metamodell für die Analyse und das System-Design. Angewandte InformationsTechnik-Verl. GmbH (1992)

333. Palmer, N.: A survey of business process initiatives. BPT Report, Business Process Trends and Transformation+Innovation (January 2007)

334. Pemberton, S., et al.: XHTML 1.0 The Extensible HyperText Markup Language (Second Edition). W3C Recommendation 26 January 2000, revised 1 August 2002, World Wide Web Consortium (2002)

335. Petri, C.A.: Kommunikation mit Automaten. PhD thesis, Fakultät für Mathematik und Physik, Technische Hochschule Darmstadt, Darmstadt, Germany (1962)

336. Philippi, S., Hill, H.J.: Communication support for systems engineering - process modelling and animation with april. The Journal of Systems and Software, 80(8), 1305–1316 (2007)

337. Pnueli, A.: The Temporal Logic of Programs. In: Proceedings of the 18th IEEE Annual Symposium on the Foundations of Computer Science, pp. 46–57. IEEE Computer Society Press, Los Alamitos (1977)

338. Porter, M.E.: Competitive Advantage: Creating and Sustaining Superior Performance. The Free Press, New York (1985)

339. Pretorius, A.J., van Wijk, J.J.: Multidimensional visualization of transition systems. In: 9th International Conference on Information Visualisation, IV 2005, 6-8 July 2005, London, UK, pp. 323–328. IEEE Computer Society Press, Los Alamitos (2005)

340. Pretorius, A.J., van Wijk, J.J.: Visual analysis of multivariate state transition graphs. IEEE Visualization and Computer Graphics 12(5), 685–692 (2006)

341. Priemer, J.: Entscheidungen über die Einsetzbarkeit von Software anhand formaler Modelle. PhD thesis, Westfälische Wilhelms-Universität Münster (1995)

342. Puhlmann, F., Weske, M.: Investigations on soundness regarding lazy activities. In: Dustdar, S., Fiadeiro, J.L., Sheth, A.P. (eds.) BPM 2006. LNCS, vol. 4102, pp. 145–160. Springer, Heidelberg (2006)

343. Recker, J.: A socio-pragmatic constructionist framework for understanding quality in process modelling. Australasian Journal of Information Systems 14(2), 43–63 (2007)

344. Recker, J., Mendling, J., van der Aalst, W.M.P., Rosemann, M.: Model-driven enterprise systems configuration. In: Dubois, E., Pohl, K. (eds.) CAiSE 2006. LNCS, vol. 4001, pp. 369–383. Springer, Heidelberg (2006)

345. Recker, J., Rosemann, M., Krogstie, J.: Ontology- versus pattern-based evaluation of process modeling languages: A comparison. Communications of the Association for Information Systems 20(48), 774–799 (2007)

346. Reichert, M., Dadam, P.: ADEPTflex: Supporting Dynamic Changes of Workflow without Loosing Control. Journal of Intelligent Information Systems 10(2), 93–129 (1998)

347. Reijers, H.A.: A cohesion metric for the definition of activities in a workflow process. In: Proceedings of the Eighth CAiSE/IFIP8.1 International Workshop on Evaluation of Modeling Methods in Systems Analysis and Design (EMMSAD 2003), pp. 116–125 (2003)

348. Reijers, H.A., Vanderfeesten, I.T.P.: Cohesion and coupling metrics for workflow process design. In: Desel, J., Pernici, B., Weske, M. (eds.) BPM 2004. LNCS, vol. 3080, pp. 290–305. Springer, Heidelberg (2004)

349. Rittgen, P.: Modified EPCs and Their Formal Semantics. Arbeitsberichte des Instituts für Wirtschaftsinformatik 19, Universität Koblenz-Landau (1999)

350. Rittgen, P.: Paving the Road to Business Process Automation. In: Proc. of the European Conference on Information Systems (ECIS), Vienna, Austria, pp. 313–319 (2002)

351. Rodenhagen, J.: Ereignisgesteuerte Prozessketten - Multi-Instantiierungsfähigkeit und referentielle Persistenz. In: Proceedings of the 1st GI Workshop on Business Process Management with Event-Driven Process Chains, pp. 95–107 (2002)

352. Rolland, C., Prakash, N., Benjamen, A.: A multi-model view of process modelling. Requir. Eng. 4(4), 169–187 (1999)

353. Rolón Aguilar, E., García, F., Ruiz, F., Piattini, M.: An exploratory experiment to validate measures for business process models. In: First International Conference on Research Challenges in Information Science, RCIS (2007)

354. Rolón Aguilar, E., Ruiz, F., García, F., Piattini, M.: Applying software metrics to evaluate business process models. CLEI Electron. J. 9 (2006)

355. Rolón Aguilar, E., Ruiz, F., García, F., Piattini, M.: Evaluation measures for business process models. In: Haddad, H. (ed.) Proceedings of the 2006 ACM Symposium on Applied Computing (SAC), Dijon, France, April 23-27, 2006, pp. 1567–1568. ACM Press, New York (2006)

356. Rolón Aguilar, E., Ruiz, F., García, F., Piattini, M.: Towards a Suite of Metrics for Business Process Models in BPMN. In: Manolopoulos, Y., Filipe, J., Constantopoulos, P., Cordeiro, J. (eds.) ICEIS 2006 - Proceedings of the Eighth International Conference on Enterprise Information Systems: Databases and Information Systems Integration (III), Paphos, Cyprus, May 23-27, 2006, pp. 440–443 (2006)

357. La Rosa, M., Dumas, M., ter Hofstede, A., Mendling, J., Gottschalk, F.: Beyond control-flow: Extending business process configuration to resources and objects. In: Li, Q., Spaccapietra, S., Yu, E., Olivé, A. (eds.) ER 2008. LNCS, vol. 5231, Springer, Heidelberg (2008)

358. Rosemann, M.: Erstellung und Integration von Prozeßmodellen - Methodenspezifische Gestaltungsempfehlungen für die Informationsmodellierung. PhD thesis, Westfälische Wilhelms-Universität Münster (1995)

359. Rosemann, M.: Preparation of Process Modeling. In: Becker, J., Kugeler, M., Rosemann, M. (eds.) Process Management: A Guide for the Design of Business Processes, pp. 41–78. Springer, Heidelberg (2003)

360. Rosemann, M.: Potential pitfalls of process modeling: part a. Business Process Management Journal 12(2), 249–254 (2006)

361. Rosemann, M.: Potential pitfalls of process modeling: part b. Business Process Management Journal 12(3), 377–384 (2006)

362. Rosemann, M., van der Aalst, W.: A Configurable Reference Modelling Language. Information Systems 32, 1–23 (2007)

363. Rosemann, M., de Bruin, T., Power, B.: A Model to Measure Business Process Management Maturity and Improve Performance. In: Jeston, J., Nelis, J. (eds.) Business Process Management: Practical Guidelines to Successful Implementations, pp. 299–315. Butterworth-Heinemann (2006)

364. Rosemann, M., Green, P.: Developing a meta model for the Bunge-Wand-Weber ontological constructs. Information Systems 27, 75–91 (2002)

365. Rubin, V., Günther, C.W., van der Aalst, W.M.P., Kindler, E., Dongen, B.F.v., Schäfer, W.: Process mining framework for software processes. BPMCenter Report BPM-07-01, BPMcenter.org (2006)

366. Rump, F.J.: Geschäftsprozessmanagement auf der Basis ereignisgesteuerter Prozessketten - Formalisierung, Analyse und Ausführung von EPKs. Teubner Verlag (1999)

367. Russell, N.: Foundations of Process-Aware Information Systems. PhD thesis, Queensland University of Technology (2007)

368. Russell, N., ter Hofstede, A.H.M., van der Aalst, W.M.P., Mulyar, N.: Workflow Control-Flow Patterns: A Revised View. BPM Center Report BPM-06-22, BPMcenter.org (2006)

369. Russell, N., van der Aalst, W.M.P., ter Hofstede, A.H.M.: Workflow exception patterns. In: Dubois, E., Pohl, K. (eds.) CAiSE 2006. LNCS, vol. 4001, pp. 288–302. Springer, Heidelberg (2006)

370. Russell, N., van der Aalst, W.M.P., ter Hofstede, A.H.M., Edmond, D.: Workflow resource patterns: Identification, representation and tool support. In: Pastor, Ó., Falcão e Cunha, J. (eds.) CAiSE 2005. LNCS, vol. 3520, pp. 216–232. Springer, Heidelberg (2005)

371. Russell, N., ter Hofstede, A.H.M., Edmond, D., van der Aalst, W.M.P.: Workflow data patterns: Identification, representation and tool support. In: Delcambre, L.M.L., Kop, C., Mayr, H.C., Mylopoulos, J., Pastor, Ó. (eds.) ER 2005. LNCS, vol. 3716, pp. 353–368. Springer, Heidelberg (2005)

372. Sadiq, W., Orlowska, M.E.: Modeling and verification of workflow graphs. Technical Report No. 386, Department of Computer Science, The University of Queensland, Australia (1996)

373. Sadiq, W., Orlowska, M.E.: Applying graph reduction techniques for identifying structural conflicts in process models. In: Jarke, M., Oberweis, A. (eds.) CAiSE 1999. LNCS, vol. 1626, pp. 195–209. Springer, Heidelberg (1999)

374. Sadiq, W., Orlowska, M.E.: Analyzing Process Models using Graph Reduction Techniques. Information Systems 25(2), 117–134 (2000)

375. Sarshar, K., Dominitzki, P., Loos, P.: Einsatz von Ereignisgesteuerten Prozessketten zur Modellierung von Prozessen in der Krankenhausdomäne – Eine empirische Methodenevaluation. In: Nüttgens, M., Rump, F.J. (eds.) Proceedings of the 4th GI Workshop on Business Process Management with Event-Driven Process Chains (EPK 2005), Hamburg, Germany, December 2005, pp. 97–116. German Informatics Society (2005)

376. Sarshar, K., Loos, P.: Comparing the Control-Flow of EPC and Petri Net from the End-User Perspective. In: van der Aalst, W.M.P., Benatallah, B., Casati, F., Curbera, F. (eds.) BPM 2005. LNCS, vol. 3649, pp. 434–439. Springer, Heidelberg (2005)

377. Scheer, A.-W.: CIM - Computer integrated manufacturing: Der computergesteuerte Industriebetrieb. Springer, Heidelberg (1987)

378. Scheer, A.-W.: ARIS - Business Process Frameworks, 2nd edn. Springer, Berlin et al (1998)

379. Scheer, A.-W.: Wirtschaftsinformatik: Referenzmodelle für industrielle Geschäftsprozesse, 2nd edn. Springer, Heidelberg (1998)

380. Scheer, A.-W.: ARIS - Business Process Modeling, 3rd edn. Springer, Berlin et al (2000)

381. Scheer, A.-W.: ARIS business process modelling. Springer, Heidelberg (2000)

382. Scheer, A.-W.: ARIS: Von der Vision zur praktischen Geschäftsprozesssteuerung. In: Scheer, A.-W., Jost, W. (eds.) ARIS in der Praxis - Gestaltung, Implementierung und Optimierung von Geschäftsprozessen, pp. 1–14. Springer, Heidelberg (2002)

383. Scheer, A.-W., Nüttgens, M., Zimmermann, V.: Objektorientierte Ereignisgesteuerte Prozeßketten (oEPK) - Methode und Anwendung. Heft 141, Institut für Wirtschaftsinformatik, Saarbrücken, Germany (1997)

384. Scheer, A.-W., Thomas, O., Adam, O.: Process Modeling Using Event-Driven Process Chains. In: Dumas, M., ter Hofstede, A., van der Aalst, W.M.P. (eds.) Process Aware Information Systems: Bridging People and Software Through Process Technology, pp. 119–146. Wiley, Chichester (2005)

385. Schneider, K., Thomas, O.: Kundenorientierte Dienstleistungsmodellierung mit Ereignisgesteuerten Prozessketten. In: Proc. of the 2nd GI-Workshop on Business Process Management with Event-Driven Process Chains (EPK 2003), Bamberg, Germany, pp. 87–93 (2000)

386. Scholz-Reiter, B., Stickel, E.: Business Process Modelling. Springer, Heidelberg (1996)
387. Schütte, R.: Grundsätze ordnungsgemäßer Referenzmodellierung. Gabler Verlag, Wiesbaden (1998)
388. Schuette, R., Rotthowe, T.: The Guidelines of Modeling - An Approach to Enhance the Quality in Information Models. In: Ling, T.-W., Ram, S., Li Lee, M. (eds.) ER 1998. LNCS, vol. 1507, pp. 240–254. Springer, Heidelberg (1998)
389. Scott, J.: Social Network Analysis: A Handbook, 2nd edn. Sage, Thousand Oaks (2000)
390. Searle, J.: Speech Acts: An Essay in the Philosophy of Language. Cambridge University Press, Cambridge (1969)
391. Software Engineering Institute SEI: Software size measurement: A framework for counting source statements. Technical Report CMU/SEI-92-TR-020, ADA258304 (1992)
392. Seidlmeier, H.: Prozessmodellierung mit ARIS. MIT Press, Cambridge (2002)
393. Selby, R.W., Basili, V.R.: Analyzing error-prone system structure. IEEE Transactions on Software Engineering 17, 141–152 (1991)
394. Selby, R.W., Basili, V.R.: Analyzing error-prone system structure. IEEE Transactions on Software Engineering 17(2), 141–152 (1991)
395. Shannon, C.E., Weaver, W.: Mathematical Theory of Communication. B&T (1963)
396. Shatz, S.M.: Towards complexity metrics for ada tasking. IEEE Transaction on Software Engineering 14(8), 1122–1127 (1988)
397. Shen, V.Y., Yu, T.-J., Thebaut, S.M., Paulsen, L.R.: Identifying error-prone software. IEEE Transactions on Software Engineering 11, 317–324 (1985)
398. Siau, K., Rossi, M.: Evaluation techniques for systems analysis and design modelling methods – a review and comparative analysis. Information Systems Journal (2008)
399. Siau, K.L., Tan, X.: Improving the quality of conceptual modeling using cognitive mapping techniques. Data and Knowledge Engineering 55(3), 343–365 (2005)
400. Silverston, L.: The Data Model Resource Book, Volume 1, A Library of Universal Data Models for all Enterprises. John Wiley and Sons, Chichester (2001)
401. Silverston, L.: The Data Model Resource Book, Volume 2, A Library of Data Models for Specific Industries. John Wiley and Sons, Chichester (2001)
402. Simon, C.: Negotiation Processes. The semantic process language and applications (Habilitationsschrift). University of Koblenz (2006)
403. Simon, C., Mendling, J.: Verification of Forbidden Behavior in EPCs. In: Mayr, H.C., Breu, R. (eds.) Proceedings of the GI Conference Modellierung, Innsbruck, Austria, March 2006. Lecture Notes in Informatics, vol. 82, pp. 233–242. German Informatics Society (2006)
404. Simon, H.A.: Sciences of the Artificial, 3rd edn. MIT Press, Cambridge (1996)
405. Slack, N., Chambers, S., Johnston, R.: Operations and Process Management. Principles and Practice for Strategic Impact. Prentice-Hall, Englewood Cliffs (2006)
406. Smith, A.: An inquiry into the nature and causes of the wealth of nations. London (1776)
407. Smith, H., Fingar, P.: Business Process Management: The Third Wave. Meghan Kiffer (2006)
408. Smith, R.F.: Business Process Management and the Balanced Scorecard. Focusing Processes as Strategic Drivers: Using Processes as Strategic Drivers. Wiley & Sons, Chichester (2007)
409. Smith, S.M., Albaum, G.S.: Fundamentals of Marketing Research. Sage, Thousand Oaks (2005)
410. Smolander, K., Lyytinen, K., Tahvanainen, V.-P., Marttiin, P.: Metaedit - a flexible graphical environment for methodology modelling. In: Andersen, R., Solvberg, A., Bubenko Jr., J.A. (eds.) CAiSE 1991. LNCS, vol. 498, pp. 168–193. Springer, Heidelberg (1991)

411. Söderström, E., Andersson, B., Johannesson, P., Perjons, E., Wangler, B.: Towards a Framework for Comparing Process Modelling Languages. In: Pidduck, A.B., Mylopoulos, J., Woo, C.C., Ozsu, M.T. (eds.) CAiSE 2002. LNCS, vol. 2348, pp. 600–611. Springer, Heidelberg (2002)

412. Soffer, P., Wand, Y.: Goal-driven analysis of process model validity. In: Persson, A., Stirna, J. (eds.) CAiSE 2004. LNCS, vol. 3084, pp. 521–535. Springer, Heidelberg (2004)

413. Sommerville, I.: Software Engineering, 6th edn. Addison-Wesley, Reading (2001)

414. Stachowiak, H.: Allgemeine Modelltheorie. Springer-Verlag, Wien (1973)

415. Staud, J.L.: Geschäftsprozessanalyse: Ereignisgesteuerte Prozessketten und Objektorientierte Geschäftsprozessmodellierung für Betriebswirtschaftliche Standardsoftware, 3rd edn. Springer, Heidelberg (2006)

416. Stevens, S.S.: On the theory of scale types and measurement. Science 103, 677–680 (1946)

417. Stevens, S.S.: Mathematics, Measurement, and Psychophysics. In: Stevens, S.S. (ed.) Handbook of Experimental Psychology, John Wiley, Chichester (1951)

418. Stone, M.: Cross validity choice and assessment of statistical predictors. Journal of the Royal Statistical Society 36, 111–147 (1974)

419. Strahringer, S.: Metamodellierung als Instrument des Methodenvergleichs. Eine Evaluierung am Beispiel objektorientierter Analysemethoden. Shaker Verlag, Aachen (1996)

420. Striemer, R., Deiters, W.: Workflow Management – Erfolgreiche Planung und Durchführung von Workflow-Projekten. Arbeitsbericht, Fraunhofer Institut für Software- und Systemtechnik (1995)

421. Taylor, F.W.: The Principles of Scientific Management. Harper and Brothers, New York and London (1911)

422. Thomas, O.: Understanding the term reference model in information systems research: History, literature analysis and explanation. In: Bussler, C.J., Haller, A. (eds.) BPM 2005. LNCS, vol. 3812, pp. 484–496. Springer, Heidelberg (2006)

423. Thomas, O., Dollmann, T.: Fuzzy-EPK-Modelle: Attributierung und Regelintegration. In: Proceedings of the 5th GI Workshop on Business Process Management with Event-Driven Process Chains (EPK 2006), Vienna, Austria, December 2006, pp. 49–68. German Informatics Society (2006)

424. Thomas, O., Fellmann, M.: Semantic event-driven process chains. In: Semantics for Business Process Management 2006 (SBPM 2006): Workshop at 3rd European Semantic Web Conference (ESWC 2006), Budva, Montenegro (June 2006)

425. Thomas, O., Fellmann, M.: Semantische ereignisgesteuerte prozessketten. In: Schelp, J., Winter, R., Frank, U., Rieger, B., Turowski, K. (eds.) Integration, Informationslogistik und Architektur: DW2006, Friedrichshafen, Germany, September 2006. Lecture Notes in Informatics, vol. 90, pp. 205–224 (2006)

426. Thomas, O., Hüsselmann, C., Adam, O.: Fuzzy-Ereignisgesteuerte Prozessketten - Geschäftsprozessmodellierung unter Berücksichtigung unscharfer Daten. In: Proc. of the 1st GI-Workshop on Business Process Management with Event-Driven Process Chains (EPK 2002), Trier, Germany, pp. 7–16 (2002)

427. Thomas, O., Scheer, A.-W.: Tool support for the collaborative design of reference models - a business engineering perspective. In: 39th Hawaii International International Conference on Systems Science (HICSS-39 2006), CD-ROM / Abstracts Proceedings, 4-7 January 2006, Kauai, HI, USA, IEEE Computer Society Press, Los Alamitos (2006)

428. Tiplea, F.L., Marinescu, D.C.: Structural soundness of workflow nets is decidable. Inf. Process. Lett. 96(2), 54–58 (2005), doi:10.1016/j.ipl.2005.06.002

429. Tjaden, G.S.: Business process structural analysis. Technical report, Georgia Tech Research Corp. (June 2001)
430. Tjaden, G.S., Narasimhan, S., Mitra, S.: Structural effectiveness metrics for business processes. In: Proceedings of the INFORMS Conference on Information Systems and Technology, May 1996, pp. 396–400 (1996)
431. van der Toorn, R.: Component-Based Software Design with Petri nets: An Approach Based on Inheritance of Behavior. PhD thesis, Eindhoven University of Technology, Eindhoven, The Netherlands (2004)
432. Torgerson, W.S.: Theory and methods of scaling. Wiley, Chichester (1958)
433. Trochim, W., Donnelly, J.P.: The Research Methods Knowledge Base, 3rd edn. Atomic Dog Publishing (2006)
434. Tukey, J.W.: Exploratory Data Analysis. Addison-Wesley, Reading (1977)
435. Vaishnavi, V.K., Purao, S., Liegle, J.: Object-oriented product metrics: A generic framework. Information Sciences 177, 587–606 (2007)
436. Valmari, A.: The state explosion problem. In: Reisig, W., Rozenberg, G. (eds.) APN 1998. LNCS, vol. 1491, pp. 429–528. Springer, Heidelberg (1998)
437. Vanderfeesten, I., Mendling, J., Reijers, H., van der Aalst, W., Cardoso, J.: On a quest for good process models: The cross-connectivity metric. In: Bellahsène, Z., Léonard, M. (eds.) CAiSE 2008. LNCS, vol. 5074, Springer, Heidelberg (2008)
438. Vanhatalo, J., Völzer, H., Leymann, F.: Faster and more focused control-flow analysis for business process models through sese decomposition. In: Krämer, B.J., Lin, K.-J., Narasimhan, P. (eds.) ICSOC 2007. LNCS, vol. 4749, pp. 43–55. Springer, Heidelberg (2007)
439. Velleman, P.F., Wilkinson, L.: Nominal, ordinal, interval, and ratio typologies are misleading. The American Statistician 47(1), 65–72 (1993)
440. Verbeek, H.M.W., van der Aalst, W.M.P.: On the verification of EPCs using T-invariants. BPMCenter Report BPM-06-05, BPMcenter.org (2006)
441. Verbeek, H.M.W.: Verification and Enactment of Workflow Management Systems. PhD thesis, Eindhoven University of Technology, Eindhoven, The Netherlands (2004)
442. Verbeek, H.M.W(E.), van der Aalst, W.M.P.: Woflan 2.0 A Petri-Net-Based Workflow Diagnosis Tool. In: Nielsen, M., Simpson, D. (eds.) ICATPN 2000. LNCS, vol. 1825, pp. 475–484. Springer, Heidelberg (2000)
443. Verbeek, H.M.W., Basten, T., van der Aalst, W.M.P.: Diagnosing Workflow Processes using Woflan. The Computer Journal 44(4), 246–279 (2001)
444. Verbeek, H.M.W., van Dongen, B.F., Mendling, J., van der Aalst, W.M.P.: Interoperability in the ProM Framework. In: Missikoff, M., Nicola, A.D., D'Antonio, F. (eds.) EMOI - INTEROP'06, Enterprise Modelling and Ontologies for Interoperability, Proceedings of the Open Interop Workshop on Enterprise Modelling and Ontologies for Interoperability, Co-located with CAiSE'06 Conference, Luxembourg (June 2006)
445. Verbeek, H.M.W., Pretorius, A.J., van der Aalst, W.M.P., van Wijk, J.J.: Visualizing state spaces with Petri nets. Computer Science Report 07/01, Eindhoven University of Technology, Eindhoven, The Netherlands (2007)
446. Brocke, J.v.: Referenzmodellierung - Gestaltung und Verteilung von Konstruktionsprozessen. Advances in Information Systems and Management Science. Logos Verlag, Berlin (2003)
447. Wahli, U., Leybovich, L., Prevost, E., Scher, R.: Business Process Management: Modeling Through Monitoring. IBM Redbooks. Vervante (2006)

448. Wand, Y., Weber, R.: Mario Bunge's Ontology as a Formal Foundation for Information Systems Concepts. In: Weingartner, P., Dorn, G. (eds.) Studies in Bunge's Treatise on Basic Philosophy. the Poznan Studies in the Philosophy of the Sciences and the Humanities, pp. 123–149. Rodopi (1990)

449. Wand, Y., Weber, R.: On the deep structure of information systems. Information Systems Journal 5, 203–223 (1995)

450. Wand, Y., Weber, R.: Research Commentary: Information Systems and Conceptual Modeling - A Research Agenda. Information Systems Research 13(4), 363–376 (2002)

451. Weber, I., Haller, J., Mülle, J.A.: Derivation of executable business processes from choreographies in virtual organizations. In: Proc. of XML4BPM 2006 (February 2006)

452. Welch, B.B., Jones, K., Hobbs, J.: Practical Programming in Tcl and Tk, 4th edn. Prentice-Hall, Englewood Cliffs (2003)

453. Weske, M.: Foundation, Design, and Implementation of Dynamic Adaptations in a Workflow Management System. In: Fachbericht Angewandte Mathematik und Informatik 6/2000-I, Universität Münster, Münster, Germany (2000)

454. Weyuker, E.J.: Evaluating software complexity measures. IEEE Transactions on Software Engineering 14(9), 1357–1365 (1988)

455. Winograd, T.: A language/action perspective on the design of cooperative work. Human-Computer Interaction 3(1), 3–30 (1987)

456. Winter, A.J., Kullbach, B., Riediger, V.: An Overview of the GXL Graph Exchange Language. In: Diehl, S. (ed.) Dagstuhl Seminar 2001. LNCS, vol. 2269, pp. 324–336. Springer, Heidelberg (2002)

457. Wintergreen Research: Business process management (bpm) market opportunities, strategies, and forecasts, 2006 to 2012. Technical Report Pub ID: WGR1352720, Wintergreen Research (October 2006), http://www.marketresearch.com/product/display.asp?productid=1352720&g=1

458. Wohed, P., van der Aalst, W.M.P., Dumas, M., ter Hofstede, A.H.M.: Analysis of web services composition languages: The case of BPEL4WS. In: Song, I.-Y., Liddle, S.W., Ling, T.-W., Scheuermann, P. (eds.) ER 2003. LNCS, vol. 2813, pp. 200–215. Springer, Heidelberg (2003)

459. Wohed, P., van der Aalst, W.M.P., Dumas, M., ter Hofstede, A.H.M., Russell, N.: Pattern-Based Analysis of the Control-Flow Perspective of UML Activity Diagrams. In: Delcambre, L.M.L., Kop, C., Mayr, H.C., Mylopoulos, J., Pastor, Ó. (eds.) ER 2005. LNCS, vol. 3716, pp. 63–78. Springer, Heidelberg (2005)

460. Wohed, P., van der Aalst, W.M.P., Dumas, M., ter Hofstede, A.H.M., Russell, N.: On the Suitability of BPMN for Business Process Modelling. In: Dustdar, S., Fiadeiro, J.L., Sheth, A.P. (eds.) BPM 2006. LNCS, vol. 4102, pp. 161–176. Springer, Heidelberg (2006)

461. Workflow Management Coalition: Terminology & Glossary. Document Number WFMC-TC-1011, Document Status - Issue 3.0, Feb 99, Workflow Management Coalition (1999)

462. Workflow Management Coalition: Workflow Process Definition Interface – XML Process Definition Language. Document Number WFMC-TC-1025, October 25, 2002, Version 1.0, Workflow Management Coalition (2002)

463. Workflow Management Coalition: Workflow Process Definition Interface – XML Process Definition Language. Document Number WFMC-TC-1025, October 3, 2005, Version 2.00, Workflow Management Coalition (2005)

464. Wynn, M.T., van der Aalst, W.M.P., ter Hofstede, A.H.M., Edmond, D.: Verifying Work-flows with Cancellation Regions and OR-Joins: An Approach Based on Reset Nets and Reachability Analysis. In: Dustdar, S., Fiadeiro, J.L., Sheth, A.P. (eds.) BPM 2006. LNCS, vol. 4102, pp. 389–394. Springer, Heidelberg (2006)

465. Wynn, M.T., Edmond, D., van der Aalst, W.M.P., ter Hofstede, A.H.M.: Achieving a General, Formal and Decidable Approach to the OR-Join in Workflow Using Reset Nets. In: Ciardo, G., Darondeau, P. (eds.) ICATPN 2005. LNCS, vol. 3536, pp. 423–443. Springer, Heidelberg (2005)

466. Wynn, M.T., Verbeek, H.M.W., van der Aalst, W.M.P., ter Hofstede, A.H.M., Edmond, D.: Reduction rules for reset workflow nets. BPMCenter Report BPM-06-25, BPMcenter.org (2006)

467. Wynn, M.T., Verbeek, H.M.W., van der Aalst, W.M.P., ter Hofstede, A.H.M., Edmond, D.: Reduction rules for yawl workflow nets with cancellation regions and or-joins. BPM-Center Report BPM-06-24, BPMcenter.org (2006)

468. Yourdon, E., Constantine, L.L.: Structured Design. Prentice Hall, Englewood Cliffs (1979)

469. Zhao, W., Hauser, R., Bhattacharya, K., Bryant, B.R., Cao, F.: Compiling business processes: untangling unstructured loops in irreducible flow graphs. Int. Journal of Web and Grid Services 2(1), 68–91 (2006)

470. Ziemann, J., Mendling, J.: EPC-Based Modelling of BPEL Processes: a Pragmatic Transformation Approach. In: International Conference "Modern Information Technology in the Innovation Processes of the Industrial Enterprises", Genova, Italy (2005)

471. Zisman, M.D.: Use of production systems for modeling asynchronous concurrent processes. Pattern-Directed Inference Systems, 53–68 (1978)

472. Zisman, M.D.: Representation, Specification and Automation of Office Procedures. PhD thesis, University of Pennsylvania, Warton School of Business (1977)

473. Zukunft, O., Rump, F.J.: From Business Process Modelling to Workflow Management: An Integrated Approach. In: Scholz-Reiter, B., Stickel, E. (eds.) Business Process Modelling, pp. 3–22. Springer, Heidelberg (1996)

474. Zuse, H.: Software Complexity: Measures and Methods. Walter de Gruyter and Co., New Jersey (1991)

Index